EITHER YOU'RE IN OR YOU'RE IN THE WAY

EITHER YOU'RE IN OR YOU'RE IN THE WAY

TWO BROTHERS, TWELVE MONTHS, AND ONE FILMMAKING HELL-RIDE TO KEEP A PROMISE TO THEIR FATHER

LOGAN and NOAH MILLER

HARPER

An Imprint of HarperCollins*Publishers*
www.harpercollins.com

HarperCollins books may be purchased for educational, business, or
sales promotional use. For information, please write: Special Markets
Department, HarperCollins Publishers, 10 East 53rd Street, New York,
NY 10022.

FIRST EDITION

Library of Congress Cataloging-in-Publication Data

Miller, Logan.
   Either you're in or you're in the way: two brothers, twelve months,
and one filmmaking hell-ride to keep a promise to their father/Logan
Miller and Noah Miller.—1st ed.
      p. cm.
   ISBN 978-0-06-176314-4
   1. Touching home (Motion picture). 2. Miller, Logan. 3. Miller,
Noah. I. Miller, Noah. II. Title.
   PN1997.2.T68M55 2009
   791.43'72—dc22

                                                            2008045802

09 10 11 12 13   OV/RRD   10 9 8 7 6 5 4 3 2 1

FOR DAD

he always wanted the best for us

Seven thoughts on our first hell-ride through filmmaking . . .

1. *Every day is the Cuban Missile Crisis: Your world could blow up.*
2. *Surround yourself with gray hair and listen.*
3. *Never wait for a phone call.*
4. *Stay relentless. Rely on no one.*
5. *There are only solutions.*
6. *Spend the financier's money as if it were your own: Don't be a scumbag.*
7. *Either you're in or you're in the way.*

What follows was written from the IGNORANCE of having only produced and directed ONE film, and the ARROGANCE of having only produced and directed ONE film.

CONTENTS

TWO GUYS WHO LOVE EACH OTHER

IT'S BEEN SAID we have an unusual relationship.

Bro is me and I am Bro. We're identical twins. We share everything; it's been like that since the womb. Before that it was an egg, and before that it's hard to say. We have one cell phone, one computer, and one car between us. Not saying that it would be a bad thing to have two of each, but right now money is tight. So for now, we share. And are blessed to have someone to share with.

We've always been best friends and have always helped each other, except when we tried to resolve our conflicts by punching one another. We stopped doing that once we started breaking noses and knocking out permanent teeth. It got expensive. So now our arguments never escalate beyond "intellectual frustration," if we may boldly say so.

Each of us would rather the other guy succeed. If there's only one trophy, we want the other to have it. If there's only one princess, then Bro can have her. We cook for each other and serve more food to the other guy.

Thought experiment: Let's just say that *we*—the Bros— had only 51 percent of a brain apiece. Unfortunate, yes, but paralyzing, no, because if we work together we have 102 percent, which is

2 percent more than any human on the planet, beat Einstein if he were still around.

People often ask us, do you *really* share everything? Yeah, just about. Then they'll usually say something stupid like, "Even underwear?" Chuckle, chuckle. Yes, even underwear, smart-ass. But it's not like one of us wears a pair Monday and then flips it to the other guy on Tuesday. We wash them first. Then we flip them.

Then the most common question: "So what's it like being twins?" And we usually reply with, "What's it like being you?" It's our reality. It's what we know. What do you know? Tough question, isn't it, it's rather broad. Hopefully by the end of this adventure you'll have a better understanding of what it is, and perhaps, so shall we. Bro is me and I am Bro.

PART I

HOLLY-WAR
(1999-2006)

THE TIME BEFORE NOW

THE MANAGER OF the building dropped dead in our apartment the day after we moved in. He was an ex-marine, wounded by a grenade in Korea, played baseball for the San Francisco Seals in the late 1940s. We had terrible credit then. He rented to us when no one else would.

The apartment was made of bricks. During the day it became a kiln. You could bake clay pots in the freezer. At night we sweated and killed cockroaches.

Pigeons roosted above our stove. Their shit and feathers fell through the air vent. We patched it with a square of sheet metal and duct tape. Occasionally the tape would lose its stickiness and drop a trapdoor of crusty pigeon shit and feathers onto our stove. The shit-cloud resembled a mushroom. It reeked of dried piss.

Our neighbor was an old man. His TV exploded through the walls. He never turned it off. It was so loud you could see what he was watching.

We spent the first few months in Hollywood on our friend Pietro's floor, warming up for the roach and pigeon palace. Pietro was renting a room in a two-bedroom apartment. There were three of us living in a room slightly larger than a shower stall. A rocker named Dave lived in the other room with his Japanese girlfriend, Roki or Soki, something like that. She didn't speak any English. They were happy. It was a happy apartment. We ate a lot of peanut butter sandwiches in those days.

We'd been on the road playing baseball for the better part of five years, lived in Iowa, Texas, Arkansas, Florida, Arizona, and hung out in every state in between. But baseball didn't work out. It had been our dream since we had dreams. We had no backup plan, limited education, no résumé for any job above manual labor. We'd never thought of the future in terms other than baseball. Now we were forced to think about it.

We didn't want to go back home to Northern California and pound nails. We'd done plenty of that growing up. We wanted to make a living at something we loved. We needed a new dream. But what could we do?

Not much in the professional world.

So we decided to write a movie.

But we'd never written a movie before. Hell, we'd never even *seen* a written movie before. We walked down to Larry Edmunds' Bookshop on Hollywood Boulevard and were informed that a written movie is called a "screenplay." We pulled the screenplay for *Casino* off the dusty shelf. It looked like some form of alien communication.

Discouraged, we put the screenplay back on the shelf, cursed our ignorance, and walked out.

A week later, our buddy Nicky Hart introduced us to a guy named Erik, who recommended the tool that could decipher the code: "*Lew Hunter's Screenwriting 434* is the book you need."

So we walked back down to Larry Edmunds and bought *434*. The book was plainly written and easy to understand. It demystified the process, cracked the screenwriting enigma.

If we ever make any money in this business, Lew Hunter should receive a percentage of our tax receipts.

We finished *434* and started writing *Touching Home,* a story about us and our father. We had a lot of pain. And writing helped get it out. *Touching Home* was written on college-ruled notepads on a park bench in the Valley. We didn't own a computer at the time, and the park had grass and flowers and other living things that didn't try to steal our food.

Half this book was handwritten. Noah still doesn't type, says it "doesn't work right with his mind," which is probably all right, 'cause last time we checked, Shakespeare couldn't type either.

It took us twenty-five days to complete the first draft of *Touching Home*. It was the most difficult thing either of us had ever done. We swore we'd never write another one . . .

Then we saw the road ahead. We tried to deny it, swore it was a hallucination. But it wouldn't go away. It was there. It was our future.

We wrote twelve screenplays and a seven-hundred-page manuscript during that first Hollywood tour. Each time we completed a screenplay, we'd grab a couple bottles of cheap wine at the corner liquor store and climb the fire escape to the rooftop of our apartment and celebrate the victory. Passing the bottle back and forth, we'd stare at the shimmering city where movies are made, envisioning the day we'd be making *our* movies.

Sometimes we drank so much we were flammable. Coming down was tricky.

Back then, we had the worst car in Los Angeles. It looked like a crushed sardine can. The passenger side had been T-boned at 45 mph by some lady that didn't see the red light. When she was done, the car had one working door. You had to climb over the stick shift to get to the passenger's seat. The passenger couldn't roll down the window because it was made of Visqueen and duct tape. There was no air-conditioning. In the summer, it became a sweat lodge; you could lose five pounds driving to the grocery store. In the winter, it became a rain forest. One night we drove in a storm from San Francisco to L.A. with a shin-deep puddle in the passenger foot bucket. It was so ridiculous we surrendered to the water and took off our shoes. Our car was so ugly people were ashamed to look at it.

Our buddy gave us the car after our other car blew up, and we abandoned it on the highway north of Santa Barbara. A salvage company sued us for $800 after they cubed it.

In those days, we worked at a bingo hall in the Valley. Our job was to walk the gymnasium floor, selling blotters, raffle tickets, fresh sheets of bingo paper, and other senile paraphernalia. One night the number caller had to use the bathroom. It couldn't wait. So Logan replaced him onstage and started pulling the balls from the basket and calling out the numbers. Logan had never performed this task, wasn't trained to, didn't know the rules of the spinning balls.

Someone yelled bingo. Logan thought the game was over and released the balls from the basket. But it wasn't over, far from it. This was a blackout game. Elderly rage exploded. Dentures shot from mouths. Words that spark riots were hurled. Our employment ended there that night.

We were fired from a bingo hall. Not many people can claim that.

Then we got suckered into the world of high fashion—modeling. It wasn't our scene. But they said that we *could* make $1,000 a day . . . *could*. But never *would*.

Noah got hired by Dave LaChapelle. (He's a famous photographer in his world.) Dave wanted to paint Noah gold and dress him up in a G-string for some MTV Awards photo. "Noah, you'll be one of my golden pillars . . . You've got a few minutes before we paint you. Are you hungry?"

"I was . . ."

"Good. Go downstairs and eat."

So we walked downstairs to the royal buffet and stuffed our backpacks with chocolate chip cookies, a pecan pie, turkey, smoked salmon, bagels, and about three pounds of ham. It was Thanksgiving in a backpack. Then we walked out the back door and drove straight to Northern California without the gold body-paint and

G-string and went camping and fishing for a week to try and rec-
oncile what we had almost experienced. We had plenty of food.

Then our apartment was burglarized. They stole everything we
had, which wasn't much: a glass jar of change, a VCR, and a .45
Springfield automatic. They let us keep our sleeping bags.

We got a new job at an after-hours club in Hollywood, a flesh-
pot called The Cosmopolitan. We worked from 1 A.M. to 8 A.M.
It was Tony Montana's playhouse. No carnal desire was out of
the question. It was all for sale. At the end of the night, the black
tables were dusted white with coke. Garbage bags of money were
loaded into the trunk of a Chrysler every morning.

The head bouncer was the toughest man on the planet. He was
a German named Rolf. He was six foot four, two hundred and
thirty-five pounds of discipline and muscle. He never smiled. He
could kick your ass in thirty different art forms.

We originally met Rolf at the gym. He taught a kickbox-
ing and grappling class there. We started taking it. One time he
cracked Noah's ribs. Another time he nearly broke Noah's jaw; it
still aches on cold mornings. We never missed a class.

"I'm looking for two reliable guys to work for me," Rolf told
us one day, in a stiff accent. "You are them."

Rolf beat us up during the day. At night, we risked our lives for
him.

Bolo was the second bouncer in command. He was a heavy-
weight boxer. He could kick your ass in *one* art form, and one
was enough. Back in the day, his father was a sparring partner for
Mike Tyson.

The club was on the fifth floor of a high-rise near Hollywood
and Vine, a few blocks from the Capitol Records Building. The
second and third floors had been gutted by a fire. They looked like
some apocalyptic horror movie set, exposed steel beams black-
ened by the blaze.

Our man-post was the underground parking garage. Jackers

and crack addicts roamed the streets. They looked like white-eyed zombies in the apocalyptic movie. Some of them lived in the burned-out levels of the building. They stabbed two people and shot another over the glorious course of our employment. Sometimes they would just appear in the hallway. We had to clear them out each night before the club opened.

Starting at 1 A.M., cars would drive up to the retractable steel gate and flash their lights. We'd ask them "How can we help you?" They'd give us some fabulously exciting name like "Johnny Eyelashes" or "Bubbles." We'd check our clipboard for their fabulously exciting name, and if their fabulously exciting name was on the list, we'd hit the button, retract the gate, and they would drive in and park. Stand in line. Then we'd frisk them. And that's where they would stay for a while if we didn't *know* them, that is, if they didn't give us at least a twenty-dollar bill to avoid the line and receive a direct elevator ride to the top with Bolo.

Unlike everywhere else in Hollywood, we didn't care if they were famous. Fame didn't pay our rent. Cheap celebrities waited in line like everyone else. 'Cause our landlord didn't care who we saw each night. Neither did the phone man or the gas man or the cable man.

All kinds of people were fond of the club. Porn stars and strippers would stop by after a long slog in a hotel room or a long slide on a pole. They spoke about their professions with forensic clarity. To one nurse, giving a blow job was no different from drawing blood. Some of them had wild fantasies about screwing twin doormen in an elevator. Rolf wouldn't tolerate any hanky-panky. The more we resisted, the more they insisted.

We ended our doormen days after two guys stole a car and crashed through the retractable gate at 40 mph in a failed robbery attempt. The car launched into the parking garage, feet from us, pinballed off a Benz and a cement wall, shotgunning glass and car parts and chunks of pulverized cement.

The night before that, a guy had pulled a gun on Logan in the elevator. We weren't living in Hollywood to get killed. We were there to make movies. But we were still several years away from that. We've done many stupid things. Many. And working at the club was one of the stupidest.

So we stumbled around Hollywood, peddling our screenplays. We lived in six different apartments and twice moved back home to Northern California, following what we thought were writing opportunities, only to return to L.A. after the prospects vanished.

Those were tough times. We felt terribly inadequate. But we also felt defiant, defiant to make something of ourselves. We started at the absolute bottom: no film school, no college degree, no family or friends in the movie business. It took us eight years to make *Touching Home*. But during those eight years we worked at our craft with monastic discipline. Books became our sport. In them we found the tools of our future.

Touching Home had been rejected hundreds of times by hundreds of agents, producers, and studio executives. Thank God.

What follows is the year the cosmic forces started working with us. It's also a year that started with great tragedy.

PART II

OUT OF THE ASHES

GOING HOME

ON JANUARY 5, 2006, our father died on the cement floor of a jail cell. He'd been in and out of jail over the past several years due to alcohol-related offenses, locked up this time since mid-December. He said nobody really messed with him in there because he was one of the oldest inmates, and the guys sort of respected him for that. He was also the resident artist. Our father spent his last Christmas and New Year's behind bars. His name was Daniel Arthur Miller. He was fifty-nine.

Earlier in the year he'd been given a seat at the table with "the guys that run the joint," as he put it, after one of them saw him drawing on a piece of paper at lunch. Valentine's Day was approaching, and the guy asked if our dad would draw him a Valentine's Day card for his girlfriend. No problem. Our dad drew the guy a card. The guy sent it to his girlfriend. She loved it. Word spread through the jailhouse, and by the time Valentine's Day rolled around our dad had drawn cards for nearly every guy's girlfriend in there. Free walls and refrigerators all over the county were displaying our dad's love-work.

From then on, he was royalty. Whenever he was in the Marin County Jail there was always a seat waiting for him at the "don't mess with us table" in the chow hall.

WE WALKED OUT of Loews Theater on the Third Street Promenade in Santa Monica after watching *Walk the Line* for the second time.

We rarely watched movies in theaters. We were broke. This was high living, and to pay for a movie twice, well, that was downright profligate.

Noah turned on our cell phone. We had three messages.

"I'll check them in a sec," he said. "Let's walk around a bit."

During the movie both of us had unsettling thoughts, premonitions we were trying to ignore, though neither of us shared these thoughts with the other. We'd been thinking about our dad, reflecting on his situation, how to help him.

About a month earlier we were going to take him to see Cash on the big screen. We had come home to Northern California for the week of Thanksgiving and made plans to spend a day with him. It had been a long time since we'd all hung out. We were going to treat him to a nice restaurant or his favorite burger joint, eat a good steak or greasy cheeseburger, maybe both, and then go see *Walk the Line,* stuffing our faces with buttered popcorn and Milk Duds, tapping our feet to Cash.

Our dad had been homeless for the last fifteen years, mostly living in his truck, until it was confiscated by the courts ten months earlier. He'd been battling alcoholism his entire adult life and was now sleeping in a thicket of scotch broom, his "hideout" on a wooded hillside in Fairfax, a small town twenty miles north of San Francisco. We had given him a pager for Christmas years earlier so we could stay in touch. If we paged him and he didn't call back within a couple hours he was either on a drinking binge or in jail. Otherwise, he was more reliable than Swiss time. He knew every pay phone in the area.

It was cold that week in November, the temperature dipping into the twenties. Early Monday morning we found our dad walking down the road, hands in his pockets, hunched over, brittle after a night in the woods. He was wearing a thick down jacket and backpack, incoherent, muttering to himself. We were supposed to meet him in town at 11 A.M. It was now 7 A.M., and we were happy to see him early, make a longer day out of it.

"Hey, Dad-o!" Logan yelled out the window as we pulled alongside him and stopped. "How you doing?"

He was shivering. It took him a moment to recognize us.

"Get in," Logan said. "We're gonna have a great day."

He got in our car. The skin under his eyes was swollen from the cold, leaves in his hair. There was no energy to him, no happiness, no warmth of life. He usually lit up when he saw us. But there was no light today.

Tomorrow, he was going to start serving a thirty-day sentence in the Sonoma County Jail. He'd never been to the Sonoma County Jail before and didn't know how he'd be treated, didn't know if some young punk would mess with him or any of the other bullshit that can hit you in jail.

He didn't know anybody in Sonoma County, and he was uneasy about it.

No worries, Dad-o, we told him.

Today was his day. We were going to spend some money on him, treat him to all the good stuff, whatever he wanted. But he said he couldn't spend the day with us, wasn't in the right state of mind to be around people, couldn't sit inside a dark movie theater. He was in a bad way, the worst we'd ever seen him, like an abandoned dog on a lonely street. We just wanted to hug him and tell him everything was going to be all right.

He'd been a roofer for thirty-five years. But no one would hire him anymore. He said he was practically begging for a job. "It doesn't feel good, you know . . ."

He'd lost his pride. And that's what was most painful to see.

"We're going to start making movies, Dad. You just gotta hang on for a few more years and then we'll take care of you."

"I can't keep starting over . . ."

"Don't worry," we told him. "We'll get through this."

"You can let me out here," he said.

We pulled over, sad, frustrated. We'd been watching our dad

slowly kill himself for more than twenty-five years. A once vital and robust man, with limitless endurance and strength, was now weak and exhausted. His teeth were rotting. His body was so dependent on alcohol now that he started having seizures when he didn't drink. He had his first seizure alone in the woods and said it scared him pretty bad, didn't know what it was. He woke up on his back, staring up at the trees, couldn't remember how he got there but knew he hadn't been drinking. Then he had a seizure in jail, and they diagnosed him and started giving him meds. The meds sedated him. It was disturbing to see him that way, a man so far behind his eyes. But when he got out, the only medication he had to prevent the seizures was alcohol. The poison had become the cure.

Alcoholism steals the soul. Perhaps the most painful aspect is that it's a gradual theft.

"I don't want you boys to be angry with me," he said, about to open the door, staring out.

"We're not, Dad. We love you. We'll get through this . . . We're proud of you."

He shrugged, frowned, as though he didn't believe us. And that killed. We felt like failures. We weren't where we wanted to be in life and neither was he. None of us could help the other, and we all felt ashamed about it.

We dropped him off in town and gave him money for a meal and a cup of coffee. It was the last time we saw him alive.

WE WERE FARTHER down the Promenade now, on the crowded corner of Santa Monica Boulevard, when Noah decided to check the messages on our cell phone.

When we were ten our mom's cousin, "Uncle Gary," was shot four times in the head and stuffed in the trunk of his car. We had just spent two weeks with him at Lake Tahoe. He was our first surrogate father. A few months later our uncle Dirk killed himself. And before we were born our maternal grandmother committed suicide by soaking herself in gasoline and lighting herself on fire in the backyard. At an early age we had a strong sense of mortality and took nothing for granted. Sudden death has a haunting energy running through it. And the phone messages had that energy.

The first and third messages were from our mom, the second from Coach Gough. Neither said why they called, something like "Call me when you get this message." But the tone in their voices said everything. There was terrible news awaiting us.

We called our mother. It was as though she didn't need to tell us, we already knew.

"Noah, is your brother with you?"

"He's right here."

"Your father passed away this morning . . . I'm so sorry . . ."

"No . . . Poor Dad . . . Poor Dad . . ."

We leaned against the side of a building and cried. People stared.

"He deserved better . . . I wish he'd had a better life."

We loved our father as much as any sons can love. We prayed for him every day and we prayed for him now.

Earlier that day two sheriffs had stopped by our mom's house in Fairfax to inform us of our father's death. At first, they wouldn't tell our mom why they were there, only that they were looking for us. So she wouldn't tell them anything either. If they wanted to know where her boys were, then they were going to have to tell her why, and maybe then, maybe, she'd tell them where we were.

We told our mom that we were driving home immediately. The next day there would be a story in the newspaper about an inmate dying in jail. We didn't want Grandma to find out that way. We needed to tell Grandma in person, sit down with her. This was her son. Our dad was more than some reporter's scoop.

We hung up our cell phone and walked crying down the busy sidewalk, around the tourists, panhandlers, and buskers. Everything was blurry.

We hugged each other when we got inside our apartment, threw some clothes into a duffel bag, and headed North on I-5. It was past midnight. We listened to memories through the darkness.

"Poor Dad . . ." Noah kept saying, shaking his head as he cried. "I wish he'd had a better life . . ."

He died alone in jail, a horrible place under any circumstances, but to die there gasping on the floor with no one who cared . . .

OUR FATHER WAS drafted into the army at eighteen and sent to Korea. He guarded the DMZ and was nearly killed in an ambush that killed two of his best friends. When he got out of the military he built a driftwood hut on an empty stretch of wind-blasted beach in Northern California. He grew out his hair and lived there for several months until a ranger burned down his hut and told him to leave. So our dad borrowed a Triumph motorcycle from a buddy and rode around the western United States, sleeping in churches and turnouts alongside the highway. After that he came back to Northern California, started roofing, and met our mother, Lynette. Our mom got pregnant, and they drove to Lake Tahoe and got married.

We were born six weeks premature with a host of complications and spent our first days in incubators. Noah had emergency surgery at three weeks after his appendix ruptured, and Logan at six weeks for a hernia; the scars are identical. Our dad said we were born fighters. When Noah was three he tried to pet a goose; it was taller than he was. The goose hissed and bit Noah's hand. So Noah grabbed the goose by the neck and punched it. No goose ever tried to bite Noah again.

When we weren't in the hospital we lived in a damp carriage house with a wood-burning stove on a dirt road in the redwoods of Lagunitas, California, a town of a couple hundred outlaws and outcasts doing their best to stay off the grid. When we were eleven months old our dad's drinking led to divorce. We stayed with our mom, moving around for the next three years and finally settling in Fairfax, just over the hill from Lagunitas. Our dad moved down the road to another tiny place called Forest Knolls.

Our mom's house had one bedroom, six-and-a-half-foot ceilings, no foundation, and a bathtub without a shower. There was grass growing on the roof. We called it "The Shack." When men walked into The Shack it shook.

Our mom worked as a gardener and waitress in those days and drove a blue mail jeep she bought for a hundred bucks. In the summer we drove with the doors open. We took pride in that jeep and got in a couple fights at school when older kids teased us about it. We didn't win all the fights, but that didn't matter.

Our dad lived in a corrugated aluminum shed that he built on a woman's property. Her name was Jean. She played the piano and harp, painted enchanting postcards of fairies and unicorns and medieval wonders. She was also an heiress to the Sterno fortune, or so we were told by our dad.

The shed had no windows, no electricity, and no running water and was bordered by horse pastures and a firewood yard with rats the size of cats. The interior of the shed was solid wood. It felt indestructible, like a cannonball, only square. Bunks were built into the walls; we shared the bottom, Dad had the top. Nothing was up to code. On winter mornings, before we crawled out of our bunk, the shed was colder than an Alaskan doghouse. But there was an open flame propane heater, and when our dad lit it with a match, it shot out blue fire like a military weapon. The shed went from arctic to tropic in three seconds. Our dad had lots of guns in those days and loaded his own ammo inside. The shed was a living and breathing powder keg.

We spent the weekdays with our mom and the weekends with our dad. Back and forth, from The Shack to The Shed . . . and we lived in one of the wealthiest counties in the world. Go figure.

We had some great times out there with our dad. When he was sober he was a beautiful man, a brilliant artist who could make anything out of wood, and perhaps more optimistic than the first astronauts. Everything was possible. If somebody else could do something, then so could we. But when he was drinking, he went to Mars, and it scared the crap out of us. The nightmares came with the bottle, and his screams were terrifying, especially in the claustrophobic darkness of the shed. We didn't understand the craziness when we were young and cried and begged him to stop, thinking it was a switch he could turn off. We developed a bizarre sense of diplomacy and learned ways to deal with extremely irrational behavior.

One drunk night he blew off the meaty part of his left hand while playing with flash powder. A doctor had to sew his thumb back on. Another drunk night he spray painted red question marks on the doors and hood of a neighbor's truck, turned it into the Joker mobile. Like we said, he went to Mars. After twelve years, Jean kicked him off her property. She'd had enough of his drinking.

From then on he lived in his truck, parking many nights at Samuel P. Taylor State Park, where we often ate dinner with him on a sturdy wood table under the towering redwoods. He called it his "Redwood Restaurant." The house special was canned ravioli. Occasionally the chef would barbecue steaks on the park grill.

About the same time our dad got kicked out of The Shed our mom moved out of The Shack. A few years after Uncle Gary was murdered an attorney called and informed our mom that Gary had left a wealthy chunk of his estate to her. Gary wasn't that fond of his other relatives, and his sister, whom he loved, had been killed in a car accident when she was nineteen. His mom and dad were dead.

So we were going to be rich. Not rich by rich people's terms, but rich to everyone else, you know, like a million dollars or something. So our mom, expecting this windfall, went to the bank and secured a home loan and bought The Shack for $45,000. She then sold it a year later for $99,000 and bought a 1,700-square-foot house, with a shower—two of them. No more washing our hair under the faucet before school. Compared with The Shack the new house was a castle. But there was one significant problem that came to light right before we became rich.

According to the FBI, Uncle Gary made his money outside the law. And according to the IRS, they owned it. Our mom was stuck with a mortgage she couldn't afford. So what do you do? Open up the house to roommates.

We recognized early on that we weren't going to get anywhere in life through privilege. It wasn't hard to figure out; it was in our faces. We always dreamed about doing great things and knew that we had to do more than just dream. There had to be action behind those dreams. Baseball was our chance to be great. We were terrified of failure and worked to become professional baseball players with frightened obsession. We always hated school and weren't mature enough to appreciate the opportunity. But we couldn't have played any more baseball than we did growing up unless God had made more hours in the day.

We feared we'd become like our dad, still do at times. He was a man of great talents who never got to realize them. This was the greatest tragedy.

In high school we never had a sip of alcohol and rarely went to parties because we were scared of becoming alcoholics. We feared that if we had one sip we might forever be addicted. We were confused about the disease, and it scared us into discipline. At night we'd break into a basketball gym called the Pavilion, turn on the lights, plug in our Wiffle ball machine and hit for hours. Afterward Noah would work on his pitching mechanics, sweating, straining, striving to become great at something, striving to feel important, striving not to feel scared. We woke up at 5 A.M. and lifted weights three times a week before school with Coach Gough and the Fairfax rough squad, a motley band of knuckleheads who found significance with barbells and steel determination. Coach Gough, a cigar-chomping ex-marine and at the time a San Francisco cop, forged seven national champion Olympic-style weight lifters and one Olympian out of that crew. It was an ultracompetitive brotherhood where teenage angst was beaten into manhood.

Although our dad roofed every day, he gambled and drank away his money faster than he could make it. Every time he'd start saving his money to get a place to stay, he'd lose it in a card room, start over, and lose it again. Such is the curse of addiction. Toward the end, he stopped trying.

THE VOW

WE DROVE NORTH all night and arrived in Fairfax at dawn. We needed to go tell Grandma her son was dead. We went over to her apartment and sat down with her and held her hand. She reacted the way any mother would.

We stayed there for several hours. We did what we could for her and then it was time to go.

It was getting colder and darker and we needed to say goodbye to our father.

On December 19, he was released from the Sonoma County Jail, took the bus out of that county, found a liquor store, got drunk, and was picked up by the police and thrown back in the Marin County Jail eight hours after being released from Sonoma. He spent Christmas in jail, and we didn't visit because we were pissed at him.

Looking back, we wish we had seen him, but that's how it was then.

The holidays can be tough, and visiting your dad in jail makes them even tougher. When you leave, you always feel worse than when you arrived. We tried to see him on January 1, just before heading back to L.A. But we never saw him. His cell mate came to the visiting booth and told us that our father was sick and that he couldn't come and see us.

That was five days earlier.

We called the coroner's office and spoke to an investigator.

They said they needed to conduct an autopsy. We told them our father wouldn't want that, asked them to let him be and not cut him open. He always told us he never wanted to be gutted like a fish. They said they had to.

When someone dies in jail, they're still not free. The deceased is only free once the authorities say so. The body remains property of the state until the state is done. Various procedures need to be performed to determine if foul play or negligence was involved. Basically, the government needs to cover its ass.

The coroner called after the autopsy and told us our father was being held at a local mortuary. We drove over there. We had dreamed about making enough money to get him a little apartment where he could be warm and watch TV, eat a hot meal, away from the cold and rain, where he could sleep and not worry, where he could wake up and not shiver, where he could be proud. But the dream was over now. We had failed our father. If we had been more successful, more involved with him, been around more—if we had been more than we were maybe he'd still be alive.

We pushed through the glass doors and were greeted by the mortician. We sat in his office and discussed the financial realities of death. He started by saying that the county classified our dad as an "indigent" and as such, would pay for the services. We declined their generosity. It was our duty and we would pay for it. He wasn't an indigent to us. He was a wartime veteran, and the government would send us a flag in honor of his service.

"We'd like to see our father now . . ."

The mortician wheeled out a cardboard coffin and removed the top. We hoped to see someone other than our father, hoped he was still alive and that the jail had made a mistake. But the man in the cardboard coffin was our father. His torso was cut open, covered with blue paper towels. There was blood smeared on his right forearm and neck where they had tried to clean him up.

Even with the blood, there was a peacefulness about him that gave him back ten years of his life. His bloated skin had smoothed away the wrinkles and rejuvenated his weathered features. His hair was combed. But there was a yellow tinge to his face and the cold of his body was death. He was gone forever. The pain swelled and was then unleashed. We held his hand, crying, told him we loved him, told him we were proud of him . . . told him we were sorry.

We thought about the last time we saw him, on that cold day in November, and what he told us in the car just before we dropped him off.

"I wish I could've been better to you boys growing up . . . I'm sorry that I wasn't. I've never been able to be there for you one hundred percent . . . And I know I never will be . . . Thanks for never giving up on me . . ."

We tried to cheer him up. "We're going to start making movies, Dad. We're really close. We're going to do some great things together; fishing in Alaska, camping in Montana, sailing the oceans, like we've always dreamed. You just gotta take better care of yourself . . ."

"I know . . . I know."

Then we remembered a few months before that, the last time we visited him in jail. He lifted up his orange shirt, revealing his lean stomach, and hit his abs with his fist. "This is where you come to get fit . . . When are you gonna make our movie?"

"Soon, Dad . . . Soon."

"Who's gonna play me? He's gotta be good-looking."

"Ed Harris."

He always reminded us of our dad.

"Yeah, he's good. I'll give him permission to be me . . . The sheriff will negotiate on my behalf."

We all laughed. It was a jailhouse dream, an *impossible* dream, something to be accomplished in another lifetime when you could start over and make all the right decisions. Ed Harris was light-years from our moment.

Our dad knew how hard we were working to break into the business. He wished he could help us and felt worthless that he could not. Years earlier, his heart was broken when we failed to realize our baseball dreams, not because he had wanted it for himself, but because he knew how much it meant to us. His heart was broken because our hearts were broken. And now ours were broken again.

We always thought we could save him. And now we had to accept that we could not.

As we continued holding his cold hand and caressing his cold head, telling him that we loved him and that we were sorry, our sadness and guilt grew into frustration and defiance.

We wanted to prove that his life was important, that he was loved, that his final chapter was not the shameful end on a jail cell floor—that his life had been worth living.

We squeezed his hand for the last time and made a vow. "When are we making our movie, Pops? . . . This year . . . this year . . ."

In death, our father gave us what he was unable to give us in life. From now on we'd be riding with the full force of his spirit. Nothing could stop us, not fear, not money, nothing. Only God could decide otherwise, and we hoped he was on our side.

From then on, either you were in, or you were in the way.

THE WEIGHT

JANUARY 2006 WAS spent on the business of death. We went to the jail a few days after the autopsy. They handed us a plastic bag. Inside was our dad's Wrangler jeans and cowboy boots, his sweater, down jacket, and the checkered wallet we gave him for Christmas when we were eight. There was a ticket stub from *King Kong* in his jacket pocket. It was dated December 19, the same day he was let out of jail and then thrown back in. We imagined him riding the bus from the Sonoma County Jail, hopping out, and walking through the rain to the nearest liquor store, drinking a pint of something cheap, and then staggering across the street into a warm movie theater to eat popcorn and be carried away from the pain for a few hours.

We cremated his body and held a wake for him at our mother's house. A couple of Fairfax cops showed up to pay their respects, dressed in uniform and all. It meant a lot to us. They were choked up. They liked our dad and felt terrible about his passing.

Then we tracked down our dad's few possessions, most of which he had stored with friends. A woman retrieved his belongings from his camp in the woods and gave them to us. She made a stone circle there in memory of him.

We knew where our dad wanted his ashes spread. But we weren't ready to let him go yet. So we placed the urn inside a wooden box he built for us when we were born and figured we'd know when it was time to set him free.

BURNING FOR BOOKS

"Our movie" was *Touching Home*. It was about the three of us, a nine- or ten-month period after Logan was released from the minor leagues and Noah flunked out of college. We came home and worked with our dad in order to save enough money to go down to Arizona for baseball tryouts, give our dream of playing in the major leagues one more shot. It was a desperate time, lots of tension, lots of fighting. It was a candid portrayal of our father's struggles with alcoholism and our own struggle for meaning.

Our dad had read the screenplay and looked forward to seeing it made into a movie one day. He thought that making movies was probably the next best thing to playing baseball for a living.

Movies, as everyone knows, cost big bucks—mountains of money. Currently, a low-budget movie is anything under $40 million. You can feed countries with those numbers. Writing, on the other hand, is comparatively free. Other than mental anguish, it costs you nothing, except for pen and paper. And if you can't afford that, there's always something you can find to receive your thoughts; a freshly painted wall, a park bench, a cave, the stall of a public restroom. And since the screenplay is the foundation of a movie, we figured (when we first got to Hollywood six years earlier) we should start at that fundamental level. After all, it was the cheapest part of the business. Start from the bottom and work our way to the top. It made sense.

During those years we "developed" (industry jargon for exploiting young writers) several scripts with producers around town. These were our ideas, scripts that we'd written independently—by way of coffee and mental pain. Producers had read them, liked them, and wanted to "develop" them with us. So we'd have a conference call here, a meeting there, incorporating some of their "notes" into the script, writing for free of course. Eventually they would try to sell our script to a studio, and when that failed, they would fail to return our phone calls . . . On to the next desperate writer.

Nothing had come of this path, largely, we thought, because someone else was in control of our future. Things were different now. We had resolved to go it alone. From now on, we'd be the producers.

ON THE DRIVE back to L.A. we listened to Bob Dylan and stared out the window at the passing farmland. When we arrived at our apartment, we threw our bags inside and walked to the bookstore. There was no time for self-pity. It was time to find out what we didn't know.

One month had already been ripped from the calendar. We needed to make a battle plan, devise a strategy for the road ahead. We wanted books by people who had actually *made* movies, not academic works on moviemaking, but practical experience from frontline soldiers. We walked over to the entertainment section and plunged in.

Two hours later:

"We need to buy these," Logan said, holding a stack of books.

"You're out of your mind," Noah said, adding up the sticker prices in his head. "We came here to read, not buy. If it's important, write it down."

"What do you want me to do, write down the whole damn book?"

"I don't know. Figure it out. You're a smart guy. We ain't buying anything."

"We're buying them."

"You got money?!" Noah yelled. " 'Cause I ain't got any money! Unless you got a stash I don't know about."

Noah has a flair for loud candor. He yells in public. He's the asshole who has the argument in the crowded elevator. It's not as if he's deliberately rude, because as soon as you point out he's yelling and disturbing others, he whispers. Yelling is just his habit of communication. He's what a therapist might call "passionate."

"I guarantee that whatever we spend on these books we'll make back a hundredfold," Logan said, pounding his fist into the cover of the *Guerrilla Filmmaker's Handbook*. He turned over the book and read the tagline to Noah. "*The Guerilla Filmmaker's Handbook* is *the* definitive guide. Buy it and save yourself thousands of dollars . . ."

The sales pitch hung in the air. Noah grabbed the book and flipped through it. We barely had enough money for rent. The business of death had drained our savings.

Fifteen minutes later Noah looked up from the book, a religious transformation in his eyes.

"We gotta buy this."

"All of them?" Logan said, referring to the stack.

"Yeah . . . all of them."

We hustled back to our apartment, brewed a pot of coffee, and dove into the stack of books, highlighting the pages, writing notes in the margins, composing a strategy in our notepads and most forcefully, in our minds.

Our mission was to obtain as much knowledge about movie production in the shortest time possible—a crash course in the business. We had the script and creative vision. Nothing happens without a script. Nothing. The script is EVERYTHING before it's something. And even when it becomes something, the script is always the bedrock. But what comes after the script? What we lacked was the list of elements needed to assemble this giant apparatus called a "production." We were ignorant, without experience, completely blind to the process of putting together a movie. We didn't know where to start. Who do we hire first? Who needs what? What goes with what? But we had instincts and common sense and soon formed a parallel between baseball and movies:

Baseball is a team sport. Making movies is team art. All we need to do is assemble the right team.

So rather than trying to understand the micro of every department—and they are infinite, as many departments as you want to create—we determined that the quickest and most sensible approach was to understand the macro, a broad-brush strategy to the enterprise. We'd heard it said many times by successful men and women: Hire the best and let them do their job. This would be one of our guiding principles. *(Admittedly, we hired some boneheads along the way, but for the most part we had a terrific team. After it was all over, we had assembled a cast and crew with eleven Academy Awards and twenty-eight nominations. But our story is a long ways from there right now.)*

THE ANGEL

A WEEK LATER Noah was buried in the *Guerrilla*, reading an interview of Lorette Bayle, a Kodak film representative.

"She sounds like a nice woman," Noah said. "I'm gonna call her and see if she can help us out."

Foolishly optimistic? Sure.

Harebrained? Yes.

Too simple? Of course.

But maybe, just maybe, naively brilliant.

Logan was skeptical, irritable. The kick from the first cup of coffee was wearing off, blood sugar dropping, eyes starting to burn. "Sure, go ahead, call her, see if she wants to help out a couple of strangers with a dream . . . Hi, I read your interview in this book and was wondering if you could help us out by donating some film to our movie that we don't have any money for, no crew, no cast, no nothing, other than a screenplay and a personal declaration."

Noah kept believing. Then Logan rolled his eyes and changed his outlook. "Why not? Let's do it."

It took us several phone calls to track down Lorette's number.

We called her and left a message. The worst that could happen was that she would say no. Big deal. We were accustomed to no. We figured that if we got enough no's we'd eventually find a yes. All we needed was one yes from which to build on. Only one. But we never thought the yes's would start coming our way so quickly.

LORETTE CALLED BACK a few days later. We were driving north on I-5 to do some location scouting back home. Cell phone reception is terrible on I-5. So we pulled off the road and into the parking lot of the restaurant with the giant windmill that serves world-famous split-pea soup.

"Tell me about your project," Lorette said.

Now, Lorette gets pitched about movies every day. Every day for almost seven years. She is a keen listener and can determine within a few sentences whether or not you have your act together.

When you're pitching a movie, you're selling. It's our opinion—take it for what it's worth—that selling a product is a war of attrition. Our primary jobs growing up were always manual labor—tearing off roofs, digging ditches, refinishing furniture, painting houses, washing dishes. There's very little selling involved in these jobs. Start digging here, dig to there. Start painting here, paint to there. Tear off the whole roof. These dishes need washing—see me when you're done.

From time to time, we'd sell *products* rather than our labor. We'd sell mistletoe around the holidays, firewood, Christmas trees, newspaper subscriptions, board games, parking spaces. To us, it just took grinding, hustling. Knock on enough doors, make enough phone calls, stand outside the grocery store and talk to enough people and we'd eventually sell our entire inventory.

It was no different now. We had a strong hunch that the same fundamentals applied to filmmaking. We needed to transmute a textual medium, our script, into a visual one, a movie. That required film. And Lorette Bayle had access to the largest storehouse of film in the world—the Kodak vault, the Federal Reserve of motion pictures.

Lorette listened to our pitch. We didn't stop talking for seven minutes. For seven minutes we rambled and digressed, finishing each other's sentences, a dizzying blizzard of swirling words and cell phone static.

"Sounds like an interesting project," Lorette said. "You guys have great vision. This is a project that Kodak would be willing to get behind . . . Now I can't give you an exact commitment from Kodak at this point, but what you should do in the meantime is call Ric Halpern at Panavision. He runs the New Filmmaker Program out there . . . Are you familiar with the program?"

"No."

"Have you booked a camera rental yet?"

"No . . ."

"Then call him. Here's his number . . . Get back to me after you've spoken to him."

We called Ric Halpern at Panavision on February 20. He was on vacation until March 1.

FOLLOW EVERY LEAD

Ricardo Galé was the first "Key" to come on board. A Key is a department head. We met Ricardo through a chain of phone calls. Each phone call went something like this:

"We're looking for a cinematographer. Do you know any?"

"No, call so-and-so. They might know one."

The first link was Gordon Radley, the only link on the chain we knew prior to the phone calls. Gordon is the former president of Lucasfilm turned philanthropist. He's a close friend and mentor. He's the only suit you'll ever meet with a tribal tattoo below his right eye from Malawi and a warrior band around his left wrist and calf from Western Samoa, tokens of brotherhood from the people he lived with during his Peace Corps years. He's read all the books on the shelf and lived in all those places too. He's Harvard Law and jungle ambassador. He's one of the few who have studied and lived it. And he just might be the toughest negotiator in the business.

Several years earlier, we met Gordon after we signed what he called "the worst contract I've ever seen" with some crooks and cowards in Northern California who hoodwinked us for the rights to one of our scripts—the notorious first-time writers, no lawyer present, carrot-in-front-of-the-starving-donkey contract.

Gordon took the initial meeting with us as a favor to a mutually dear friend, Gale Gough. (Gale is Coach Gough's wife. She was Gordon's assistant at Lucasfilm.) Gordon thought we'd go away after the initial consultation. But we didn't. We clung to him like desperate mountain climbers hanging from a ledge. He would become one of the executive producers of *Touching Home*. But not early on. First we had to prove ourselves. Gordon doesn't do anything for you that you can do for yourself. That's the genius of his instruction. He points you in the right direction and then kicks you in the ass.

We asked Gordon if he knew any cinematographers. He said no, "Call so-and-so. Here's her number."

We called so-and-so. Here's what she said: "Don't know any. Call so-and-so."

And so it went for three or four phone calls until a "so-and-so" gave us Ricardo's telephone number. We called Ricardo, met for coffee, gave him our script. He called the next day. "I want to shoot this movie."

Although supremely talented, Ricardo had given up on Hollywood in 2000. He was tired of the grind, the nasty, soulless aspects of the business. He had moved back to his native Miami and got a job at Restoration Hardware. He thought he'd never shoot again. His career was over. He was ready to sell his light meters, which, for a cinematographer, is akin to a painter selling his brushes. But then, as he was roaming linoleum floors, hawking bed linens and faucets, he received a call from a producer of a Swedish soap opera. They needed a cinematographer. And thus began his new voyage west, back into the belly of the beast—and us.

100 PERCENT LUCK

Anthony Sanders called us from Tucson a few days after we spoke to Lorette. He DID NOT KNOW we were making a movie. Anthony was Logan's roommate when they played minor league baseball for the Toronto Blue Jays. Years earlier, Anthony's family took us in when we were living in Tucson trying to get picked up by a major league club. At the time, we were staying at a transitional housing complex on East Twenty-second Street, the In N Up. It was a shithole. According to one newspaper, the In N Up's tenants consisted of "the evicted, addicted, convicted, and afflicted and their children," helping them, "avoid the streets, institutions and death." It was so dangerous it had its own police station. The city was trying to close it down.

As residents of the transitional housing complex, we were required to attend one meeting a week, a choice between Alcoholics Anonymous, Narcotics Anonymous, Anger Management, or Men's Group—where you discussed all three, sort of like an addict's free-for-all. We told them we weren't addicts. Of course, we were in denial. Forced to pick one, we chose Men's Group on Saturday mornings. It was a no-brainer. They served free pancakes and sausage. The syrup was amazing.

Anyway, you won't find better people than Anthony and his family. Anthony named one of his sons Logan Noah Sanders.

So Anthony called to tell us that he'd just signed with the Colorado Rockies and that he would be home in Tucson for spring training in case we wanted to visit. The profound effect of this phone call cannot be overstated. Coincidentally, the Colorado Rockies was the team Lane (Logan's character) plays for in *Touching Home*! Reid Park is where the Rockies hold spring training. We'd practiced on those fields with Anthony dozens of times when we lived in Tucson. If he'd signed with any other major league team, our movie might not have come together.

In strict numbers, the odds of Anthony signing with Colorado, as opposed to any other team, were 1 in 31. But there was nothing to guarantee that he *would* be signed by a team, let alone the Colorado Rockies. And the odds of Anthony signing with the team in the script, at the same time that we were putting our movie together, are well beyond our mathematical abilities to determine. Let's just say, astronomical.

Our immediate thought was: go down to Tucson for a day and shoot one of the spring training scenes in our script. Then cut the footage together and show it to prospective investors. We had to shoot something to demonstrate that we could direct *Touching Home*. Anything, even if it was just a few minutes.

We immediately called Ricardo and told him we had a connection with the Colorado Rockies.

"Get your gear ready, Ricardo. We're going to shoot a day of spring training. We leave in a week."

We started calling vendors and booking gear. We drove out to Tucson and scouted locations, worked with Peter Catalanotte at the Tucson Film Office and secured our permits. We didn't sleep much. Thank God for truck stops. We drove back to Los Angeles with everything in place.

And then our plans were nuked.

Ricardo called and told us that he couldn't shoot spring training; he'd just got hired on a low-budget slasher flick in Georgia. He was broke, needed the money. We saw disaster on the horizon. Was our movie doomed to fail? If we couldn't pull off *one* day of filming, how could we pull off an entire movie? It felt as though our ship had been torpedoed in the harbor.

But it wasn't sunk yet.

Ricardo would be back in a month, which at first thought, didn't do us much good, because spring training would be over by then. There wouldn't *be* any baseball to shoot. We needed more than cacti and Indian casinos. Ricardo felt horrible.

We hung up the phone and pondered our situation.

We needed to shoot spring training this year. Not next year, but this year.

What was the solution? There had to be one. As we would come to learn and adopt as a means of survival—everything was improvisational. We needed to accept and understand this concept as our *new* reality. When problems arose, we couldn't just throw money at them like larger productions. We had to be an adaptive force. Flexibility and quick thinking would be essential; make immediate decisions and act upon them—and work with the consequences, painful though they may be.

Should we call some other cinematographers?

"What about *extended* spring training?" Logan asked. "There will still be guys down there."

"For how many months?"

"Until mid-June."

It was now late February.

"How many players?" Noah asked.

"Forty or fifty . . . Enough to look like spring training in a movie. No one will know the difference."

We called Ricardo and told him we'd wait until he came back from Slasherville. We'd dealt with delays and setbacks before. Hell, our whole life up to this point felt like one big delay and setback. So we convinced ourselves that the delay would make us better, allow us to gather more knowledge, more time to prepare, compose a more thorough game plan. We'd be better by then. It was the luckiest failure we ever had.

A PANAVISION WITH VISION

IT WAS NOW March 1.

"What do you think, should we call Ric Halpern at Panavision?" Logan asked.

It was Ric's first day back from vacation.

We vacillated. Should we call or not call? He'd be swamped.

"Never wait for a phone call," Noah said, opening our cell phone. "We'll be the first phone call on his first day back. Somebody has to be that guy."

So we called Ric.

He answered. Not a secretary or assistant or voice mail, but the only man we needed to talk to, the man with the power—Ric Halpern. This event is so rare in Hollywood that it stalls the brain. It's never happened before or since. It may never happen again. You just can't get through to the Mifwic. Everyone has an assistant. Even the assistants have assistants. And if you get the assistant's voice mail, well, you're doomed. You never made that call. You don't even exist.

Our logic was that we'd call Ric in March to get a meeting in June, but probably more like July. When you're nobody, everyone cancels on you, whether they're busy or not. It's just part of the drill. "How many times have we rescheduled this thing?" "Five, sir." "Okay, cancel the meeting one more time and we'll take it next month."

"This is Ric."

He wasn't supposed to answer the phone. We didn't say any-thing.

" . . . Hello, this is Ric."

" . . . Uuuuuhhhh . . . Hey, Ric. This is the Miller Brothers."

"Who?"

The brain cleared. Thoughts were transmitted to our tongue.

"Lorette Bayle from Kodak told us to give you a buzz. We pitched her on our movie and she really likes it."

"My three o'clock meeting just canceled. What are you guys doing this afternoon?"

We looked at each other, bewildered. Does he want us to come out there today? TODAY? He can't possibly mean *today*. We're supposed to wait at least a few months for this sort of opportu-nity. How do we know this guy is even Ric Halpern?

"Hey, if you guys can't make it today, we can just schedule something for later—"

"No-we'll-see-you-at-three," we said rapid-fire.

We hung up the phone, slammed our laptop shut, ran out of our apartment, jumped in the car, and gunned it. Panavision was only thirty minutes away. Our meeting was in six hours. But we wanted to make sure we were there on time. You never know what can happen on the streets and freeways of Los Angeles, Califor-nia. Six-hour traffic jams? They happen.

THE PANAVISION NEW Filmmaker Grant could give us *credibility*, a commodity we lacked in spades. Of course this depended on us *receiving* the grant.

It would take a miracle to realize our movie in the time we wanted—to realize it at all. Because at this point, we were zeroes, nonentities, ciphers—the proverbial nobodies from nowhere. We needed to raise money—several million dollars by our calcula-tions—in a few months. In order to do this we needed things that we could sell other than ourselves—events, people, awards, who knows. We needed to build leverage out of nothing, 'cause right now, that's what we had—NOTHING.

It was one thing for us to set out to raise money with a script and a vision. That would be well received in the gumption department, but that was where it slammed into the guardrail and died. Past recipients of the Panavision New Filmmaker Grant included *Napoleon Dynamite* and Steven Soderbergh's first film *sex, lies, and videotape*. Both movies generated tens of millions of dollars at the box office and launched careers. If we could associate ourselves with these successes—by receiving the grant—we would significantly increase our chances of raising money. It would give us credibility.

We had to receive the grant. We needed this as much as anything we'd ever needed. And we knew this driving out there.

THE CATALYST

The receptionist told us that Ric wanted to meet in the espresso lounge. It was down the hall and to the right. We sat at a table. A bunch of technicians were leaning against the counter behind us, taking their afternoon coffee break and talking shit about everyone that walked by. We were sitting in the crosshairs of their ridicule, certain to be next. We had on collared shirts and khakis, backpacks, and oversize daily planners, a hybrid of schoolboy and Sherpa.

Waiting there for Ric felt like medieval surgery.

Ric showed up. We shook hands. He sat down. "Tell me about your movie."

No pleasantries, no "Where are you from," none of that crap. He wanted to hear our pitch. We got the firm impression that he wasn't looking for any new friends.

So we broke into our pitch. It was miserable. Our words collided. We stuttered, paused blindly. We were all mishmash and hogwash, balderdash and claptrap, bosh, piffle and hokum—the verbal fluency of a backfiring go-cart.

We were floundering and we knew it.

We started sweating.

And Ric sat there with his arms crossed and didn't say a word. For thirty minutes.

For thirty minutes he didn't say a word.

His face was expressionless. He was watching us drown. He was the *Omen* child.

We felt like ending the struggle, stop the pitch, shake his hand, thank him for his time, and leave. Never see the guy again. Hopefully he'd forget about ever meeting us. Our prospects of receiving the New Filmmaker Grant were irretrievably lost. We felt like failures, minds blasted with the events that led us here: our father's death, our vow to make our movie this year, all those years of hard work and struggle to get to this moment, and we were now failing. It was all some ridiculous plan.

We're making our movie this year. Sure, good luck guys. Why don't you go borrow your neighbor's home video camera and enter the YouTube Olympics?

Who were we to think that we could make a *real* movie?

All those years of discipline, and we had now failed.

Then Ric lifted us out of the water, mysteriously, inexplicably—MIRACULOUSLY.

"This is a movie that needs to be made," Ric said. "Panavision is going to back you one hundred percent."

What?

A man rushed over to Ric and whispered in his ear.

"Guys, I gotta go take care of something," Ric said to us. "I'll be back shortly."

And Ric was gone.

What the hell's going on? We'd just pitched ourselves and our movie for thirty minutes, miserably, convinced that we couldn't have performed any worse, when the man in charge stops us, and tells us the best possible result, "Panavision is going to back you ONE HUNDRED PERCENT," without even so much as opening the script, and as soon as those words leave his mouth, he disappears.

What would you think?

We stood up and looked around.

The espresso bar was now closed. It was silent in our corner of the building, as though everyone had gone home for the night, laughing their way through the parking lot at the gullible twins in the espresso bar with their collared shirts, backpacks, script, and oversize daily planners. How many times had they played this trick on aspiring filmmakers? The guy we just met wasn't even Ric Halpern. That's why we met him at the espresso bar instead of his office—because he doesn't even have an office. He's an imposter!

It had been too good, too easy. "Hey, come on out this afternoon. I'm free." He was free because he was a fraud. We'd heard *no* and been rejected thousands of times, and now suddenly, the cosmic fortunes were going to be in our favor?

Hardly.

We slumped into our chairs.

We waited five minutes. Still no Ric.

We waited ten minutes . . .

Then . . .

"Hey, guys. Sorry about that." Ric appeared from who knows where. "So as I was saying, Panavision is going to back you one hundred percent. You guys need a break, and I'm going to give it to you. Sounds like you haven't had many."

If there are earthly angels, then Ric Halpern is certainly one of them. We'd been working to meet this guy our entire lives.

"The grant doesn't provide you with any money, only equipment: cameras, lenses, camera bodies, and other gear, based on availability. Over the course of a feature-length film, however, it could save you hundreds of thousands of dollars . . . Now if I give you guys a camera package, are you going to promise me that you'll complete this movie, no matter what, no matter how little money you raise?"

"Yes."

"Good. Let's go meet some people."

He marched down the hall, narrating Panavision's celebrated history, pointing to the black-and-white photographs on the walls and the filmmakers and stories behind them.

"This is this and that is that," he said, all movement driving forward, nothing wasted laterally. "You guys want a crane? What about a Technocrane? Of course, you want a crane! We'll make this movie of yours look like a big-budget film."

Technocranes are an expensive and exquisite piece of equipment. They cost about five grand a day, prohibitive on our change-jar budget.

"Let's go see Rich Amadril. He's in charge of our remote systems." Ric made a hard right into the reception area. "Where's Mr. Amadril? Is he in his office?"

The secretary didn't have time to reply. Ric was already in Amadril's office.

Now, Ric Halpern is not a large man, at least not in the physical sense. But as you can tell, he's got the heart and balls of a rodeo king.

Rich Amadril, on the other hand, is a very tall man, standing nearly a foot taller than Ric.

"I'd like you to meet the Miller Brothers," Ric said, arms crossed, looking up at the face of Mount Amadril. "They have a very special project. We're going to back them one hundred percent. What can you do for them?"

Amadril was caught off guard, Ric, firm, staring up at him, looking like a young Teddy Roosevelt.

"Uhhhh, yeah, sure . . . Whatever they need . . ."

"Can you show them the Techno?" Ric asked.

"Sure."

There was a Technocrane in the corner of the loading bay, about twenty feet from us. Mechanics were wrenching on it. Amadril led us over to the crane and gave us a tutorial.

Then Ric took us on the grand tour of Panavision.

The building is an industrial labyrinth, single storied, covering several acres, hundreds of thousands of square feet. We explored the deep recesses and secret lockers. It was King Tut's tomb to the archaeologist, Cooperstown to the baseball nut. We looked through lenses that shot some of the greatest movies of all time.

We sat back down at the espresso bar. We still hadn't seen Ric's office.

"I'm going to give you guys a letter of endorsement. It's up to you guys to create the snowball. I'm also going to give you the telephone numbers of several vendors who work in coordination with the New Filmmaker Program. There's Lorette Bayle at Kodak, whom you've already spoken with, there's Allan Tudzin at FotoKem, the world's leading developer of negative, and there's Frank Kay at J. L. Fisher. Call them. Have lunch with them. Get the best deals you can. It's up to you guys to make it happen. I'm counting on you."

It's rare that the significance of an event is recognized immediately. Sitting there in Panavision, however, we knew instantly that our lives had changed. From then on, things would be different. We now had credibility. An industry leader believed in us. And we weren't going to let them down.

SOUND RANGER AND BOOM MAN VOOT

UNLIKE A HOME video camera, motion picture sound is not record-ed in the camera. It is recorded by a sound team, a discrete unit with its own instruments.

Ricardo was our cinematographer. So we had "Picture." To consummate the marriage, we needed "Sound." A *good* sound man. Make that a GREAT sound man, or rather, a team. The sound mixer is only as good as his boom man. The boom man is the guy that collects the sounds. His instrument is a long pole with a microphone on the end, "the boom." You typically see him in tai chi-like poses, his boom suspended inches above an actor's head, trying to find the ideal spot to capture sound. But this is a futile, Platonic quest. There is no ideal spot in this cave called Earth. He's always searching for pure sound, and invariably, there's always interference. He'll spend his life searching for an ideal take, and it will never happen, never, 'cause that microphone of his is so damn sensitive it can pick up the crunching of a Neanderthal walking on ice twenty thousand years ago. Like a philosopher seeking true knowledge, boom men and their brothers in arms, the sound mixer, are forever tormented. They'll NEVER find the perfect sound recording environment, and they know it. Yet they courageously persevere, day after bloody day.

Except for a few minutes of baseball in Tucson, *Touching Home* takes place in the pastoral landscape of West Marin, where we grew up. The sonic landscape needed depth, resonance, shades, and features to accompany its visual beauty. The rhythms of base-ball, the cacophony of a rock quarry, the tranquility of a redwood forest were characters, the sounds of which could intensify the emotional experience.

Poor sound is one of the distinct flaws of independent and low-budget movies. But it doesn't have to be this way. To their det-riment, many filmmakers overlook the sonic aspect of storytell-ing. They're preoccupied with picture, the moving image, what the camera is doing and seeing, a tricky shot or interesting angle. The movie doesn't necessarily *look* low-budget, but it sure as hell *sounds* like it. Poor sound has an insidious effect on the audience. It's not always perceptible to the average moviegoer, but they know something is off. The experience just doesn't feel right. Bad sound can kill a great performance, no matter how good the actor.

We called Richard Hymns.

Richard is a three-time Academy Award–winning supervising sound editor. *Jurassic Park, Saving Private Ryan, Indiana Jones*, that's him. He lives in Northern California and works at Sky-walker Ranch. We met Richard through a friend a few years back. One of the beauties of Northern California is that the filmmaking community is tiny. It's also tight-knit. If someone can help you out, they will.

Richard recommended several sound men. All highly distin-guished. They had worked for titans like Lucas, Spielberg, East-wood, Coppola, and so on. We started calling. The next day Richard fired us an e-mail with one more name: *Try this guy, Sound Ranger. He doesn't have the résumé of these other guys, but I just did a small movie with him and his recordings were excel-lent. Also, you probably can't afford the other guys, but you can afford him.*

So we called Sound Ranger. We met him for lunch at some greasy diner in the Valley and sat outside so he could smoke. The table was on the street, one of those endless boulevards that only

Los Angeles can produce, not quite freeway, not quite residential, long and straight and loud, throbbing with traffic and feral drivers, a jungle of radio stations and cranky horns. The table vibrated from the roar of that steamy cement swamp. And we were three of its creatures.

We ordered. We talked. We ate. Each bite was all-American slop mixed with hot exhaust.

Sound Ranger is a hardened veteran of low-budget horror movies. As he explained in his raspy, smoker's voice, "I just fell into them. They've paid the bills for twenty years." But he wanted to get out of that hamster wheel, wanted to make movies with substance, ones he would be proud of. He also wanted to work with Richard again, whom Sound Ranger called, "A sound god."

After the meal, Sound Ranger lit a cigarette, shifted in his seat. It was time to talk price. The uneasy moment had arrived, where all parties tacitly recognize that the friendly conversation is over and the negotiation has begun. And since nobody has invented a non-oily, subtle way of doing this, the best transition is usually no transition—cut out the crap and go to it.

"This is a non-union gig, right?" Sound Ranger asked. If the gig was union, there wouldn't be much of a negotiation; the rate was enshrined in a union contract, roughly $800 for a twelve-hour day.

"Yeah, non-union . . . If we could afford union rates, we'd pay them. But we can't."

"So what are you paying then?" Sound Ranger asked. "Are you going Favored Nations?" Favored Nations means different things in different industries, but in this case, he was referring to the practice of paying all the "Keys," the department heads, the same rate.

"We're paying our Keys three hundred a day. Flat rate. No overtime."

"Twelve-hour day?"

"Yes."

Sound Ranger took a drag. "Look, I'll give you guys a great deal. Fact is, I want to work with Richard again. It's a huge career move for me . . . But look, if I do this four-day gig for you, will you promise to bring me back when you shoot the rest of the movie—whenever that is?"

"If you do a good job, we'll bring you back."

"Will you put it in writing?"

"Sure."

"That's fair . . . I've got some hard costs that I can't get around. I need to cover my equipment rental, which includes microphones, mixing board, and my boom man Voot. I gotta take care of Voot. He works for me. I can take a pay cut, but he can't."

"Deal."

"I don't know how you boys got to Richard Hymns . . . ," he said, taking another drag from his cigarette, then chuckling, shaking his head—*what am I getting into?*

It's as though your movie is this giant electromagnet. If you have influential—magnetic—people aboard, whose names mean something to someone, for whatever reason—a name like Hymns's has little currency outside the sound world—then that magnet (your movie) attracts names like iron fuzz. You can get good people for cheap. If you don't have names attached, people will run from your movie like a stick of dynamite in an outhouse. And what stinks worse—you'll be forced to pay top dollar for mediocrity. Just about everyone in this business is a mercenary, and has to be; they are all independent contractors. They are on your show for a blip. You're just another plastic bumper on the assembly line.

We settled on a package deal with Sound Ranger; $3,000 for seven days (four shooting, two travel, and one prep), not including gas, per diem, hotel, and other incidentals.

We wrote and signed a piece of paper that said: "In the event that both parties are satisfied with the work rendered in Arizona, the Miller Brothers intend to hire the Sound Ranger (Randall Lawson) for the remainder of principal photography in Northern California."

After our lunch with Sound Ranger we drove back to Tucson and decided to expand our operations.

PART III

DESERT SHOOT-OUT

PONYTAIL DUDE
AND THE ROCKER

THE INITIAL PLAN for Tucson was to shoot pretty images of spring training with a long lens from outside the fence, cut it together, and make a trailer to show prospective investors. This would be a tool to raise money, nothing more. It would most likely be shot on video, unusable for *Touching Home,* which we planned to shoot on film, preferably 35 mm; if we couldn't afford 35 mm, then 16 mm. At that point, we just didn't have the financial resources or manpower to produce a quality piece of work. But now, three weeks later, our production had undergone a tectonic shift; we now had Panavision cameras, Kodak film, a veteran cinematographer, and an ace sound team. We were no longer going to waste our time recording unusable images. We had the firepower now. If we were shooting, then it was going to be in the movie.

We still had *extremely* limited funds, but we'd figure out a way to surmount this short-term obstacle.

So we decided to shoot ten pages of the script, all the scenes that take place in Tucson. This decision increased our workload exponentially. It demanded multiple locations: a college, interiors and exteriors, a dean's office, a library, a motel, baseball fields, access to highways and city streets; oh, and a rather important element, known in the industry as "actors." It was a prodigious undertaking for two guys. A typical production would have dozens of people in multiple departments handling this.

We started hustling around Tucson and soon met another angel.

We had scouted Pima Community College a few days earlier

and thought the location, perched on a hill overlooking Tucson, was visually stunning. In addition, there was ample parking and room to maneuver equipment, a significant production concern; if you can't get to it, you can't shoot it.

So we called Peter Catalanotte at the Tucson Film Office, and he gave us the phone number to the Pima Community College Film Department. We left a message with the head professor and didn't wait for him to call back.

We drove immediately to Pima and walked into the professor's office unannounced.

We gave him our pitch. He thought we were out of our minds. Don't think he'd ever heard guys talk so fast.

He was a big dude with a ponytail and he wanted us out of his hair.

"That's great guys. But we gotta go talk to the dean. Let's go see where she's at."

We followed him upstairs.

Victoria Cook was in her office. Once again, we had barged into someone's space without an appointment. She smiled and asked us to sit down. She looked amused. *Who are these guys? Twins?* People either immediately like us or immediately hate us. It's just the way it's always been. Nobody is ever on the fence with us. It's probably our energy. Like a rock concert at full blast, some can take it, some can't.

Our first impression: Vicki's a rocker.

We pitched our story. By the end, she was in tears. She had just emerged victorious from a two-year battle with cancer, her ear-length hair fighting its way back down to her shoulders. She had taken on death, and beat him. Put simply, she inspires.

"I think our school should be involved in this," Vicki said. "This would serve as a great example for our students. This is what education is all about. Can our students participate? I'm sure our film students would love to gain some hands-on experience, don't you think?" Vicki looked at the film professor. He was standing at the door, one foot out.

He nodded. "Of course." He still wasn't impressed. He was also a filmmaker.

"I need to get back to class," he said. We never saw him again.

"Where do you guys want to film?" Vicki asked.

"Well . . . pretty much everywhere," we said with a questioning smile. It was a massive stretch of a request.

"You just tell me the specific locations, and I'll put in a request with the board. It shouldn't be a problem."

Vicki took us on a tour of the campus and introduced us to baseball coaches Edgar Soto and Keith Francis. As mentioned, we had scouted Pima CC on our own a few days prior. Now we had the guided tour. The location was perfect for our movie. We thanked Vicki and went back to planning.

Another invaluable lesson was impressed on our minds, a lesson employed time and again throughout the making of *Touching Home:* always, always, whenever possible, meet in person. It's worth ten thousand phone calls and a lifetime of e-mails. Get face-time. Otherwise they'll only half believe you.

Never underestimate the human element.

OUR GRANDMOTHER LEFT us a message on our cell phone when we were with Vicki.

We called her as we pulled out of Pima Community College parking lot. Grandma told us that she phoned to apologize for not coming to our father's wake. He was the second son she'd lost.

"We understand, Grandma. So does Dad. We don't want you to worry about that. It's all right. Dad never wanted you to worry."

Nobody from our dad's family showed up for his wake. But we had no hard feelings. Our dad wasn't a man who held grudges. There was no point. Everyone grieves in their own way. And they preferred to grieve alone.

"I know he's so proud of you two," she said. Then her voice broke and she started crying. And so did we. Logan pulled over to the side of the road and we stayed there for some time.

Balancing our emotions turned out to be one of the greatest challenges. The loss was so fresh. Early on, the pain could hit at any time. But we had to push on. We had to be leaders.

When we got off the phone we cried some more, the red-rock sunset flooding into our car. We felt completely isolated, struggling to accomplish a vision that only we held, personal and perhaps foolishly idealistic, and in all likelihood, a failure. But there was an energy that we held in those lonely moments, a bond with Dad, a spiritual frequency that came to life after his death. Staring west across the desert and beyond that to the unseen world where the sun was heading filled us with a sense of power and a sense of the everlasting; that time holds no preference for anyone, it moves with or without you, and while you're here, you might as well be making good time and going after your dreams. Our dad would want that.

We wiped our eyes and drove thirty minutes across town to Anthony's house in Sabino Canyon at the base of Mount Lemmon. We were staying with him and his wife, Claudia, and their three sons, Logan, six, Marcus, three, and Troy, two. Exhausted, we opened our laptop and got to work, the kids jumping on us, videogames blaring, footballs and toys flying.

There was still a Herculean number of labors to complete before we started filming. And we had only two weeks. We had no actors, no secured locations, no permits, no shooting schedule, hotel rooms, food, insurance, equipment, travel arrangements for our crew 470 miles away—and a multitude of other as yet uncompleted requirements. And this was just the production side. We were also the creative force behind the movie. We needed to act and direct, each with its own manifold responsibilities. Where would the time come from? It was the one thing we could not produce.

Over the next two and a half weeks we spent four thousand minutes on our cell phone.

SERAPHIM

Tucson was floating with angels.

We wanted to film spring training. The real deal. Professional ballplayers. Not some fake re-creation with actors swinging sissy sticks. To accomplish this, we needed the okay from the City of Tucson, and if humanly possible, the okay from the Colorado Rockies. The former was likely, the latter, extremely *unlikely*.

Reid Park is city property. It's also the home of the Colorado Rockies Spring Training. It is managed and run by the Tucson Parks and Recreation. Peter Catalanotte started processing the paperwork for our permits to the fields, assuring us that filming there would not be a problem, so long as the Rockies weren't practicing at the time. But we told him that we WANTED the Rockies to be on the fields, that we WANTED to film them practicing. He smiled, chuckled—thought we were crazy—and told us that he would try to help any way he could. For starters, Peter didn't know anyone with the Rockies. And even if he did, it would still be nearly impossible to get permission to film the players. We told him to let us take care of that.

We were ex-ballplayers. We knew how the system worked. The front office, president, executives, the "Suits" would never, ever, not in Mother Charity's finest hour, allow two no-named filmmakers with no money to hop the fence and throw a movie camera and crew into the middle of spring training. For a large chunk of change—they'd certainly consider the request. But for free, and in the short time given for clearance—NEVER. You've never seen real baseball like this in a movie because IT DOES NOT HAPPEN. Major league teams are gearing up for the season, their core business. They don't give a rat's ass about some movie, and rightfully so. But we needed to depict reality. And that demanded we get on that field—at all costs.

So we started working the back channels through Anthony. He spoke to his friend and Rockies minor league coach, P. J. Carey, about our movie. They had known each other for years. Both are Tucson residents. P. J. had watched Anthony play since Anthony was in Little League, cranking homers all over town. And now, they were both part of the same major league organization.

P. J. was in charge of extended spring training, had been for years. Coincidentally, we had tried out for him years earlier when we were living in Tucson pursuing our baseball dreams. P. J. told Anthony that he would meet with us and see if he could help us out.

Anthony has experienced great tragedy in his short life. He lost his first son and wife, in separate instances, then his aunt was murdered by her husband, all in a six-year span, and we'd been through it with him. He'd do whatever he could for us, and we for him.

Anthony had a monster spring training, led the Rockies in home runs and RBIs, and on the last day, they released him. Yep. Leads them in *everything* and is released. It all came down to dollars. They had signed Anthony a month prior to spring training for a box of Cracker Jacks and a Diet Coke. It was a pittance, a nominal investment—an *expendable* investment. Conversely, they had substantial money invested in other players, and when it came time to free up roster space, well, you got it, money was supreme. They offered him a coaching job.

We were scheduled to have lunch with P. J. and Anthony the following day. P. J. had three days off before the start of extended spring training.

Anthony getting canned the day before our lunch with P. J. didn't bode well for our enterprise. We didn't sleep that night. We had the uneasy feeling that our train was about to be derailed. Anthony tried to relieve our anxiety by telling us that P. J. was good people, and that Anthony's release from the Rockies would not have a negative influence on our situation.

Several days earlier, Anthony had given our script to P. J. We figured that if P. J. read the script he would be compelled to help us. But the odds of him reading it during the height of spring training were slim.

Going into lunch, we felt as though our entire movie hinged on P. J.

WE MET P. J. at Chuy's Baja Broiler on the north side of town. Anthony was with us.

"So I read your script and started thinking—it was very good by the way," P. J. said. "Had me and my wife choked up."

P. J. breathes sincerity and compassion, an old-fashioned tobacco-spitting charmer from a Pennsylvania steel town, skin weathered from a lifetime spent on baseball fields under the sun.

"So anyways, I was thinking . . . What if we threw Lane, which one of you plays Lane?"

"I do," Logan said.

"What if we threw you in a Rockies's uniform and let you practice with us for two days? Would that work for your movie?"

He had to be kidding.

But he wasn't.

We tried to suppress our smiles, but they exploded.

"Yes, sir. That would definitely work," Noah said.

It felt as though the ghost of our father was staring at us through his eyes.

"I think it would be a great experience for our young ballplayers, get them used to being in front of a camera. I trust you kids. If Anthony named his son after you boys, then you gotta be good guys . . . Your script touched me. I've had my own battles with alcohol. I tell people you're allowed twenty thousand beers in your lifetime, and I had mine before I was thirty . . . I think your movie will touch a lot of people . . . Of course, you'll eventually need to get this approved by the front office."

THE FRONT OFFICE

Our primary concern, or more accurately, our primary fear, was the Colorado Rockies front office. The nightmare of them getting wind of our movie before we finished filming spring training was relentless. It threw us into severe paranoia.

What we were trying to pull off was equivalent to borrowing the marines for two days without the Pentagon finding out. Yes. This was our grand plan.

Who would even attempt something so stupid?

It was going to fail.

And yet it had to work.

Perhaps it was so stupid, so bold—remember: one person's bold is another person's stupid—that nobody would see it coming . . .

We told P. J. that we would contact the front office. We didn't say *when*, only that we *would*. We were the producers. It was our responsibility. We'd call them when we were done. But not before. Our survival depended on timing.

If someone from the front office in Denver called down to extended spring training in Tucson—which happens several times a day—and the man in Tucson, a clubee, coach, player, agent, groundskeeper, fan—pick one—intentionally or unintentionally mentioned that there was a film crew on the field making a movie with the ballplayers, we'd be arrested, thrown in the slammer, kicked off baseball fields forever.

The conversation might have gone down like this:

FRONT OFFICE GUY, smiling, upbeat, the sun shining in Denver: "How's everything going down there?"

COACH, smiling, chewing tobacco, sun shining in Tucson: "Great. Guys are working hard. The movie crew is having a blast out here, getting the shots they need, bought us all lunch. It's a pretty cool process. Didn't know it was so slow . . . But we're working around them."

FRONT OFFICE GUY, mouth open: "Movie?"

COACH, still smiling, spits a muddy stream of tobacco: "Yeah, the movie. The guys making the movie."

FRONT OFFICE, jaw clenching, a cold wind sweeping down from the Rockies: "What are you talking about?"

COACH, chuckling, he's having a ball: "The guys shooting a movie on the field with our players . . . Yeah, gave me a couple lines. I'm gonna be in a movie, can you believe that shit?! Holleewooood!"

THE FRONT OFFICE: NUCLEAR.

Our anxiety meters were pinging.
We had to keep this impossible secret, secret for a week.
Permission was inconceivable. We'd ask forgiveness later.
We weren't trying to cheat or swindle anyone. We were just trying to make our movie, a couple of guys with a dream, following their instincts to achieve it. After it was done, those involved would be proud, whether they had knowingly or unknowingly participated at the time.

Our father had been dead for just two months. We'd held his cold hand at the mortuary and swore we'd make our movie that year. We had made a vow. And we would do whatever it took to realize that commitment.

We were borrowing the marines. And there wasn't a damn thing the White House could do about it.

TRUCKIN' IT IN A CAR

WE DROVE BACK to Los Angeles (470 miles, one way). The fourth time in three weeks. We had to finish hiring our crew and booking equipment. Yes, we had Panavision cameras and Kodak film. But we also needed a bunch of other stuff: a grip truck and gear, lighting package, insurance, etc. . . .

So we went out to the Valley and negotiated deals with hard-bitten vipers of the moviemaking underworld. This is who you deal with when you don't have any money. You just hope you make it out of their hole without them sinking their fangs into your ass. These guys have been burned, ripped off, and underpaid countless times. It happens to everyone in this business, even the best. If you make it through the fire, you come out crafty and hardened, like a mobster who has survived a couple purges in the ranks.

These guys don't care about your story or the quality of your movie. They just want your money.

Typical conversation:

FIRST-TIME FILMMAKER: "Good morning, sir. How much are your lighting packages?"

HARD-BITTEN VIPER: "How much you got?"

FILMMAKER: "Well . . . uhhh . . . what's your cheapest package?"

VIPER: "It all depends."

FILMMAKER: "On what?"

VIPER: "How much you got?"

And so the negotiation goes . . . Never tell them how much you got. Make them tell you how much it *is*.

Our Tucson filming almost collapsed the last day in Los Angeles, hours before shipping out. Source of the problem: a Hardbitten Viper.

But that's another adventure. All you need to know is that it wasn't easy to get *here* from *there*.

ACTING SCHOOL FOR NONACTORS

Actors are important. And we had none. Other than ourselves, that is, and we had never been in front of a camera before, *or behind it*—but that's the director's position. We're talking acting now. We needed five baseball coaches (three with speaking roles), a community college dean, a tutor, and a few hundred extras.

Early on, we made phone calls to actors we felt would be suitable for the Tucson roles, actors we knew from L.A., actors suggested by *friends,* actors we had seen in movies.

One actor was mildly interested, told us to call his agent. Fair enough. So we called her. The wonderfully charming agent told us to call back when we "knew what we were talking about." Even the assistant was a bitch. This actor would later appear in *Touching Home,* in a much smaller role than we were currently offering.

He's no longer with that agent.

With no money and no SAG (Screen Actors Guild) contract in play—better have one if you plan on filming anything other than your cousin's wedding, actors are *very* serious about their union—we decided not to cast L.A. actors in the Tucson roles. Conclusion: hire locally, Tucson actors. Save money.

Now, our approach to acting is simple: tell the truth. That's it. Do that and you win. That's all the audience asks for: TRUTH. Bad acting is false. It's untruthful. No one likes to be lied to, whether in person or on the big screen.

Somewhere along the stretch of desert highway from L.A. to Tucson, possibly delusional from diesel fumes and sun, we seized upon this quixotic notion: Why not hire the real people? We met the real-life characters on our last trip to Tucson. Why not cast the real people as themselves? They play the part every day. Vicki can play the dean, P. J. the Rockies' coach, Edgar Soto and Keith Francis, the community college baseball coaches, and we'll find a tutor somewhere . . . perhaps . . . the school? The place should be crawling with tutors.

All we had to do now was sell this brilliant idea to these actors who had NEVER ACTED BEFORE.

"No way," Vicki said. She was petrified. "I'll ruin your movie."

"All you have to do is be yourself, Vicki. You play a dean every day. You *are* a dean."

We reminded her that she had just beat cancer. If she could beat cancer, then she could certainly act in our movie—she could be the dean. She slept on it, called us in the morning, and said she'd try. We assured her she was in good hands and that we wouldn't let her ruin our movie.

P. J. was also concerned about his acting ability. We told him the same thing. "All we're asking you to do is be yourself, P. J. Can you be yourself?"

"Sure . . . I think so . . . I've never tried to be myself. It's just something I do."

"You're hired."

Coach Soto and Francis, the community college baseball coaches, were easy. They loved the camera. They wanted to be stars. We promised them they would be.

Now all we needed was a tutor. So we strolled through the Pima CC drama department with our backpacks and oversize daily planners, odd, out of place.

We found the theater and stood at the door. A professor was giving a lecture. He looked over at us, a hundred heads followed. Then he said, "Can I help you?"

"The dean sent us down here." A partial truth. She gave us directions. "We're making a movie and we need an actor."

"Do you want to make an announcement?"

"No, sir, just a question. Who's your best actor?"

"Evan." The professor pointed.

"We'll take him."

REHEARSALS: FIRST, THE PHONE

Baseball, and sports in general, taught us the importance of fundamentals. Start simple and gradually build toward more complex movements. The best hitters in the world, Ichiro, Manny, A-Rod, still take batting practice, still hit off a batting tee before games, same as a five-year-old.

Why would acting be different?

The first drill: READING. Actors read the script before they perform, some more than others, some hundreds of times. No different than hitting off a batting tee. We needed to create a safe, controlled environment for our actors, an environment conducive to repetitive exercises, one that would build their trust and confidence.

We held our first rehearsals over the phone. Our actors were in Arizona, and we were in L.A. No one besides Evan had any acting experience, and none of them, including Evan, had ever acted in front of a camera. So we started with a simple exercise by reading the dialogue in the script with no emotion. Back and forth over the phone, ten times each, just to get them comfortable with the lines, the natural rhythm and cadence of the writing.

"Don't try and act, we're just reading the words on the paper . . . No emotion. We don't even know what ACTING is right now."

The first rehearsals were challenging. Our actors' inexperience was painful. So was ours. This was just an experiment, mind you. They'd never acted, and we'd never directed.

So we read with them over the phone, in the morning and in the evening, every day for a week. When we returned to Tucson, we rehearsed in person for another week—twice a day, driving to our emerging actors, all over town, wherever they might be. We rehearsed with them before they went to work, on their coffee break, over breakfast, at baseball practice, everywhere we could.

Were we nuts? Maybe. But we had confidence in our abilities as directors and confidence in our actors' abilities to be themselves.

THE 10:1 TO ZOOMA

OUR FIRST ASSISTANT director, Connie Hoy, cinematographer, Ricardo, his first assistant, Lenny, Sound Ranger and Voot, two grunkeys and a box truck, and several buddies from back home constituted our Arizona crew. The bulk of financial contributions were provided by an army of credit cards we'd accumulated over the past several years. During that span, every time we received a solicitation from a credit card company in the mail, espousing the glorious benefits of free money, we promptly filled out the application and sent it back. A week or two later we'd receive a new credit card. Like poverty, it was the gift that kept on giving. It was guaranteed success in an unsuccessful time.

Armed with seventeen of these plastic time bombs and ten grand borrowed from a couple buddies back home, we drove out to Arizona for four days of filming.

We were worth forty-five thousand dollars.

The day before shooting we conducted a location scout with our skeleton crew. The first part of the day went smoothly. It was now late afternoon, and a warm desert breeze carried the sweetness of sagebrush as we stood in the bullpen of the Pima CC baseball field, the last stop on the scout.

"FUCK!!!" Ricardo screamed, collapsing onto the grass, twisting in pain, forearm across his brow. We thought he was dying. "I need a zoom! I can't do it without a 10-to-1 zoom, guys. I can't do what you want me to do . . . Damnit, I need a zoom. Fuck me, you idiot!" Then the Spanish cuss words started flying.

"I'll call Panavision," Noah said.

"They don't have any!" More Spanish cuss words. "They're all booked. I asked for a zoom before I left."

"We gotta try," Noah said.

Ricardo was despondent, staring at the sky. "Even if they have one now, it'll never make it out here on time. It won't make it out here till midday. There's no way we can make our shooting schedule with prime lenses. No way."

Noah pulled out our cell phone. There was no reception. So he ran to right field, waving the cell phone overhead, nothing there, onto left field, nothing there either, then to second base. Still no reception.

He ran across the infield and climbed on top of the dugout. "I got reception!"

He called Ric Halpern at Panavision.

"Ric, we're screwed. We absolutely have to have a 10-to-1 zoom for tomorrow."

"We don't have any."

"We're dead if we don't get one. We need a zoom."

"We don't have any. We're all out. I'd give it to you if we had one, but we don't."

"Are you sure?"

"I can check down at the receiving counter . . . But I KNOW that we don't have any."

"Please. Could you please do that for us? Could you at least check?"

"I'll call you back in five."

It was silent on the field. Our crew sat on the grass: Ricky, Lenny, Connie—downcast, hopeless. Without a 10-to-1 zoom, tomorrow was doomed. (Don't worry about all the jargon, zoom lenses, prime lenses. All you need to know is that WITHOUT A ZOOM, TOMORROW WAS DOOMED.)

Ric called back. "I got one."

Noah started jumping atop the dugout. "He's got a zoom! Ric's got a zoom!"

"It doesn't matter!" Ricardo yelled to the heavens, still lying on his back. "It will never get here on time! Is anybody fucking listening to me?!"

Atop the dugout: Noah was still jumping, the phone to his ear.

Ric said, "You're not going to believe this. But I was walking back from receiving, empty-handed, and I passed some guy pushing a cart with a 10-to-1 zoom on top. And now it's yours. I can't believe it. I can make FedEx, but it won't get to you until mid-morning, which is probably too late. When's your call time?"

"Five-forty-five."

"Yeah, it'll never make it."

"Let me make a phone call," Noah said. "I'll call you right back."

Noah yelled down to us on the grass. "I'm calling Sound Ranger. His shop is right down the street from Panavision. Maybe he hasn't left L.A. yet."

Sound Ranger was supposed to be on the road three hours ago.

Noah called Sound Ranger. "Sound Ranger, where you at?"

"Dude, look, I'm sorry, but I'm running a little behind. I got held up at the shop. Don't worry, though, I'll be out there tonight."

"Perfect. We need you to pick something up for us at Panavision."

"I'm *at* Panavision."

"You're kidding?"

"No, I'm here right now. That's crazy . . . I haven't been here in ten years. What do you need?"

"A zoom."

LITTLE ANGRY

Our crew had witnessed scores of confident first-time directors charge headlong into a tidal wave, swallowed forever. As a consequence, they were emotionally reserved, skeptical of the two greenhorns leading them onto the field in the morning.

"Does anyone know what we're doing?" a senior member of the crew asked over drinks the night before shooting. Let's call him Little Angry. "It would be nice if *someone* knew. That way they could tell *me* what we're doing so I can be prepared. Because it sure as hell seems like nobody has a clue what we're doing tomorrow."

We were sitting at an outdoor table in a grove of palm trees at the Old Pueblo Grill. We hardly knew any of these people.

Little Angry was older than us by three decades and angry about it. He had insulted us in front of the crew, tried to project an air of dominance, undermine our leadership at the moment we were trying to establish it. Under normal circumstances, Little Angry would have been fired, stripped naked, and hog-tied to a cactus. But he knew our situation prevented that. We were 470 miles from base camp. He had all the gear; without him, no show.

Connie told Little Angry the little plan for tomorrow. It quieted his anger for the night. Little Angry could now sleep happily.

WE WALKED BACK to the hotel. We were sharing a room with our buddy Pierson, a talented film editor, sailor, and real-life Eagle Scout, as solid as they come. He's also one of the first people we met in Los Angeles, seven years earlier, on a Jennifer Lopez video shoot. He was working as a production assistant, a month out of film school. We were extras, our first and last time in that role. In between takes, the extras were sent to a holding stage the size of an airplane hangar. Pierson was in charge of detaining the extras. He saw us writing on our notepads, arguing about a scene. He asked what we were doing. We told him writing a screenplay, *Touching Home*, the same screenplay that he was now helping come to life after years of struggle.

We drank a Budweiser and reminisced about the low times and the broke times, and all the times in between when it felt like it would never happen. It was good to be there with someone who'd been there from the beginning. We all went to bed, smiling.

Pierson slept. But we didn't, not a wink. Our nerves were humming. Too many things could go wrong tomorrow.

TWIN CHAOS AND THE BATTLE OF THE GREASY GRASS

EVERYONE MET IN the lobby at 5:45 A.M. It was still night outside. We hopped into our cars and headed to Reid Park, the spring training home of the Colorado Rockies.

FIRST SHOT: Capture the sunrise over the baseball fields.

The camera was set, the sun peaked over the mountains, the dew sparkled in the first rays, and we rolled film. Our first shot as directors was complete. We rolled a second take for insurance. It was intoxicating. We had seized destiny by the throat and strangled the courage out of it.

We loaded our gear onto a golf cart that we had borrowed from the grounds crew and sped over to the stadium clock for our second camera position. An hour later it was time to put actors into the frame.

LOGAN:

I had never been in front of a movie camera before. I was nervous, same as before a big game. But I wasn't hesitant, wasn't afraid. There are two types of nervousness: one that wants to delay the action and another that's eager to get it on. I was eager to get it on, eager to confront the challenge.

"Action," Noah said.

I walked through the center-field gate with my equipment bag and onto the damp field. "Cut." There was a technical error. So we shot it again. After a few takes my nerves calmed.

I also made a valuable observation at that moment, one that would inform our decisions not only as actors, but perhaps more importantly, as directors: The actor isn't the only person who can screw up the scene. Any number of technicians can butcher the take and render it unusable. It's a bracing concept. It mitigates your stress. What's even more emancipating is that you shoot more than one take per scene. You get more than one try. If you don't get it right the first time, try again. If you can bat three hundred in filmmaking, you're kicking ass. (Similarly, the actor can pull off the greatest two-minute performance of his or her life and it can be unusable for the above-mentioned reasons, be they man-made or machine-made.)

Then the Rockies came out of the locker room. I sat on the grass and stretched with them. They started giving me shit. A guy in the back row, in a girlie voice: "Oh, he's pretty. I bet he's an actor. I wanna be in the movie. I wanna be in the movie." He stood up and pranced and skipped and paraded around the grass like Pippi Longstocking. "Weeeee."

Fifty guys laughed. A few started mouthing off.

By their estimation, I hadn't earned the right to be out there. For all they knew I was some Hollywood dick pretending to be a baseball player. These guys had worked their entire life to get here. I hadn't suffered through eighteen-hour bus rides, slept in one crappy motel after another, traveling so much that you don't even know where you're at, what town you're in, bloated on shitty food that's been sitting under a heat lamp at a gas station for two days, eating this fried jerky-thing because it's late and all the restaurants are closed, battling diarrhea the next day as you try to survive the game in the blurring humidity of some southern state, sleeping on buses, forced to live with guys you just met whose mama never taught them how to pick up after themselves.

Nevertheless, all that cruel and unusual punishment still didn't give them the right to be assholes. But it's easy to understand why they were. If you had an ulcer at nineteen, you'd be in a bad way too.

I kept my mouth shut. What they didn't know was that I was a former minor leaguer. I had been in the same position as them years earlier, fighting for a job, fighting for the dream.

I knew that once we started playing catch they would shut up real quick. I could still hold my own on a baseball field, could still throw better than 75 percent of them.

The laughs played off the other laughs. Every guy was now funny and tough. We couldn't play catch soon enough.

Even the biggest pussy in the group was talking smack.

Finally, we stopped stretching. Everyone grabbed a partner and started playing catch. I grabbed a ball, but nobody would throw with me.

Noah, pissed off, surrounded by shit-talking ballplayers and a skeptical crew, yelled at me.

"Logan, play catch with someone! Let's go! We need a shot of this!"

But I couldn't find anyone to play catch with. All the players were standing on the foul line throwing with other guys. Noah spotted a catcher playing three-way. He ran over to him.

"Hey, will you help us out and play catch with my brother?"

The guy nodded grudgingly. Having to play catch with the Hollywood dick was humiliating for him.

I stood on the line and he started backing up. He said something smart as he walked backward into the outfield. Then he threw me the ball. I caught it and threw it back with a little speed on it. It nearly hit him in the chest. His eyes widened, surprised.

"Back up," I said after a few throws. Then I started throwing bullets. The players started glancing at me, trying not to show too much interest. They could hear the ball whizzing out of my hand, the pop of the glove I was throwing into. Hollywood dicks aren't supposed to throw like that.

We played catch for about five minutes. A coach called everybody in from the outfield. One of the players asked, "Did you used to play ball?"

"Yeah . . . I played in the minor leagues for the Toronto Blue Jays."

"No shit?"

"Yeah, no shit."

I jogged over to my equipment bag and started putting on my catcher's gear. For the next couple hours, I traveled from station to station, running through the drills with the catchers, grinding it out with them in the dust and the heat, blocking balls, throwing to bases, working as hard as I could as the camera rolled.

By the end of the drills, I had earned their respect. The next day, I was one of them. They turned out to be a terrific group of guys, and we'll always be grateful to them for helping us out. We had a lot of fun. My arm is still killing me. Thanks, fellas.

NOAH:

My day started off unexpectedly smooth and pleasant. But the earthquake, tornado, and hurricane were on their way, galloping in all their career-ruining glory alongside the Four Horsemen— the perfect storm of personal disaster. But that's still a couple hours away.

Back to the smooth and pleasant morning.

We arrived at Reid Park at 5:50 A.M. The parking lot was empty, just us and our film crew: fresh coffee, muffins, doughnuts, songbirds greeting the dawn.

All was at one, the world in harmony—fat pills and caffeine in every belly.

We rattled off a few beauty shots before the minor league players took the field. All was still calm.

In the preceding weeks, we had composed a detailed shot list and taken hundreds of photographs with our digital camera to demonstrate the movements of each scene. We were prepared. We knew what we wanted. However, this brilliant plan was soon to be thrown out like so many other brilliant PLANS the moment it met reality. The turbulence of the day would impose its own style of shooting: improvisational, unrehearsed—all instincts from here on.

There are two preconditions to narrative filmmaking: *time* and *control*. *Time* to set up your equipment, and *control* of the environment, that is, your actors, props, and crew.

We operated under the conditions of *time* and *control* for the first hour of filming. But they were about to evaporate.

Now, the average day of spring training consists of drills in the morning followed by a game in the afternoon. In the morning session, the players move around the field to various stations: fielding ground balls, taking batting practice, base running. The players are typically divided into groups according to their defensive positions. Each group spends roughly fifteen to thirty minutes at each station.

Today, they were spending only TEN.

And that's where the moviemaking equation starts to fail. The movie needs FIFTEEN minutes. That's right, FIFTEEN. The Rockies were only giving us TEN. Square peg, round hole. The beginning of chaos.

If you're operating at light speed, you can execute one camera position, "a setup," every FIFTEEN minutes. Anything faster than that is assumed to be physically impossible. You can't just point and shoot. There are numerous measurements and calculations that need to be performed before you can successfully roll film through the camera. If not, the image will be unacceptable; the audience will laugh your movie out of the theater.

Even more troubling, sound is recorded separately. So you need to have *both* sound *and* camera departments, with all their accompanying gear and personnel, operational before you can film. It's an interdependent relationship—unless you want to shoot a silent movie.

Sure, a few movie crews have moved faster than FIFTEEN minutes. But they are not human. We humans need FIFTEEN.

I was getting massacred. I felt like Custer at Little Big Horn, the players—the Lakota and Cheyenne—circling me on their warhorses, howling, dizzying, as we tried to follow and capture them in the camera.

Lenny, our skinny first AC, lugging around the eighty-pound camera, straining under the weight, was the first to become unhinged. "Where's the camera going next, Noah? You're the fucking director! Where's this fucking thing going?!"

His feet were sinking into the greasy grass, a tomahawk in his back, about to lose his scalp. No wonder he was pissed. I'd led him into a trap.

"Wherever he goes," I said, pointing to my brother, who was now reliving his dream of professional baseball as I was being riddled with verbal arrows from our crew.

We finally got a shot of Logan stretching with the players, kicking his leg in the air, a shot that made it into the movie. All these shots are called "oner's," that is, you only get one chance to get the shot. If we didn't get the shot, we'd be screwed, no going back and reshooting. This was a one-time opportunity. We didn't have the luxury of multiple takes or video playback, standard for narrative filmmaking.

The ballplayers were moving around the field too quickly for us to follow, working for only ten minutes at each station. We needed fifteen. The crew was witnessing disaster.

Adapt or fail.

So I started predicting where and what drills the players would do next, anticipating their movements, gambling, giving up one set of drills to capture another. Not trying to film everything. Being selective. If it paid off, we'd get a shot. If not, oh well, same outcome as if we tried to move with them. Had to gamble. Had to risk everything.

The environment became exhilarating for our crew. It was novel. Here we were, running around the spring training complex, five fields in all, with a full-access pass, throwing the camera in the middle of the action, shooting a narrative film in a documentary fashion.

Ricardo knew less about baseball than any American we'd ever met: *pitcher, hitter, third base* were all foreign words. But this was a *good* thing for us. He'd put the camera wherever we wanted. His ignorance made him fearless of the destructive powers of a screaming line drive. He did a great job, a *brave* job.

We threw the camera behind the pitcher's mound during batting practice, alongside the catcher's in the bullpen, extremely hazardous and yet fantastic positions to film from. An errant line drive or throw would have ended the shoot. But the stakes made it all the more exciting. If we were going down, at least we'd go down with our balls on the anvil.

By the time the Rockies broke for lunch, we had twenty-five setups in the can, the equivalent of a day and a half of work. At 9 A.M., the crew had no confidence in its directors. By lunchtime, they'd follow us anywhere.

THE STADIUM AND A
MAN CALLED HONCHO

IT WAS A dramatic set piece; finely manicured grass, stadium seats, towers of lights, and a wooden outfield wall with old-style billboards painted on it. We saw it and had to shoot it. We wrote a scene for it on the spot.

It would add considerable production value; make our little movie look like a big movie, or at least not an impoverished one.

We phoned Peter Catalanotte at the Tucson Film Office.

"Peter, we wanna shoot at the stadium."

"It's gonna be expensive, guys."

"We need it for free."

He laughed. "I'll see what I can do, see if they'll waive the fee for you guys."

"Give us the phone number and we'll tag team them. We don't have much time."

Peter gave us the number.

We phoned the guy in charge of the stadium. Let's call him "Honcho." He wasn't in his office. We left a message. Honcho returned our call at 6 A.M. the following morning. No joke. That's right. 6 A.M. on the nose. This guy was tough, ate cow teeth and vampire piss for breakfast. We were working out at Gold's Gym in Tucson and the call went straight to voice mail. Here's what he said:

"This is Honcho. I got word you wanted to film inside the stadium, wanted some kind of discount. No discount, guys. You either come up with the money or find a way to make your movie without it."

The stadium cost $1,500 for the night. Sounds cheap. But on our budget, impossible. A studio would have written a check for ten times that amount, without so much as a chili dog burp from one of their accountants.

So we called back Honcho and persuaded him to meet us down at the Rockies spring training complex, in person. This was no easy task, even though his office was a hundred yards away. It took fifteen minutes of pleading over the phone.

"You must be the movie guys," Honcho said as he stepped out of his golf cart. His sunglasses were huge.

"Yes, sir," we said, shaking his hand.

"I know you movie guys. You cry broke when you're swimming in cash."

"We are broke."

"Sure you are. I know you movie guys. You roll into town like you own the place. Well, guess what? There's no red carpet here."

"We're not a studio, sir. We're an independent film company."

It didn't register with him. All movie guys were the same.

We pitched him on the merits of the project, about our sponsors and endorsements: Panavision, Kodak, FotoKem, yada yada yada. Surely he could flow with the spirit of the film—the spirit of giving. We needed to shoot inside the stadium, at a discount—the 90 percent-type discount.

"Find the money," he would say. "I know you movie guys."

"If we could, we would, sir. The stadium is worth ten times what you're asking. We're not a studio. This is an independent film, a grant project."

"Find the money."

"We used to live in Tucson."

He didn't hear that one. No matter what we said, he repeated his mantra: "I know you movie guys."

We continued pleading.

He wasn't budging.

It was looking bleak.

And then our dad intervened again.

Jon, the head groundskeeper, walked over. "Hey, Honcho . . . Hey, Logan, hey, Noah."

Honcho hadn't felt a shock like this since the lightning storm of '92.

"Jon, you know these guys?" Honcho threw up his hands. "You don't know any movie guys, Jon . . . How do you know these guys? . . . Why didn't you tell me you knew these guys?"

"These are Anthony Sander's friends. He named one of his sons after them. My dad is married to Anthony's mother-in-law. Logan and Anthony played ball together with the Blue Jays."

Anthony is a Tucson legend, an all-American high school football player, major leaguer, and Olympic gold medal winner. His name is high currency. It's backed by gold, literally.

Honcho paused. He turned and walked a few paces, looked down at the green grass and then up to the blue sky, mentally wrestling with colors. He wasn't in the charity business. He had a reputation for being a hard-ass, was paid to be a hard-ass. He needed to maintain that image.

He took a deep breath, held it in, then sighed. His sunglasses were huge.

"Can you make your film without the stadium?" Honcho asked.

"No, sir."

"C'mon! Why not?! A field is a field."

He knew this wasn't true.

Then Noah said, "At this moment in the movie, sir, the brothers are living their childhood dream. They're on their way. Just imagine it, alone in a stadium under the lights, taking batting practice with your brother, a dream that you've shared together your entire life. Every kid dreams of practicing in his own private stadium. It's a magical scene . . . We need that stadium, sir."

"The stadium does look pretty damn good right now," Jon added.

Honcho sighed, looked down at the green grass again and back up at the blue sky.

"Let's take a walk, Jon."

They walked and talked. We watched them for five minutes. They came back. Honcho spoke.

"You guys are lucky that Jon is a good man." Honcho had found a way to save face and be a nice guy at the same time. He had to maintain the perception that he was a hard-ass. And Jon could rescue him from his reputation.

"Can you guys afford five hundred dollars?" Honcho asked.

"No, sir." It was the truth. We couldn't.

Honcho shook his head. *What can I do with these guys?* He looked down to green, looked up to blue. *Make them go AWAY.* He frowned, put his palm on his forehead. Then he said:

"Fine. Here's what I can do for you. You're lucky Jon likes you two, 'cause I don't. The only reason I'm doing this is because of Jon. He's a great worker . . . Jon said he's willing to stick around Saturday night and open up the stadium for you. You gotta be out of there by eleven-thirty. City ordinance."

"No problem," we said.

"How much can you guys pay? I'm not going to let Jon do this for free, you hear me?"

"That's all right, Honcho," Jon interrupted. "I don't mind helping these guys out."

"No way!" Honcho said, slamming the heel of his cowboy boot into the grass. "These guys are gonna come up with something to pay you, Jon. They need to pay you *something*." Honcho pointed at Jon, then at us. "I know you movie guys."

We stood there silent.

Honcho threw his arms in the air again, exasperated. "You'll pay Jon two hundred and nothing less. You hear me, Jon?" He looked hard at Jon. "I don't care if you boys have to sell Kool-Aid to come up with the money. If anyone asks, I don't know about this. I don't know who you are. If someone calls me about a film crew inside the stadium, as far as I know, you guys are trespassing . . . I don't know any movie guys."

Honcho turned his back to us and climbed into his golf cart. "Good luck with your movie," he said over his shoulder as he drove away.

SOMBREROS IN THE NIGHT: ME TEQUILA, YOU TEQUILA

It glowed magical under the lights. The electric hum wrapped the stadium in a sonic shell, muting the city noise. It was as though we alone existed. Our crew was mesmerized, we were mesmerized. Our own stadium. We were living the dream as we walked through the left field gate and across the outfield grass.

We didn't have time for a technical scout with Ricardo, which is a big deal. You just don't shoot without a technical scout and expect greatness, or even mediocrity. You expect disaster.

Ricardo's main concern was the lights. Cinematographers are paid to control light. He wouldn't be able to control the stadium lights, and that worried him. "Guys, there's no guarantees here," Ricardo said. "I don't know anything about these lights. This scene could look like ass."

He pulled out his light meter, held it in the air.

"Jeez . . . Never mind, this place is perfect."

In the movie, the brothers give the groundskeeper a case of beer in exchange for an hour on the field. It's night, the stadium empty. The brothers take batting practice. It's an important moment for them, the last rise before the fall, before their baseball hopes are dashed . . .

So we shot the batting practice scene from six or seven camera positions, smooth, effortless, Logan cracking the ball all over the park. It was now time for the "martini." (The martini is the last shot of the working day. In this case, the night.)

There was a visual trick we wanted to pull off on this last shot. Here was the idea: Logan hits the ball over the fence and circles the bases as the lights go out, in order, from right to left. When he touches first base, the lights on the right side of the field turn off. When he touches second, the lights in center field turn off, and so on as he circles the bases until he lands on home plate and the entire stadium crashes to black.

All this needed to be performed on the field, what's called "in camera," one miraculous take, no special effects, no computer wizardry to aid the shot. Very, very difficult! The stadium lights needed to be turned off manually. The timing had to be perfect. We would only have one chance. And the human chain required to pull this off made it even more difficult. It required everybody—EVERYBODY—even the drunks.

THE HUMAN CHAIN OF DRUNKENNESS

The muscle we brought to Tucson, two of our good buddies from Northern California, modern-day Celtic warriors, Nate and Taylor, and two of their buddies from Southern California, Brooks and Andy, got thirsty and started shotgunning beers and shooting Cuervo in the bleachers after they unloaded the equipment. They had been working in the desert sun since 6 A.M., for free. They were volunteers, and they were now voluntarily going to get drunk. This was a working vacation for them.

We asked them not to swim too deep into the booze. We still needed them for the last shot of the night. They assured us they would be able to perform.

In between takes, one of us would yell up to the muscle in the stands, "Guys, you okay?"

"Yeah, yeah, we're fine up here," someone would reply, an empty beer can cartwheeling down the cement steps.

"Why don't you guys slow down?"

"Don't worry about the lights," Jon, the head groundskeeper, would say. It was Saturday night. He was hanging out and drinking with the muscle. "We got it covered. No problem. Quit worrying."

They would rag us in between takes. "Miller, you're a bum. Get him out of the game . . . Hey, Noah, you throw like a girl. Hey, Logan, your brother's ugly."

We started filming around 8 P.M. It was now 11 P.M., time for the final shot. The camera was placed behind home plate, all the way against the backstop.

We called the muscle down from the stands. They were wearing huge sombreros. Some of them were cross-eyed. They had to lean against the wall to stand.

Noah sighed, dropped his head. He didn't bother asking where they got the hats.

"We're ready, Captain," Nate said, standing at attention. He saluted. They all saluted.

"We've been rehearsing all night . . . in our minds," Jon said. "My boys are trained." He was just as drunk as they were. "C'mon, boys, let's show 'em what we got!"

We climbed into the stands and followed Jon and his staggering crew. Their trail of breath was like jet vapor.

"I thought you guys stopped drinking?" Noah asked.

"We did. Now we're drunk," Nate replied.

The switchboard for the lights was in a bunker underneath the stadium, down a maze of dark cement hallways. It looked like a serial killer's workshop. There was no cell phone reception down there. We didn't have walkie-talkies. This meant that the signal to turn off the lights needed to be orally relayed, from the field, through the maze, and into the bunker. This required a human chain.

"Who's the least drunk?" Noah asked.

"I am," Taylor said.

"No you're not," Nate said. "I am."

"You're right. I lied. I'm a pirate."

Here was the plan: Nate would be in the stands watching Logan circle the bases. Just before Logan touched each base, Nate would yell "NOW" down the hallway to Brooks. Once Brooks heard "NOW," he would yell "NOW," down *his* hallway to Andy, who, once hearing Brooks's "NOW" would then yell "NOW" into the bunker, where Taylor and Jon would manually turn off the lights. Each section of lights corresponded to a specific base. First base had its own quadrant, second base had its own, third base, and home plate.

Before all this could happen, Noah needed to pitch the ball to Logan, who needed to hit the ball over the fence. No small feat. Ricky needed to capture the image. Sound Ranger and Voot needed to capture the sound. Everybody needed to be perfect, especially the human chain. One take was all we'd get to pull off a fantastically complex operation, anchored by a bunch of cross-eyed drunks.

Where in history has this combination produced success?

So we rehearsed it a few times. Logan would stutter-step just before hitting each base, cueing Nate to begin the drunken chain of yells.

Finally, we were ready to go. Or at least as close as we could be, considering . . . This was one in a hundred, and everyone knew it. But even though it should *not* have been, confidence was fairly high.

"WE'RE READY AMIGOS!" Nate yelled from the stands, waving his sombrero in the night.

Noah pitched the ball and Logan hit the ball over the fence. Logan rounded the bases, and with sober precision, the lights went off, one after the other, POOF . . . POOF . . . POOF . . . crashing to black at home plate—the final POOF. We howled. Our crew howled. The drunks HOWLED.

Somehow, by some godly touch of sobering intervention, we had pulled it off.

WE COULDN'T SEE. We could only hear, temporarily blinded by the darkness. The electricity was off, but we were not. Stumbling, groping for a shadow, everyone hugged and congratulated one another, tripping over equipment, rolling in the grass, laughing at the absurdity of the achievement, the drunks rioting in the bleachers as the stadium lights slowly began to glow again.

We all started packing up the gear. The final shot was a paragon of collaboration. Everyone was buzzing, except one.

A LITTLE ANGRY

His toxic frustration had reached the Vesuvius level. His anger was now volcanic. He was going to bury the operation. We were succeeding marvelously and he hated us for it. Everyone was having a blast and their joy clashed with his ash.

Little Angry was now VERY ANGRY.

And he was leaving, taking off with all his gear, driving back to L.A. in the morning. Our movie was sunk. We had two more days of filming, impossible without him and his gear. He said he had a SMALL problem with us and a BIIIGGGGG problem with Ricardo. He hated the Cuban, wanted to smoke him. Little Angry was so angry he was making flour out of his teeth.

INTERDEPENDENCE

How can your world blow up at any moment, you ask? How did Little Angry have such big power? It's easy. Everything on a movie set is interdependent—people, equipment, it all forms this long chain of production that culminates with the camera rolling film on the actors. It's TEAM art. This implies multiple people and parts working toward a unified goal.

The locations department arrives at the set first. Sometimes they sleep there to make sure that everything is ready to go in the morning. Then the trucks arrive: grip, camera, art, catering, and so on. All of the trucks, people, and equipment funnel goods and supplies toward the camera position, and when lights, sound, grip gear, C-stands, and a multifarious assortment of industry goods are in place, then and only then, can actors speak, car chases speed, and sex scenes burn an image onto film.

Large productions have redundancy measures. If one link in the chain is broken, they have the resources to replace it. Not true on our budget. If the grip truck got a blowout or a generator failed or the camera broke, we were finished. If someone got lost, if a light broke, if the sound department ran out of batteries, if a boom microphone was struck by a baseball (it happened), if the film stock wasn't delivered, if any of a ridiculously large number of variables in a prodigious equation failed, our movement ceased. The convoy was stuck in the mud.

Now, considering that Little Angry owned the only truck on our Tucson shoot, which was loaded with all our equipment, and we mean all of it—grip, lighting, sound, and camera—he had the ability to wipe us out. We couldn't allow that to happen. We didn't have the time, money, or industry resources to fire Little Angry and hire a friendly replacement by morning. We HAD to shoot the next morning or else all was for naught.

Little Angry was threatening to destroy years of determination and hard work. Yeah, we felt like introducing Little Angry to TWIN ANGRY. But that would only make MORE ANGRY, a human eruption we were trying to avoid. Right now we needed to shrink VERY ANGRY back down to Little Angry. Make him dormant. Make him safe.

So we pleaded with him for forty-five minutes in left field as our now faithful crew waited in the parking lot, throwing worried glances at us, hoping that we could stop the lava and save the village.

Eventually, we persuaded Little Angry to stick around and work the next day. The show would go on.

We encountered more of his tribe along the way. Little Angry was just the first.

BORDER TANGO

IN CASE YOU'VE been smoking the reality TV pipe for the past decade, we have a crisis down there, a virtual war zone manned by choppers and border patrol agents with machine guns. So why not film there? The location was interesting. Sound was a problem; the Black Hawks probing the desert made it difficult to record dialogue. But as Connie's boyfriend Buck would later say in the driving rain of Northern California, "What are you guys, a bunch of Hollywood pussies? Shut up and shoot it."

So we did.

IN THE MOVIE, the brothers are on their way home from Tucson, canned from baseball. They are parked in a turnout, taking a break from the road. Clint (Noah) is doing push-ups in the dirt. Lane (Logan) is leaning against the car, despondent. Clint finishes push-ups, stands, and tries to break Lane out of his funk. There's some heated dialogue. The brothers get in the car and drive away.

Like many great locations, we found this one by chance. We were looking for a lake and found a shrine instead. We'd driven eighty miles into the desert along a two-lane road to find out the lake was a mud puddle. It had been a time-warping trip, checkered with half-dead Indian reservations, abandoned cars, trailers, and gas stations, stray dogs and coyotes, with relics of once good ideas and busted hopes. The road hugged the border, Mexico on our left, the United States on our right. It felt as though Pancho Villa might ride out of the heat waves, chased by a chopper.

On our way back to Tucson, we pulled off the road to take a piss. The turnout overlooked an arroyo. There were hundreds of footprints in the sandy riverbed made by caravans of illegals heading north from Mexico.

There was a shrine built to honor a saint, maybe the Virgin Mary, can't say for sure. It was an interesting backdrop. We surveyed the ground. There was ample room to park a grip truck and situate our equipment. But this was outlaw country, a dangerous stretch of road traveled by drug smugglers, human traffickers, and banditos. Shoot-outs and murders were commonplace. We ran the risk of getting robbed for our gear, or worse.

We considered the hazards. The location was perfect. We'd come back and film in a week.

PICTURE CAR, THE PERFECT CAR

We needed a car for the brothers in the movie. One week out and no car. We were the transportation department, and we didn't have a car. The directors would fire us if we didn't get one quick. Our personal car, the one we planned on using when we first wrote the script, was abandoned by us on Highway 101 north of Santa Barbara after it blew up. It was now a hundred Chinese bicycle frames.

So we searched the Internet at Anthony's house and found several potential cars, but after further inspection, we concluded that none of them were right for the movie. So we drove around to every junkyard and used-car lot in Tucson. We kicked tires and checked under hoods. After five days, still nothing. Two days out now and still no picture car. Stress was building. If we hadn't been the directors, we would've been fired by now. We searched online again and found a prospect. We called the owner.

He'd moved out to Tucson from New York six months earlier. He was now selling everything and moving back. At least that was the story he gave us. He was shady, prickly. Let's call him "Shady Cactus."

So we met Shady Cactus in a dirt alley behind some Mexican groceria on his side of town. We brought our pistola. Physically, the car was perfect—a total heap of shit; it was the kinda car we used to drive, the kinda car that ain't worth fixing, the kinda car that when it blows up you don't call the tow truck, you just pull the license plates and leave it where it dies. We knew these kinda cars.

We drove the Perfect Car around the block. It swayed and creaked. It had no license plates. (Shady had a great story for that one.) The upholstery looked like you kicked a lion in the balls and then threw him inside. The rear window was busted out, looked like you threw a horse inside after the lion. The backseat was portable, the radio had been ripped out, and there was a Cadillac hubcap in the trunk in case you felt like going to the club.

"Do you think it will make it back to L.A.?" Noah asked. The only honest answer: no way in hell.

"For sure," Shady replied. "I'd drive this thing cross-country . . . It just had a tune-up."

We laid five one-hundred-dollar bills on the hood. Shady took the dough and disappeared down the alley.

PLANET ZORTON AND BIZARROVILLE

One week later we were heading back to the shrine to shoot the pullout scene. The Perfect Car stalled at the gas station on mile one. It took fifteen minutes to restart. The day certainly didn't start off with the smell of success.

The Perfect Car rattled and shook down the highway, as if we were driving a vibrating bed from some cheap motel. We didn't want anybody else to ride in the Perfect Car in case the wheels fell off. We stuck to the slow lane. Top speed fifty. Anything beyond that was suicide.

We rehearsed our lines and discussed the coverage for the scene as we drove south toward Mexico.

Finally, the Perfect Car gurgled into the dirt turnout. Our crew looked around the alien landscape as if they'd just got off a rocket ride to planet Zorton.

"It's an interesting location," Noah said, selling the place to our disoriented crew. "It helps express the brothers' emotional desolation at this point in the movie."

Eyes rolled. "Sure guys . . . You couldn't find anything closer to town . . . or safety?"

"Not like this . . . ," Noah said. "This place is Bizarroville."

A Black Hawk shrieked over the mesa, chasing things illegal.

"Whatever it is, let's just shoot it and get the hell out of here before we get abducted," Ricardo said. "I happen to like my freedom."

We set up the first camera position, the master shot, and rehearsed the scene for the crew. It took about four minutes.

The camera was far from the action, emotionally distant. It would eat up several minutes of film. It seemed wasteful to most of our crew. "You don't need to shoot the entire scene from here. You'll never be in this shot very long."

It was sound reasoning. But we had a distinct vision for the scene that contrasted with their experience. We felt the distance of the shot expressed the dramatic mood without being heavy-handed.

Our gut told us to shoot the whole thing, all the way through. Don't edit in the camera. Always shoot the entire scene. So what if it took a few extra minutes? We could decide in the editing room what to eliminate.

Thank God we went with our gut, 'cause one take with a working car was all we'd get. We would have been irreparably screwed if we hadn't listened to our innards and filmed the brothers driving away.

TAKE 1: We played the scene: Push-ups, dialogue, we jumped in the Perfect Car and drove down the road. CUT.

We turned around and parked the Perfect Car on its mark. It was running strong, like it did back when leg warmers were hot. We moved the camera closer.

TAKE 2: Push-ups, dialogue, we jumped into the Perfect Car and Noah turned the ignition.

The engine strained, growled, shook for a few seconds, fizzed, and then smoked. And the Perfect Car went silent. Nothing. Total car death. Not a shocker, but a problem. We now had a 4,000-pound corpse on our hands.

We finished shooting and packed up the gear. The next location was Patagonia Lake, outside the border town of Nogales, forty miles southeast.

We had established the Perfect Car and needed it for the rest of the movie. It was now a character. We had to get it fixed and then out to California. So we called a tow truck in Tucson. But we couldn't leave the Perfect Car unguarded on Zorton and expect it to be in one piece when the tow truck showed up in a couple hours. There were too many scavengers roaming this part of the desert.

Pierson volunteered to stick around. We gave him our .40 caliber HK automatic pistola and told him that if they don't have no stinking badges, start blazing. Pierson is an Eagle Scout. He waited on Zorton. The tow truck showed up and he met us at Patagonia Lake.

IN THE AFTERNOON a storm swept across the desert. Black clouds and electric veins darkened and flashed. Rain and dust scoured the plateaus, hurling muddy torrents down the riverbeds. We stood on the shore and watched the turquoise waters seep into liquid coal, whitecaps swelling and colliding. We called off shooting and headed back to Tucson.

Pierson hopped in the rental car with us. We bought some beer and chewing tobacco in Nogales and drove toward the sunset, purple thunderheads swirling against orange bursts of fire, mesas silhouetted black on the horizon.

We floated on alcohol and nicotine and a straight shot of asphalt with glowing yellow lines. We reminisced about the long road behind and visualized about the unknown road ahead. Six years earlier, Pierson was in the room when we completed our first typed draft of *Touching Home*. We didn't own a computer back then and he helped us out with that.

At the time, Pierson was editing a television show at a postproduction house on Cahuenga Boulevard in Hollywood, working the night shift a few blocks from our roach apartment. He would sneak us in at midnight, set us up on a computer, disappear into his editing suite, and come get us at dawn.

It took us a week to type the screenplay from our notebooks onto that computer. We finished at 4 A.M., called Pierson into the room and drank a beer together. Pierson went back to work and we lay on the floor, staring at the ceiling as we listened to "Bridge over Troubled Water," floating on a raft of accomplishment.

And we had the same feeling now as we rolled down the highway with the sweet sagebrush. We had come far. But we had no idea how far and how fast we'd go in the next few months.

DON'T KNOW HOW, WHERE, OR WHEN

THE NEXT MORNING we felt like the lords of the desert. We strutted across the street from our hotel and had coffee with the crew before hitting the road. Morale was high. We joked about the enormous uncertainties going into the operation and the band of threats riding our tails every minute we were out there.

Ricardo had been terribly undermanned. He had one light to work with and *it* was busted. He fearlessly shot from an obsolete and perilous crane nicknamed "the widow maker," and despite these handicaps, captured steady and beautiful images. Typically he would've had a semi truck full of lights, a four- to five-person camera crew, and eight to twelve grips and electricians assisting him in his art, roughly twenty people at his disposal. On this shoot, he had only three. Two of which, counted less than one. And still, we averaged over twenty-eight setups per day. In baseball terms, he hit .500.

Sound Ranger's recordings, especially those in the stadium, were remarkable. Prior to Tucson, he'd never recorded baseball, knew little of the game, and was now fascinated with its rich and distinct sounds. You could place the CRACK of his bat and WHOOSH of his ball against any that have ever been recorded. He and boom man Voot are perfectionists, with a keen obsession for sonic nuances. Sound men live on planet Onomatopoeia. What you see, they hear. On their planet, you're blind.

Connie was especially helpful in the scenes in which both of us were acting. We trusted her opinion and consulted her often. She was a rallying force of womanhood, commander of men.

Lenny, our first assistant camera, pulled excellent focus. Every shot was pin sharp.

And Pierson was the indispensable component, the fulcrum upon which the world moved.

They asked us when we were planning to shoot the rest of the movie. "By the end of the summer," we said.

"Where are you going to get the money?"

"Don't know how, where, or when. But we're gonna get it."

They'd all heard this bold claim from many directors and producers who had failed. But it appeared, in the haze of that sunny-sun-shiny morning, that they believed we just might do it. Just might. Tucson had turned skeptics into half-believers.

We were physically exhausted but mentally uplifted. We'd written, produced, directed, and acted in a four-day shoot. Mission accomplished. Granted, it was only four days. But as any veteran producer will tell you, shooting for a week requires just as much legwork as shooting for a month.

We remembered what Coach Gough, our surrogate father growing up, said to us three days before filming: "It's midnight . . . The enemy is creeping under the wire. You gotta keep your cool."

Coach Gough is a Khe Sanh marine, was there for the siege, living in a muddy hooch, isolated, a world of thunderous explosions, bullets, and blazing fire, bombarded and attacked for seventy-one days straight. And that was his wisdom at zero hour. *The enemy is creeping under the wire. You gotta keep your cool.* We repeated this in our minds whenever things got hectic, repeated it to each other throughout the tumult of filming.

AND ON THE FIFTH DAY, THE CASH WAS BURNED AND THE PLASTIC TIME BOMBS EXPLODED

American Express, the first company to take a gamble on us, Visa, Chase, MasterCard, Washington Mutual, Discover, and a host of other credit issuers were now our best friends. They started sending us mail every week, sometimes twice, wrote us more than all our other friends combined. And they did it the old-fashioned way—on paper and through the United States Post Office.

When we checked out of the Randolph Park Clarion in Tucson, Logan's stack of credit cards—rubber-banded in his pocket—had mysteriously stopped working. The exercise went like this: Logan would hand the clerk a card, she'd run it. Denied. Sorry about that, try this one. Denied. Whoaa, shit. Uhhh, shuffling through the stack, trying to remember which cards had a chance. The blue, the green, they all weighed the same. Oh, here it is. Yeah, the red one should work. It's good luck in the Orient, you know. And again. Denied. He smiles. She doesn't think the game is funny anymore, and she's cute, so it's even more embarrassing for Logan. He had ideas of asking for her number, not anymore. Noah has slipped out of the lobby, the car packed, engine running, in case we gotta drive out quick. Logan hands her another card, a big, desperate, uncomfortable smile.

This is it.

This is the one.

Has to be.

She fakes a smile before she runs the card. Are you sure? Logan smiles, brighter than the desert sun: definitely. That's right. Money. Only a wealthy man would have such a large bundle of credit cards. Lunatic rich is what he is. Only he doesn't know it. He thinks he's Park Place. She knows he's Freddie Mac.

She runs the card. And again. Denied. The shame. Should he split? He gives it a thought. Bro is in the car, ready to speed. It's fast. It's new. It's a rental. He's wearing sunglasses. She'll never get the plates. No. He can't. She's got his ID, knows who he is. He thinks . . . He could always blame it on his brother . . . He looks at her. Damn, she's cute. Can't run from that. There's still hope. Still more credit cards to run. He digs up another card. And again, and again, until a purple one accepts the burden. Phew . . .

We shuffled cards all over the desert.

TUCSON TAUGHT US many financial lessons, among them:

Receipts are no longer trash that builds up in our pockets.

Plastic friends are better than no friends.

And happiness in America is being comfortable with debt.

Post-Game Analysis: We got ripped off on a couple deals, even on most, and ahead on a few. Most importantly, we accomplished the objective. The travel days killed the pocketbook—we had to pay for wages, meals, and fuel—but we made up for it by establishing the core of a strong team: Ricardo, Connie, Taylor, Pierson, and Sound Ranger and Boom Man Voot.

In total, we were roughly $45,000 in debt. A heavy pile. And it would only get heavier before we climbed out.

We had a hot lead on some money in Northern California. Things were kindling, a small flame pressing up and around the edges. We didn't want to go back to L.A. and risk losing the heat. So we drove west and then turned north with the belief that we could steal the fire burning over the horizon.

BAD BROCCOLI[*]

Noah got food poisoning somewhere in the desert between Blythe and Chiriaco Summit, right around Patton's tank. It attacked his bowels until we reached the Bay Area the following afternoon. The potential financier turned out to be blowing steam. But without this jackass leading us on, it's doubtful that we would have been home for the San Francisco International Film Festival. In all likelihood, we'd have left Tucson and returned to L.A.

But we hadn't. And that would make all the difference.

---

[*] Broccoli in a bag in your car in the desert goes bad quickly. It can turn from a wholesome vegetable into an intestinal inferno in a hot afternoon. Tiny demons with daggers will be slashing the walls of your gut. So beware of broccoli in a bag in your car in the desert. It doesn't last long.

PART IV

THE AMBUSH

HONEST PETE DETERDING AND THE BEGINNING OF SOMETHING GREAT

HONEST PETE DETERDING had been following our unsuccessful writing career for several years. Pete is the founder of Diamond D Construction in Sacramento. He's got thick forearms and workingman's hands, wears jeans and boots, drives a truck, eats red meat, and doesn't need to pour his beer into a glass; the bottle is just fine.

We'd usually see Pete during the holidays at the Lafranchis'. Pete's beautiful wife, Dee, is the sister of our mom's boyfriend, Randy Lafranchi. The Lafranchis have been dairy ranchers in the Nicasio Valley for over a hundred years, a few miles from where we grew up. After dinner, we'd walk outside with Pete and have a chew and beer together on the hilltop overlooking the dairy.

"Always take the high road, gentlemen," he'd say. "Quality counts. You build your career on quality, on word of mouth from your customers. I suspect your business is the same . . . How's it going in Hollywood?"

"We just finished a new screenplay."

"You've written quite a few of them, haven't you?"

"Yes, sir."

For years, we never had much to show for our hard work other than a dozen scripts on our shelf. And you don't bring those to Christmas parties; they're a lousy gift.

EASTER SUNDAY 2006

Our mom is having Easter dinner with the Lafranchis. Pete asks our mom, "How are your boys doing?" Our mom tells him that we're finally making a movie. "They're down in Tucson filming spring training right now."

She tells Pete about the Panavision Grant, Kodak, etc. "It's been hard for me to keep track of what they're doing because all of this has come together so quickly."

We'd last seen Pete at Christmas, had our customary beer and chew together, and now, a few months later, we were shooting a movie.

"They finally got their big break," our mom says.

"Are they looking for investors?"

" . . . I think so."

"Let me know if they are," Pete said. "I might know some people in Sacramento who can help them."

Our mom calls us the next day in Tucson and says we should call Pete. "You never know. It might lead to something."

So we called Pete when we got back from Tucson. He told us to send him a few business plans. He'd pass them around Sacramento to see if he could find us some money. We had a good feeling about it. The capital has a legacy of gold seekers and dreamers, a risk-taking appetite that swirls in the confluence of the American and Sacramento rivers.

Only one problem: we didn't have a business plan yet. So once again, we consulted the books and Internet, figured out the general structure and language, wrote a detailed plan, and called Pete three days later. We told Pete we'd drive up and deliver the business plans in person.

"No need to drive all the way up here," Pete said. "Just throw them in the mail."

"We're in the car. We'll see you in a few hours."

Two hours later we sat down with Pete in his office. He was blown away by our progress. But it made sense to him. He told us about his big break in the construction business, how he'd struggled for years, barely getting by, when one day, while sitting in a bar, Pete's brother asked him to take over the construction management of a large development in Sacramento. The job changed Pete's life. But the overnight success was a decade in the making; the only thing that happens overnight is the check clearing in the bank.

We shook hands with Pete. "Thanks for driving up guys. I'm glad you did. It says a lot about your character . . . I'll see what I can do."

WHEN POOR IS GOOD

The San Francisco International Film Festival was honoring Ed Harris with a lifetime achievement award. It was a two-day celebration: Thursday, April 27, and Friday, April 28. Thursday night was a $500-a-plate black-tie gala, an intimate affair, Bay Area socialites schmoozing with the stars. It was a great environment to rub elbows with celebrities, a great environment to talk to Ed Harris, pitch him on our movie, and give him our script.

Yes, Ed Harris. The movie star we wanted to play our dad on the big screen. The actor we had talked about at our jailhouse casting session, when we were three fools laughing at the impossible.

Ed Harris was coming to the city near us. And we were going to be there.

We called Gordon Radley, our mentor.

"Gordon . . . Did you know that Ed Harris is coming to San Francisco for the film festival? We just read about it in the *Chronicle*."

"Yeah, I heard something about that . . . Why?"

"We're going to talk to him and give him our script."

"How are you going to do that?"

"Wait in the lobby of his hotel and buttonhole him as he walks by, maybe corner him in the elevator, something like that."

"NO! You guys are insane! You can't do it that way. It's gauche. Wait until you get the money and call his agent. You've gotta go through the proper channels."

"We'll never get the money without an actor like Ed on board. He's the number one guy to play the role of our dad."

"Get the money first!"

"If we use conventional methods, we'll get conventional results . . . What about the Thursday night black-and-white gala thing?"

"What about it?"

"You going?"

"No."

"Do you know anybody who is? Do you know who's in charge? What about talking to Ed there?"

"Guys, guys, guys, listen to me!" Gordon can yell with the best of them. And he was yelling right now. "GET THE MONEY FIRST! You guys are too damn impulsive. Get the money and then go through the agents!"

For some reason known only to science, we have NEVER had any success with convention, or conventional settings, even when we've tried our king's best to fit in and make it work. Maybe it's a twin thing. We're a genetic deviation. Perhaps this interferes with conventional energy or structure on some unconscious level. For us, the front door has always been locked.

So we came up with a pitch and called the festival: "Hi, we're a couple of local independent filmmakers and we're shooting a movie in the Bay Area this summer. We'd love to attend the gala. It would be a wonderful learning experience for us, only we can't afford it. We think this presents a great opportunity for you to waive the fee, support the starving filmmaker, give back to the community, the very spirit of your festival. In turn, we'll come and speak at the festival when our movie comes out. In March, we received the Panavision New Filmmaker Grant and just concluded a four-day shoot in Arizona. We'd LOVE to come to the gala . . ."

And anything else we could throw at their benevolent side.

The Person with the Festival: "Wow . . . Sounds like a noble venture . . . Don't see why we can't bend the rules and support a couple of local filmmakers."

It sounded reasonable to us.

Festival: "I'm fine with it. You need to call the person above me. Tell them I gave you their number."

Great. Progress. Moving up. Next phone call. Same pitch.

Festival: "Don't see why we can't get behind a couple of locals . . . That's the spirit of independent film, right?"

"Right."

Festival: "I don't have a problem with letting you in, but it's not my call. You need to talk to my boss."

We worked our speakerphone all afternoon, climbing the marble steps to the Film Festival Ticket Queen. Two hours later, everyone below had signed off. It was all roses and dandelions, rolling plains of pretty flowers, pixies and posies and butterflies with wings.

Only the Queen was unimpressed. "No."

"C'mon."

"No."

"We're locals."

"Guys, there's seven million locals. We haven't waived the fee for anyone. I wish I could. But this is our only fund-raiser of the year . . . I'm sorry."

"What about a two-for-one? $500 for the both of us? C'mon, let's make a deal."

We looked at each other. We didn't have the money. If she said yes, we'd find a credit card to throw it on.

Queen: "Sorry guys. I can't do it. Good luck."

No black-and-white gala. Thursday night was out. We didn't have a thousand bucks. It's a good thing we were broke.

THE AMBUSH

ON FRIDAY NIGHT Ed Harris was going to appear at the Castro Theatre for a career retrospective and interview prior to the screening
of *A Flash of Green,* one of his first starring roles. We'd ambush
him there, at the Castro, and detain him in conversation. How?
We had no idea. We'd never stepped foot in the Castro. But the
Castro was now our only hope to speak face-to-face with four-
time Academy Award nominee Ed Harris. To boost our confidence
in this far-fetched mission, we used a syllogistic argument:

*Men conduct business candidly, face-to-face. Ed Harris is a
man. We are men. Therefore, we should conduct business with
him face-to-face.*

We convinced ourselves that Ed Harris *needed* to be in our
movie. This was the role he'd been waiting for his entire life. The
only reason he had an agent was to find him a role like this one.
It would help not only us, but also him. We were *helping* him. *We*
were helping Ed Harris.

Of course this probably sounds grandiose and delusional.
(Ed Harris needs *us*? We're helping *him*?) And it was. Times two.
Because there's two of us. So the delusion was twice as strong.
One guy is gathering wood as the other one is throwing it on the
fire. It keeps feeding and feeding, the twin fires of psychosis.

We called Gordon back.

"Gordon, they're going to honor Ed Harris tomorrow night at
the Castro, a big interview onstage."

"And? . . ."

"We're going to talk to him there."

"How?"

"Don't know yet."

An interminable pause.

"Gordon? . . . You still there?"

No response.

"Gordon?"

"I'm thinking! . . . If . . . If you're going to TRYYYYY to talk to Ed, you'd better have your pitch down. An elevator pitch."

"We thought you said no elevators?"

"Elevator Pitch, guys. Elevator PITCH! Your thirty-second pitch . . . Give me your pitch."

"Now?"

"Yes, now."

This is like asking a writer to saw off his writing arm and beat himself with it. There's no worse question—summarize your child, your life, in thirty seconds. Can you do that? Suits are always asking writers to pitch their story. Writer's write, editors abbreviate. But if you want to be a working writer, you'd better learn to edit your work, and more importantly, learn to pitch.

We stumbled. "Uhhhhmmmm . . ."

"C'mon, guys. You got thirty seconds. Your time's up. You'd better work on it."

"We're gonna do it, Gordon. We're going to the Castro. We're gonna talk to Ed Harris."

"Very well. Let me know how it goes."

We started planning.

Shit, what if it's already sold out? It's probably sold out. Damnit.

We called our friend Chau. She's like family, lives with her husband Josh in San Francisco, half a mile from the Castro. She walked down Market Street and bought three tickets. Step One complete: make sure we get in the door.

Step Two: presentation and detention.

How are we going to present our movie? How are we going to detain Ed Harris?

A week earlier, Pierson cut a beautiful two-minute trailer from the Tucson shoot, dreamy baseball sequences to Nick Drake's *Pink Moon*.

We printed a fresh copy of our screenplay and paper clipped our business card and Panavision endorsement letter to the cover and then placed all this inside a manila envelope. *What else do we need to bring?* Our laptop. The goal was to show Ed Harris the trailer on our laptop—demonstrate that we had a vision for *Touching Home*—pitch him and then get him to read the screenplay, call us, and say, "Hey, guys. I'm in."

The odds of all this happening? A million to one . . . on the luckiest day ever.

BRAD DOURIF FIRST

We met Chau at her house on Friday afternoon at four and headed west on Market Street, marching with bold optimism and a backpack full of movie-pitching materials.

Chau was the ideal companion for this mission. In 1979, her family built a forty-foot boat out of the floorboards in their house and sailed from Vietnam to Malaysia with seventy other people, desperate to escape the horrors of communism. They spent one year in a squalid refugee camp before making it to the United States. Chau remembers those rough years vividly. If anyone believes in the impossible, it's Chau and her family. Talking to a celebrity? Big deal. Sailing the high seas in a tiny boat and making it to America? That's tough.

"This is so exciting," Chau said. "What are you guys going to do? How are you going to do it?"

"We're not sure yet. We need to do some reconnaissance first, case the joint, scope it out."

The light turned green. We crossed the street. Our cell phone rang.

"Brad Dourif is in," said the guy on the other end. (You'll meet this wonderful piece of foul-smelling humanity later, not Brad, but the turd on the phone right now. You'll meet Brad later as well, but he's terrific. The piece talking right now is not.) "He read the script and loves it. He wants to play Clyde."

Clyde was the role of our uncle in the script, our dad's brother.

"Great . . . ," Noah said. "We're on our way to meet Ed Harris. Gotta go."

RECON: AN ARMY OF TWO

We arrived at the Castro Theatre at 4:30 P.M. We looked through the glass doors at the concession stand. The lights were off inside. Nobody had showed up for work yet. We bought Chau an ice cream at the coffee shop next door and then stood in front of the theater and formed the line, first ones there.

The Castro District, one might say, is *not* ordinary. All around us, packs of grown men were holding hands. There was a bar across the street with Harleys parked out front where muscular dudes in leather pants and handlebar mustaches were also hold-ing hands. Some were canoodling. We heard the crack of a leather whip in the distance. Yes, not ordinary, one might say. The Castro is definitely *not* ordinary. But it happened to be the place that we were at today, 1,440 miles from Kansas.

A few theater employees threw irritated glances at us as they showed up for work, tapping their watches. "We're not open yet."

"Thanks."

We'd smile and wave, standing with our backpack, tall and

proud at the front of the line. Finally they opened the doors and we went inside and set up operational headquarters five rows back from the stage. It was the closest we could sit. The first four rows were cordoned off for the press and film society members.

Chau watched our gear as we launched our reconnaissance. We needed to find out when and where Ed would enter the theater. There were several entrances and exits. Logan cased the right side of the building, Noah the left. We opened exit doors, peered into alleys, janitor's closets, the balcony, discovered the storehouse of candy bars and popcorn, shared a Twix.

Noah walked downstairs to the men's room to take a leak and struck up a conversation with the guy at the urinal beside him. The guy was wearing a headset and microphone, looked like Secret Service.

"You do this a lot?" Noah asked.

"What, take a piss?" He didn't turn his head, focused downward on his aimer.

"No, security detail."

"Only the festival. Worked it the last three years."

"When's Ed coming?"

"Don't know." He zipped up his fly and walked out.

Meanwhile Logan bought a bag of popcorn, wanted to look natural, just another movie junkie at a festival. He posted up next to the front door where the red carpet stretched to the curb. There was a security guy there too.

"So is, uhh, Ed, just gonna walk down the carpet right here?"

"Probably not . . . He doesn't really like the spotlight."

"You know him?"

"Not really."

"Kinda?" Logan asked, chewing on popcorn, casually looking around, nodding and appreciating the ceiling.

"Not really."

"Limousine?"

"Don't know."

"Do you know who knows?"

"You gotta go, buddy. You gotta move out of the doorway, you can't stand here."

"Okay . . . No problem. See you around."

We reconvened at our seats and held a debriefing, whispering for secrecy.

"What do you got?" Logan asked.

"Nothing. There's tons of ways to get into this place, probably twenty doors, maybe even a secret tunnel somewhere. He could come in from the alley on the right or the alley on the left. There's a parking lot adjacent to the alley on the right . . . Who knows? There's probably an entrance backstage. What do you got?"

"They rolled out a red carpet in front."

"Do you think we should wait out there?"

"It's already packed. And the security is heavy."

"I think we should do one more round of recon, talk to whomever we can. Get some hard intel."

"Roger that."

Chau listened intensely, smiling, her head swinging back and forth from one of us to the other. "This is so exciting!"

After ten more minutes of recon, we met back at our seats.

"I saw him," Logan whispered.

"Where?"

"Just a glimpse as he came down the balcony steps with a few people."

"Should we go up there and talk to him? Let's rush the balcony."

"They walked out one of the side doors."

"You should've stopped him."

"Couldn't. Didn't have time. They were across the lobby from me and moving quick."

PUSHING THROUGH THE CURTAIN

The Castro was filling up. We were sitting in the aisle seats on the right, fifth row from the stage, looking over our shoulders, scanning the balcony, studying every face spilling in, ready to pounce on opportunity. There was still a chance we could buttonhole Ed Harris on his way to the stage, pitch him with frantic passion, show him the trailer on our laptop as we hustled alongside him.

If Ed Harris walked down the right aisle . . . he was ours.

Then Graham Leggat, the executive director of the San Francisco Film Society, took center stage. He was wearing a black blazer, shaved head, sharp features. The crowd hushed.

"Thank you all for coming . . . It's our great pleasure . . . Please welcome, Ed Harris."

Clapping, cheering, whistling.

The curtain on the left side of the stage ruffled as two men swam through it. Film critic Pete Hammond appeared, followed by Ed Harris. They walked across the stage, paused in the middle, waved, and then sat in comfortable chairs, a coffee table with glasses of water between them.

The theater inflated as we deflated. One thousand, three hundred and ninety-eight people rose from their seats and cheered as twin brothers sunk into their chairs. Why? Because Ed Harris came in from backstage.

How the hell are we going to get backstage?

The prospect of us talking to Ed was nil.

It probably sounds obvious to the reader of this adventure that Ed Harris would enter from backstage, right? But in our mania, in our deluded optimism and foolishly impractical confidence, we figured he would enter from the street, walk down the red carpet into the theater, down the right aisle, shake our hands, slap us high fives—might even postpone the interview to watch our two-minute trailer on our laptop; he'd been waiting his entire career to be pitched on *our* movie. This was the role of a lifetime.

The interview began.

Pete Hammond asked his first question, something like, "Tell us about your background. You grew up in Jersey . . ."

Ed described it as the all-American, 1950s-era neighborhood: white picket fences, two-parent households, kids playing in the street. He talked about how he was a jock growing up, played football and baseball—dreamed of playing in the major leagues.

Major leagues?

We sat up.

A star high school athlete, Ed went to Columbia University to play football and baseball and quickly realized that he wasn't big enough, fast enough, and "couldn't hit a curveball." He explained how he'd never done anything related to theater or art, nothing creative, until he saw a theatrical play while visiting his parents in Oklahoma during his freshman summer break. The cast received a standing ovation. The applause lavished on the actors was the same applause an athlete received for an outstanding performance on the field. It seemed as though this new type of performance could fill the void left by athletics. Thus began his journey to where he was now.

These were favorable parallels to our journey. We had taken similar paths into the creative world. Still, our confidence faded with each question and each answer.

How are we going to talk to him? How are we going to get backstage?

Forty minutes later Pete Hammond said, "One more question and then we're going to pass the microphone around the audience for a Q&A."

Logan grabbed Noah's arm, whispered, "Bro, I'm gonna get the mic. We're gonna talk to him, put him on the spot in front of all these people."

"What are you gonna say?"

Logan squeezed his brain for thirty seconds and extracted the juice, whispered to Noah. "Hello, Mr. Harris. Me and my brother are local independent filmmakers. We're shooting a movie up here this summer and were wondering if we could talk to you for two minutes afterward?"

"Sounds great."

The interview ended.

Then Pete Hammond said, "Now we'll take some questions from the audience."

Two ushers, one on each side of the theater, stood with microphones.

"Please raise your hand if you have a question, and we'll do our best to give you an opportunity to ask it."

We ejected from our seats, the first ones in the theater to raise their hands, gesturing with fanatic intensity. An usher with a microphone was two seats in front of us. He scanned the theater for fans with raised hands. But he couldn't see the twin maniacs. So we switched tactics and became a two-man fitness video, vigorously calling attention to ourselves with jumping jacks. And when that didn't work, we switched to military tactics; signal men landing F-16s on the deck of an aircraft carrier.

The usher looked at us. We locked eyes. *Right here, dude. Land it, man. Land it.*

He nodded.

That's right, dude. Right here, give us the mic . . . We have an audience with destiny.

He walked toward us.

Yes. Destiny.

Logan smiled, nodded, held out his hand to receive the microphone. And the usher walked right past him and up the aisle. Logan swiveled in shock as destiny abandoned us.

The usher handed the microphone to a yoga-sedated woman.

She asked one of those deep, philosophical *acting* questions that only Buddha could answer. Ed did his best.

Then the microphone was passed to someone else. They asked a question. Ed answered. The microphone was passed again. And again. Everywhere but us.

We remained standing, waving our hands, desperately gesturing for the microphone.

"Over here!" We'd cry. The sadistic usher would look us in the eyes, nod, grin, step around us, and find someone less desperate. It was as if we embodied the usher's entire frustrations of his youth. And tonight was the reckoning.

"Okay. We've got time for one more question."

The last question was hurled at Ed Harris. They never gave us the microphone. Festival staffers have a preternatural ability for spotting derangement. And they had spotted us that night.

We felt like rioting, throwing chairs, burning cars.

"Thank you," Pete Hammond said.

THE INJUSTICE!

The house stood and clapped, smiled, and whistled. A deafening ovation. Ed Harris waved and then disappeared through the curtain. Our world dimmed and slowed. Our hearing muted.

The audience became a grove of giants. We had failed. We felt heavy and insignificant, embarrassed and humiliated that we'd hatched such a laughable scheme. Sure, go to the Castro Theatre along with fourteen hundred other fans, talk to Ed Harris, pitch him on our movie, show him our trailer, and give him our script. Sure, it's possible—YOU IDIOTS! Only a couple of idiots would buy into such a wild and outrageous plan. Only a couple of idiots would waste time organizing such a far-fetched undertaking.

It had all been useless, ridiculous. WE WERE RIDICULOUS.

Our chance to speak to Ed Harris was gone.

It *was* an impossible dream.

The world was silent.

Then Noah rose from his chair and stepped into the aisle.

"Where are you going?" Logan asked.

Noah turned around, fierce. "Fuck this! We're going backstage to talk to Mr. Harris."

ONWARD AND UPWARD, BROTHER! was our battle cry as we stormed the stage. EITHER YOU'RE IN OR YOU'RE IN THE WAY!

We strutted down the aisle like intoxicated prizefighters and turned left at the front row, past security in yellow jackets and San Francisco cops in blue, up the steps and onto the stage, the theater still undulating with appreciation. We pushed through the curtain and bumped into a woman on the other side, startling her.

"Uhhh, excuse me," she said. "What are you doing back here?"

"We're the independent filmmakers," Noah said. "And we're here to talk to Ed Harris."

The words echoed with self-styled importance: We are THE independent filmmakers.

Act like you belong and you might have a chance.

We stepped around her, attention forward, barely acknowledging the handler. We were important. We had an appointment. We sensed in her hesitation that she didn't want to be the one that prevented Ed Harris from meeting with "THEEE independent filmmakers."

"*Who* are you?" she asked.

"We are THEEEE independent filmmakers, and we're here to talk to Ed," Noah repeated.

THEEE independent filmmakers just came out naturally. It made us sound important . . .

Then it registered that we were imposters.

"Absolutely not! You're not going anywhere! Get outta here!" She shoved Noah back through the curtain and onto the stage. He didn't resist. The weight of being a fraud was now crushing him.

The theater was bustling, noisy, the stagehands hurrying to clear the stage in the ten-minute intermission before the screening.

Desperation set in. So Noah told the truth. "Look, we're local independent filmmakers. We're shooting a movie up here this summer, and we want to speak to Ed about it. Would you please see if he'll talk to us for two minutes? Please, just two minutes?"

She paused, softened. "Where are you guys from?"

"Across the bridge, forty-five minutes north, a small town you've never heard of."

"I'm a filmmaker as well," she said.

"Where are you from?" Logan asked.

"Arizona."

"We used to live in Tucson. We just filmed down there a couple weeks ago."

"Really? I love Tucson."

"Could you please see if Ed will talk to us for two minutes? Just two minutes of his time. That's it."

She squinted, examined our faces. Could we be trusted?

"Wait here," she said. "I'll go ask."

She disappeared through the curtain in front of us.

Behind us, cops and security guards, the ones we just walked past on our way up stage, were watching us. We felt dangerously vulnerable, as though the wooden shampoo or the security guard necktie was on its way. And we also figured that the young woman was coming back with the cops. We were surrounded by cops and security, onstage and backstage. Our run was over.

HAD HIM, THEN LOST HIM

No more than twenty seconds after she disappeared behind the curtain, Ed Harris walked out. He looked at Logan, then at Noah, then again at both of us, a double take. He grinned, chuckled, amused by the twin thing.

"Ed Harris, what do you boys got?"

Ed extended his hand and Logan shook it, then Noah. He had a firm handshake. It seemed honest.

It was loud onstage, fourteen hundred people chatting behind us, moving up and down the aisles, grabbing a Coke or hitting the bathroom before the show. We started our pitch.

"We're local independent filmmakers and we wrote a story about us and our father."

"You guys twins?"

"Yes, sir."

Ed smiled. "Keep going."

"Our father was homeless for the last fifteen years of his life, battling alcoholism. It's really a coming-of-age story about a father trying to make amends with his sons as they pursue professional baseball . . . We had always dreamed of playing in the major leagues, but it didn't work out."

"How far did you get?"

"High A ball for the Toronto Blue Jays," Logan said. "I had two surgeries on my arm, and then they let me go."

Logan rolled up his sleeve, showed Ed the zipper on his elbow. Then a man called to Ed from the seats below. Ed turned and looked down at him. "Hey, Phil . . . Hold on. I'll be right there."

Ed looked back at us and said, "Hey, guys, that's Phil Kaufman. Let me go talk to him for a second. I'll be right back."

(Phil Kaufman directed *The Right Stuff,* casting Ed as John Glenn, the role that made him a star.)

We had him and then lost him. We figured he wasn't coming back. He'd walk out the Castro with Phil and go have a drink or something, anything to get away from the twin nutcases who had so rudely forced their way backstage.

CORNERED IN AN ALLEY

"I'm gonna grab our script and laptop so we can show Ed the trailer," Logan said.

"I'll keep my eyes on him. If he leaves, we'll follow."

Logan sprinted back to our seats, where Chau was guarding our stuff as Noah kept his eyes locked on Ed and Phil Kaufman talking at the base of the stage, a crowd gathering around them.

"Logan, what's happening?" Chau asked. "I saw you guys talking to him."

"I gotta get back up there," Logan said, pulling our laptop out of the backpack and then fishing for our script buried underneath our jackets and popcorn buckets and empty soda containers.

"This is so exciting," Chau said.

"I know," Logan replied as he ran back across the theater with our gear and vaulted onto the stage. He turned on the laptop, handed Noah the manila envelope with our script inside.

Then, miraculously, Ed walked back up the steps.

"Sorry about that guys . . . I haven't seen Phil in a long time . . . So you guys wrote a story about you and your father, and you're shooting it up here?"

"Yes, sir."

We started pitching our movie again—way too excited—speaking in tongues like a couple of meth-heads, "Jibberish nonsense movie, nonsense jibberish twins, nonsense jibberish Panavison, jibberish—Amen." There's no way he could decipher half of what we were saying. But we could tell that he was amused. We were a circus act, a carnival sideshow, talking over each other, hands and arms running all over the place. We felt rushed, like we had thirty seconds to tell our life story, sure to be cutoff at any moment by security or someone more important than us, more important than a couple crazies trying to pitch a

four-time Oscar nominee on a little movie. Any distraction could
ruin our attempt.

The stagehands kept bumping into us. Logan held the laptop
for Ed.

"Here's the trailer we just put together."

Logan pressed play, tried to angle the screen for Ed. But Ed
couldn't see or hear anything. The stage lights washed out the
image, and the commotion and chatter from the audience silenced
the music.

"Excuse me, Mr. Harris," Noah said.

"Call me, Ed."

"Ed, do you mind if we show you the trailer backstage?"

"Sure. Let's go."

Ed pushed through the curtain. We followed. It was cramped,
crowded with festival people, stagehands. We huddled in a corner
and pressed play on our laptop. A stagehand bumped Logan with
a chair, almost knocked the computer onto the floor. Backstage
wasn't any better than front-stage.

So Noah searched for opportunity, a better place to watch the
trailer, one without distractions.

The door was open to the alley.

"Ed, do you mind if we go into the alley?" Noah asked, pointing
to the open doorway. It was dark and quiet out there, no people.

"Sure . . . ," Ed said, moving toward the open door.

Then a tall woman swooped upon us, near six feet of rage,
thin glasses, red hair, white skin, freckles, looked like the boss of
something. She was all fire and flame, smoking nostrils. "You two
have two minutes and then you're outta here!" She finished with a
right hook toward the door. "Outta here!"

Her job was to keep stalkers like us away from stars like Ed
Harris. We'd breached the wall and were now digging handfuls
out of her wedding cake, our faces covered in frosting. This was

her soiree, her cave, her night with Edward Harris, celebrated actor and director. *Who the hell are these assholes?!*

"Two minutes and you're—outta here!" She raged. "OOOOUUUUUUUTTTTTTTTTTAAAAAA HERE!"

Ed bravely confronted the Red Dragon and adroitly smothered the fire. He turned to her, an unlit cigarette between his fingers, held it up to his mouth. "Excuse me, but could you please get me a match?"

Dragon sighed, wings fell, smoke releasing from its nostrils like a car's last sputter of exhaust. Nice Dragon now. "Absolutely, Mr. Harris."

"Ed."

"I'm sorry, Ed," she whimpered, and then flew away screaming, "Maaaaaaaaaaatttttttttccccchhhhhh!!!!!"

We stepped into the dark alley. We searched for a place to screen our trailer. There was a greasy Dumpster beside the door. So we set our laptop on it and hit play. Ed moved closer to the screen, the music playing to dreamy images of baseball. He took a drag on his cigarette and blew the smoke into the night.

"This looks beautiful. Looks like you guys know what you're doing."

ON THE TRAILER: Logan was catching. He popped out of the hole and threw a frozen rope to third base.

"Nice throw. That was you, wasn't it?" Ed asked, pointing to Logan.

"Yes, sir."

"See, I can tell you guys apart already . . . I used to be a catcher. Like I told the guy onstage, I always dreamed of playing in the big leagues. Didn't make it as far as you though, only made it to college."

Ed continued watching the trailer, focused, bringing the cigarette to his lips, the inhale tightening his concentration. He nodded a few times.

The trailer ended.

"Did you guys go to film school?"

"No, sir."

"Neither did I."

"We just went out and did it."

"Yeah, that's probably the best way. Where are you guys planning on shooting the rest of this?"

"Up here . . . Across the bridge. Do you know where Nicasio is?"

"No."

"Fairfax, Lagunitas, Point Reyes . . . West Marin?"

"Maybe . . . I probably drove through it a long time ago when I was doing theater up here."

"It's beautiful country," Noah said. "It's rural. Lots of oak trees and rolling hills and redwood forests."

"Do you boys have any actors attached?"

"Brad Dourif."

"Wow . . . You guys must be getting this out there. Brad Dourif is excellent, love his work."

To say we had Brad Dourif attached was a stretch. Not dishonest, but very elastic. Expressing interest over the phone through a third party (Brad's agent) was months away from a formalized deal. But it was one of the only pieces of leverage we had at the moment, and we needed to exploit it, even if it was extremely tentative and just a few hours old. Actors always want to know the other actors involved, who else is on the team; good actors tend to elevate each other's performances. And bad actors, well, they tend to do the opposite.

The manila envelope with our script inside was on top of the greasy Dumpster, next to our computer. Ed grabbed the envelope.

"Is your script in here?"

"Yes, sir."

"What about your contact information?"

"It's all in there. We typed our phone number on the script, attached our business card as well. There's also a DVD of the trailer you just watched."

Ed took a long drag from his unfiltered cigarette, thinking. He blew out the smoke.

"I'm pretty busy right now . . . Give me . . . A week . . . Yeah, a week."

A week? Nobody reads your script in a week. Not even your mother. Established writers, yes. They demand it. But a couple of nobodies like us? Your script grows fields of dust on its cover page, becomes a doodling pad, and when spring cleaning rolls around, it rolls off the desk into the trash can. In the winter, it starts fires, keeps houses warm, kids cozy. Nobody reads your script in a week. NOBODY.

A group of festival staffers had made their way into the alley and were now standing behind Ed, their backs to the busy street fifty yards down. They were waiting to escort him to his next engagement. Ed put out his cigarette on the Dumpster, threw it inside.

"Good show, fellas," he said, shaking our hands. He smiled and then turned and walked down the alley with his people.

We watched them grow small, black outlines shrinking into the blur of streetlights. They turned the corner and disappeared. And we stood there beside the Dumpster, listening to the sounds of the city, staring at the cars streaking by the mouth of the alley. We didn't want to move, didn't want to step out of the dream.

THE REFLECTING ROAD

AS WE DROVE through the fog across the Golden Gate Bridge, leaving the city and Ed Harris behind, we started thinking about our father, alone with his truck in the woods, eating canned food on his tailgate, lantern beside him. Then he was walking the back roads, hands in his pockets, muttering to himself, beat up by life, hunched and shrunken, not proud, not hopeful, not happy, alone with his struggles and abandoned dreams.

Thirty minutes later the highway approached the jail where he died, and a mile from that horrible tomb was the bank parking lot where Uncle Gary's body was found in the trunk of his car, and this same strip of asphalt had just carried us to Ed Harris and past them.

We arrived home, heads spinning, the night an overload of fantastic images and swirling voices, punctuated by one distinct moment in a San Francisco alley. We were back in the woods now, and all was quiet in the trees.

We sent Gordon an e-mail at 12:58 A.M.:

> We talked to Ed Harris for about ten minutes in the alley outside the Castro, gave him the pitch, showed him the trailer. He thought it looked beautiful. He took our script and said to give him a week . . . Also, Brad Dourif's agent called and said that Brad read the script and absolutely loves it. Call us when you get a moment. We need to talk . . .

We'd accomplished our mission, achieved everything within our control. Now it was in Ed's hands. It was hard to sleep though. We feared that pitching Ed Harris in the alley would be the summit of our adventure, a bitter story that would grow old and gaudy with embellishment, a story of how we *almost* made it, a story every grandfather has about coming within an arm's length of fame. Yes, the thought of us coming that far and then failing to attain the rest of it was tormenting, a retrospective sting that would increase throughout our lives whenever we searched for a reason why fortune never left the alley.

We finally managed to sleep a few hours, but the anxiety followed the dawn, pistol-whipped by the thought of Ed losing the script, leaving it in his hotel room, or giving it to one of the festival staff, or worse, the Red Dragon, who might conveniently misplace it or torch it with her fire. Or perhaps Ed would open his eyes in the morning to the absurdity of these two guys pitching him on some super-long-shot movie with a one in ten million chance of getting made. Ed Harris was a movie star, an American icon. In all likelihood, he had a dozen scripts at his house waiting to be read, each with a seven-figure offer on the table. And he's going to spend two hours reading OUR SCRIPT? That would be an excessively bad waste of time. We had no financing, no studio underwriting our movie, nothing. We *were* the studio, a studio with no track record except a two-minute trailer.

Ed's agent might call the next morning and ask about the Castro. And if Ed mentioned that he had been cornered in an alley and pitched by a couple of aspiring filmmakers and was about to start reading their script, well, his agent, after choking on his earpiece and murdering his assistant, would do everything he could to prevent Ed from biting the apple. Two guys off the street peddling unsolicited scripts to clients is a radioactive superpill. An agent couldn't imagine a more toxic scenario. It was the agent's job to keep guys like us away, find his client big-dollar roles that advance careers upward on the money chain. These high-paying jobs are found on studio lots, not in San Francisco alleys. Opportunity doesn't knock there, only despair.

GORDON CALLED AROUND 9 A.M. He doesn't excite easily, but the Ed Harris episode had him jumping on a trampoline with four shots of espresso and a chocolate kicker.

"He'll call you."

"You think?"

"Yes . . . My gut tells me he will. It's a great script, a good role for him. Actors don't get these kinds of roles very often, even ED HARRIS. If he reads the script, which I think he will, he'll call. I don't think that will be the hard part, I really don't. But when he calls, he's going to immediately ask questions about the production side, how far along you are, scheduling, that sort of thing. It's going to be your job to navigate this area. You don't have any money, no schedule."

"We're filming the movie this summer."

"C'mon, guys. You don't have a penny. You can't have a starting date for principal photography without any financing."

"We'll get the money."

"Guys, we're talking about—at the very least—a few million dollars to do this movie right. It's not that easy to raise millions of dollars."

"What about George Lucas?"

"Guys, guys, guys! George doesn't invest in other people's movies!"

"Will you ask him?"

"No."

"Give us his number and we'll call him."

"Guys, great job. Let's see if Ed calls."

STRESSFUL PLEASURE AND THE ART OF PACING

We drove back to L.A. the following morning, our brains at war with themselves; the lofty vision of Ed calling and saying he wanted to make the movie was brought down by the alternate vision of Ed not reading the script and never calling, or worse, reading the script, hating it, and telling us he didn't want to be in our movie. Up and down, the battle of wild dreams and practical failure. Both sides fought without intermission.

The week passed like a kidney stone, long and painful. The phone was our pipeline to both deliverance and damnation. Every time someone called, the space of each ring was filled with the bipolar suspense of hope and failure. We'd scrutinize the caller ID, attempting to divine and shape prophecy.

NINE DAYS LATER

It was 9 A.M. Monday morning. We were reading at our desk when the phone rang. Noah checked the caller ID.

"Who is it?" Logan asked.

"It's restricted."

"Answer it."

There was only one phone call we wanted—Ed Harris. That's it. Eight days of disappointment. Our average heart rate: 189 per minute. We couldn't survive another week. What made things worse, was that friends would *call* to see if *Ed* had called. Selfishly, we only wanted to speak to Ed. He was the only call that mattered. We were terrible friends that week.

But this new call was promising: RESTRICTED. There was only one number that consistently came across our caller ID as RESTRICTED—and that was Gordon. And we were not expecting his call. Noah answered.

"Hello."

"Who . . . who's this?" A rugged, manly voice asked.

"This is Noah."

"Hey, Noah, this is Ed." A long pause. "Ed Harris."

Noah recognized Ed's voice from the first syllable. It was unmistakable. Especially since our life's new focus was directed toward his destiny-shifting presence on the other end.

"Hey, Ed . . . How's it going?"

Ed has a tendency to speak slowly on the phone, a mixture of perplexity and great thought; a Hemingway man, at once tough and vulnerable.

"So I read your script."

To say that we were excited would miss half the story. Yes, we were excited that he called, overwhelmed. But we were also terrified.

Ed continued, "It's good. I liked it."

"Can I put you on speakerphone so Logan can hear?"

"Sure."

Ed was now on speakerphone.

"Hey, Logan."

"Hey, Ed."

"So I like the script."

"Thank you."

"It's well written . . . Now, where are you guys with this thing? You've shot some of it, when are you finishing it? When are you shooting the rest of the movie?"

The right answer would have been "Whenever you can make it, sir" or "What's your schedule like, sir?" But in our hasty inexperience and frazzled judgment, we blurted out, "We're planning on shooting in June."

"That's too bad . . . You see, I'm busy then. Gonna be back east shooting Ben Affleck's movie."

We heard the drumroll of our execution, the axe raised overhead. Our final words had to be persuasive.

"Well, the date isn't exactly firm," Noah replied quickly. "We'll work around your schedule."

"Well . . . You guys want to shoot your movie when you want to shoot it."

He was slipping away fast.

"Look, Ed. You're the only actor we want to play the role of our father."

"I'm not trying to fudge my way out of it," Ed replied. He started thinking out loud. "Who else could I see in this role, who could I call to help you guys?"

"Ed, you're the only actor who can pull it off . . . Why don't we sit down in person and figure this out?"

"Where are you guys? You in San Francisco?"

"No, we're down here. In L.A. . . . In Santa Monica."

"I'm in Malibu."

"Why don't we get together this week? What's your schedule like? What about tomorrow?"

"No . . . I can't do tomorrow or Wednesday," Ed said. "I got people in town. Thursday would work . . . Does that work for you guys?"

"Absolutely. What time?"

Our pens were ready, daily planners open.

"You guys wanna come by my house at around eleven?"

"Uhhhhh . . ."

He was inviting us over to his house? Were the angels of mercy shining on us?

"Sure, we'll come by your house."

Ed gave us directions. "See you guys at eleven."

We turned off the phone. EXHALED. Opened up the medicine cabinet and drank a bottle of high blood pressure pills. Walked into the kitchen and started pacing.

We'd lived to fight another day.

The plan for Thursday was clear: find out when Ed will be available to act in our movie and get him to commit. We're not leaving without a commitment. Do not relent. Do not let him back out. But above all else, don't show him you're desperate. Desperation never sold anything. Not even bandages to the wounded.

There's only solutions.

PUMPING UP TO PUMP DOWN

We worked out at Gold's Gym Venice Wednesday evening, after dinner. It was our third workout of the day: a run in the morning at 5:30 A.M., a pile of push-ups and pull-ups midday, and now, weights. The system was surging, unable to concentrate.

Our cell phone rang. It was the RESTRICTED number. This was not good. A phone call now, the night before our meeting . . . WAS NOT GOOD. After our conversation with Ed on Monday, we didn't want another phone call from anybody—and especially Ed—until after our meeting.

Our gut thought: Ed was canceling.

Logan answered the phone. "Hello."

"Hey, this is Ed."

A CATEGORY 5 just made landfall. And our sand castle was beachfront.

Ed continued, "Which one is this?"

"Logan."

We're screwed, it's over. He's come to his senses.

"Hey, Logan."

Yes, it's definitely over. He talked to his people and they brought him back to reality. YOU'RE A MOVIE STAR, ED. These guys, these twins, ARE NOTHING, NOBODIES. C'mon, Bruckheimer just called last week. National Treasure 2, baby! Let's follow the treasure, Ed. Follow the treasure . . .

Ed continued, "I need to run some errands in the morning so

we're not going to be able to meet at my house. I'll come to you. Where are you in Santa Monica?"

Breathe, remember to breathe, Logan. Look in the mirror, you're still here.

Logan said, "We're at Ninth Street, north of Wilshire. A block south of Montana. Can we buy you lunch?"

"Not necessarily . . ."

"Do you know where the Starbucks is on Seventh and Montana?"

"Sure do."

"Let's meet there."

Logan hung up and relayed the call to Noah.

The crop duster ride through a tornado had just begun.

We finished our workout, speculating about the change of location. What did it mean?

Our theory: Ed called us at Gold's Gym around 8 P.M. The family had all sat down to a nice dinner, talked about the day, what's happening tomorrow. And Ed says that some guys he met in an alley in San Francisco are coming over to the house. And his wife flips out. Rightfully so. Ed comes to realize that this might not be such a good idea. They could be lunatics. "Probably are," his wife says, "especially from San Francisco."

So Ed picks up the phone and calls us to change locations for the meeting. It was the most logical inference we could form at the moment. But damn if it didn't feel like we were playing Russian roulette with five in the chamber.

LET'S SHAKE ON IT

THE VERDICT WAS pending. The future of our movie hung in the balance. And the jury would soon enter the courtroom.

We walked to the Starbucks on Seventh and Montana with our daily planners and grabbed a table on the sidewalk. We wanted to isolate our meeting with Ed, cut off potential interruptions. So we moved all the tables on one side of the building over to the other. Now there was only one table on the Montana sidewalk, and it was ours.

Ed showed up on time—Wrangler jeans, white T-shirt, and a windbreaker. We bought him an orange juice and a zucchini muffin. We got a cup of diesel, and the three of us walked outside. Ed wanted to talk baseball. We obliged. It immediately turned the wheel of power in our favor.

We had no acting experience. No screenplay sale. We had not directed a feature film. No credits to our name, not even fake ones. In Hollyworld, we had nothing. But in the baseball world, we had achieved quite a bit. We could talk with authority on the subject because we had done it.

Our baseball experience added weight to the first fifteen minutes of our meeting as we exchanged Little League stories and other great baseball moments.

Then the talk shifted smoothly into the trailer we shot during spring training.

"I was impressed," Ed said. "It really looked good."

He still hadn't mentioned his role in the movie. So Noah forced the issue.

"You've always reminded us of our father. Ever since we were little kids, watching *The Right Stuff, Places in the Heart,* every time we saw you we thought of our dad. And looking at you now, in person . . . You have similar mannerisms."

"Well, I like the role of him in your script. He's a good guy. He's just got some problems. He's conflicted . . . Now, if I was to help you out." Ed sighed, wiped his forehead with his hand. "You see, I'm so damn busy for the next six months . . ." You could tell he wasn't bullshitting us. He was genuine, a real person, a guy you could grab a cheeseburger and beer with.

He started thinking out loud. "I'm helping Ben Affleck with his movie, the first one he's directing, leaving in a couple days for Boston. I finish with Ben in the last week of July and then I'm taking my family on vacation, riding horses in Montana. Then I'm off to New York to do this one-man show until after Thanksgiving . . . When did you say you wanted to shoot this thing? How long do you need me?"

"We'll shoot whenever you can make it. You're our number one guy. We don't want anyone else to play our father but you. Period. You're the only actor that can do it."

During our first phone call with Ed, we made the mistake of saying that we were shooting in June. We thought that having a firm shooting date would make us appear more professional. But now, the schedule revolved around Ed. Whenever he could make it was when we were shooting.

"You guys got a calendar in those things?" he said, motioning to our oversize daily planners.

Noah turned to the calendar section and slid it over to Ed.

"Let's look at August," Ed said. "So I'll be with my family for the first two weeks. Sorry fellas. I can't push that." He smiled. "I love my family."

"We understand."

"But . . ." Ed studied the dates. "If you guys can push your shooting—how many days do you need me?"

"Fifteen."

He sighed. "That'll be tough . . . What kind've weeks will you be working? Five or six days?"

"We're planning on five-day weeks."

"It would sure help me if you could do six."

"No problem, we'll shoot six. Hell, we'll shoot seven days straight if you want. We don't need to rest."

The skies were parting. We could feel the light from above. We might not need to sell our teeth for this one.

Noah handed Ed a pen. Ed circled August 21–September 2 in Noah's calendar.

"If you guys can move your schedule from August twenty-first to September second, then I can give you two six-day weeks." Ed shifted in his chair, thinking. "But that's not going to be enough. You guys said you need fifteen."

"We can shoot you out in twelve. Absolutely. You give us twelve days, and we'll get it done."

How could we shoot all of Ed's scenes in twelve days? It wasn't enough time. But we figured we should commit to it now and figure it out later.

"So . . . do we have a deal?" Ed asked.

Do we have a deal?. . .

Hold on.

Ed Harris is asking *us* if we have a deal?

"Ed . . . ," Noah said, a grin turning into a laugh. "We're supposed to be asking YOU if we have a deal."

"Do we?" Ed asked, firm, straight-faced.

"Hell-yeah, we have a deal!"

"Good," Ed replied. "Let's shake on it."

Let's shake on it? This was our kinda guy, the men we knew growing up, the salt of the earth, the blue-collared boys from back home. Ed rose from his chair and extended his hand to Logan. Logan rose from his chair and shook it. Ed tightened his grip, smiled, looked Logan in the eyes. Logan smiled, looked Ed in the eyes. Ed turned to Noah, who was now standing. Another firm handshake.

"You know we're going to pay you, right?" Logan said. We hadn't talked money yet, and Ed hadn't brought it up.

"I figured you'd pay me scale," Ed replied, taking a bite of his zucchini muffin, as if money was an afterthought.

When Ed said he'd "help us out," he meant it. He was under the impression that he was going to work for "scale." Scale is the lowest amount of compensation he could accept under the SAG agreement, without getting into trouble. And it ain't much, $1,500 a week. Ed was willing to act in our movie for three grand.

In our initial budget, we had allocated X number of dollars for cameras. (Remember, this budget existed on PAPER ONLY. We still hadn't raised a dollar of financing. *And nobody could know this*.) But after Panavision awarded us the New Filmmaker Grant, that *theoretical* money was freed up to disburse to other departments and line items. We felt it only right to give Ed that money. No matter what we paid him, it would still be considerably less than his usual rate.

Noah said, "Ed, we have X amount set aside for your role. The Panavision grant freed up a lot of money. You should have it."

Ed smiled. "Even better . . . Now all you guys need to do is call my agent at CAA [Creative Artists Agency] and get a copy of the script to him. He's expecting your call. I already told him I was doing your movie."

He already told his agent? Wow. He'd made up his mind to do our movie before sitting down with us! His gut told him he should do our movie, and that's what he'd listened to. Like any great artist, he believed in his instincts. But maybe he also felt he got to know us from the script, and that if we had the nuts to rush the stage in San Francisco with fourteen hundred people watching and an army of security, cops, and press blocking our way, then we had the nuts to pull this whole thing off.

It didn't seem real though.

How could it be real? This isn't how deals are done in Hollywood. Ed Harris is one of America's finest actors. And who were we?—just two guys with a dream. But in the beginning, that's all you got.

We refilled our coffees and talked for another hour. Ed gave us big hugs when we left. We felt important, confident, unstoppable.

Ed Harris was going to star in our movie. And the deal was cemented with a handshake.

AGENT MAN

CAA's building is called the "Death Star." The name says it all. And we might as well have been Luke Skywalker and Han Solo.

CAA is the most powerful and intimidating agency in Hollywood. They do not compromise. They do not negotiate. They demand. And they usually get it. You want them as your representatives. But you do not want to go against them or piss them off. And they DO NOT waste time talking to guys like us—EVER. In fact, we were so far below them they couldn't even see us.

So we called CAA after our meeting with Ed, excited.

Agent Man answered, sick to his stomach.

"This is the Miller Brothers. Ed Harris told us to call you. He's doing our movie."

"I know," Agent Man said. He walked over to the wastebasket and puked. "Send me the script."

Agent Man hung up, screamed, and threw his phone out the tenth-floor window.

And we sent him the script.

NO THANKS, I'LL TAKE MY DINNER BEFORE THE NUKE

We were living off pots of oatmeal, beans and rice, milk and sardines. Meat always came out of a can. But tonight we needed to celebrate, blow some plastic money, pause and reflect on the range of emotions over the past few months: our father's death, the lift and encouragement of the Panavision grant, the thrill of shooting in Arizona, the rush of the ambush—Ed Harris shaking on the deal.

Seven years earlier, we had started at the lowest possible position in the industry: ignorant of the trade, uneducated and unskilled, no family or friends in the business, not one person we could call— NOT ONE—nothing to announce our arrival in the city of movies but an address in a crummy apartment off Hollywood Boulevard. But now we had strong-armed our way through the gate and were about to make a bold entrance into the exclusive club.

We got an outdoor table at Rosti on Montana and asked for their cheapest bottle of red wine. The waitress said they didn't serve alcohol. So we walked up the street to Fireside Cellars and asked the guy behind the counter to give us his finest "Ten-dollar bottle of red wine," threw it on a credit card, and sat back down at our sidewalk table.

We each ate half a chicken, a loaf of garlic bread, mashed potatoes and gravy, and watched beautiful people and cars pass by, drinking our wine in the easy weather of Southern California. This was the last space of comfort before the frontal assault, and we knew it. Ed was now on board, and that would radically change the dynamics. It was real now. The pressure was mounting, and so we savored this brief interval like soldiers the night before battle.

The next morning, the world exploded.

CLOUDS OF MUSHROOMS

Ed called at 10 A.M. Here's what he said: "I'm sorry, guys. But I can't do your movie."

We were working at our desk. Before Noah answered, our guts told us this was a *very* bad phone call. As you produce a movie, your instincts become keenly aware of the *good*, promising phone calls, and the *bad*, not-so-promising ones. You know when you see the caller ID whether it's a victorious call or whether one of your cities has just been nuked. This call was an incoming missile. It wasn't to say thanks for coffee or some creative question about the script. We knew disaster was on the other line.

Noah stood from the desk, instant vertigo, the room with white walls started spinning.

Ed continued, "I screwed up. I'm sorry. The dates I gave you won't work. I have to go to the Toronto and Venice Film Festivals to promote this movie I did last year. I'm going to be there the last week of August and the first week of September, the same time I was gonna do your movie."

CUT TO: AGENT MAN—IN HIS OFFICE

Grinning, scheming, rubbing his palms together in front of his face, Ha, ha, ha . . .

BACK TO OUR APARTMENT

Logan saw the death of our movie in his brother's eyes. Noah came back with, "Ed, you're doing our movie. You have to do our movie. We're counting on you. You can't do this."

"Guys, I'm sorry. I messed up. I'm not the kinda guy that goes back on a handshake. I made a mistake, I'm sorry."

"When *can* you do it?"

"That's the problem. There's no time I *can* do it . . . I'm doing Ben's movie until August. Then I'm with my family, and as soon as I come back I'm in Venice and then Toronto. And right after that I'm in New York doing the play."

"Do you absolutely have to go to the festivals?"

"I have to. I put a lot of hard work into that role. They're counting on me to be there . . . Look, guys, I'm not trying to fudge my way outta your movie. If I could do it, I would."

"Ed, you gotta do our movie. We'll figure it out."

"Guys, I can't. I feel terrible."

"What about the play? Is it happening for sure? Are the dates set?"

"Let me call the guy and check."

He hung up.

CUT TO—AGENT MAN IN HIS OFFICE

A look of confusion, trouble brewing. What is this? I thought we were finished with these hooligans? The agent throws his hands in the air. "What the fuck, Ed?!"

BACK TO OUR APARTMENT

Who would put us through this kind of torture? If there was a layer of Hell for this type of emotional carnage, it would be called WHIPSAW, sandwiched between Purgatory and Limbo. We paced our apartment, cursing, sweating, manic and dizzied. We felt like peeling off our skin, ripping out the concrete walls with our teeth, shattering windows and denouncing the heavens. How could we get this close and then lose it? Ed had given our movie life and then chopped off its head.

Ed called back. "It won't work, guys. I start rehearsals first week of September."

AGENT MAN

Ha, ha, ha . . . He leans back in his chair, throws his feet on the desk.

OUR APARTMENT

"Ed, it has to work," Noah said. "It's going to work. You're doing our movie."

"I know, guys. I hate it. I don't break my word. But there's no way I can do it this year."

"When's the play over?"

"Thanksgiving."

"What if we push our movie until after Thanksgiving?"

"You don't want to do that."

"We'll do whatever it takes, Ed."

CUT TO—AGENT MAN

Oh, no you're not, Ed!

OUR APARTMENT

"You gotta do our movie, Ed."

"But . . . we won't have time for rehearsals . . . It's going to be rushed, guys."

It was insane for us to consider filming in Northern California in December, especially with the large number of daytime exterior scenes in our movie. It can rain the entire month. Most of Ed's scenes took place outdoors. And if it rained, we were finished. It's also cold. The days are terribly short. The sun doesn't rise above thirty degrees latitude, and consequently, we'd be limited to eight hours of daylight shooting—maximum—which wouldn't be sufficient to complete all of Ed's scenes in twelve days. If we pushed to December, we'd be faced with an almost impossible challenge. On the other hand, if we didn't push to December, Ed wouldn't be in our movie. We had to decide immediately. Ed was slipping away. You could feel it in his voice. Our little movie was turning into a big hassle for him. We needed to find a solution NOW. Tomorrow would be too late. We'd probably never hear from him again. He was five seconds away from hanging up.

Then Noah asked, "So you're free after Thanksgiving, right?"

CUT TO—AGENT MAN

No, no, NOOOOOO!!!!!!!!!!!!!!

OUR APARTMENT

"Yeah," Ed replied. "I'm free after Thanksgiving."

"Are you sure the play won't go beyond Thanksgiving?"

"I told them that's all I'm giving them."

"Great. So you'll do our movie if we push until after Thanksgiving?"

"You sure you want to do that, guys?" Ed asked. "I don't want to be the one to hold up your movie."

"Ed, you're our number one guy. Nobody else is playing our father. NOBODY. We got a deal. We shook on it."

CUT TO—AGENT MAN

Fuck a handshake! It'll never hold up in court!

OUR APARTMENT

Ed said, "If you guys can push until after Thanksgiving, I'm yours."

"Done. We'll push until after Thanksgiving."

"Thanks, guys." Ed got fired up. "All right, my boys!"

"All right then, Pops."

CUT TO—AGENT MAN

The phone, the chair, and the desk are flying out the window onto the street, glass bouncing on the pavement. A screaming man can be heard throughout Beverly Hills.

OUR APARTMENT

We sprouted gray hair during that conversation. From then on, every day was the Cuban Missile Crisis. At any moment our world could blow up.

PART V

DANCING AROUND THE FIRES OF GREED

MONEY,
WHERE DOES IT GROW?

NO MONEY, NO movie.

Raise money.

Raise money.

We gotta raise money.

How the hell do we do that?

We don't know anybody with big money.

Nothing, nothing, nothing, nothing, nothing, nothing in this entire struggle came close to exceeding the anxiety produced by the hunt for money. Nothing.

Most movies, at least most of the movies that make it into a theater, are the product of a studio: Fox, Universal, Warner Bros., Disney, Sony, etc. These studios have production companies responsible for manufacturing movies. Typically, a producer is the head of one of these production companies. The studio is essentially the bank. The producer secures a loan from the studio and makes the movie.

So why not take our movie to a studio and secure a loan? Because we had no credit. The studios are not in the subprime, easy lending business. We would not qualify for one of their loans under any circumstances. Nobody in Hollywood was going to give us a chance to direct and act in our movie. Nobody. It was too risky.

A production company *might* buy the script from us with Ed Harris attached. Might. But then the production company would, in all likelihood, marginalize our involvement, or get rid of us entirely, bring on a new writer or writer(s) to mutilate our script, and then, five years later, if ever, get a loan from the bank and produce our movie. Chances are we wouldn't even recognize our story once it was thrown on the big screen.

We could live with failing on our own terms, but we couldn't live with failing on someone else's. If *we* made our movie and it failed, *we* could live with that. But if *someone else* made our movie and it failed? Well, that wasn't an option.

We would need to be the studio *and* production company. And in order to accomplish this, we needed money.

But where to find it?

Everybody loves movies. Most people are fascinated with celebrities and the mystery behind making a movie. Most people, that is, except those in Hollywood. It's what they do every day. The charm has worn off. But people *outside* of Hollywood? They can't get enough.

We needed to find an investor that wanted to rub elbows with famous people, hang out on set and watch the camera roll, someone who would mount the poster on his wall like a Picasso. Someone far from the jaded world of filmmaking. Someone who still felt the magic each time he watched a movie. And that was the opportunity we could provide him.

What's more, there was a new tax incentive. Prior to 2001, movie financiers had to write off their investment by amortizing it over ten years. A pain in the ass. But now a financier could write off the entire investment in *one* year. This write-off also carried with it the prospect of gain. If the movie was successful, the financier would make money on a wad of cash he had already written off.

So we packed our bags for Northern California, determined to stay until we raised the money. Our mom said we could move back in with her. Not exactly a confidence builder—moving back in with our mom, that is. But we are fortunate that she loves us. It was the fifth time we'd moved back home since we'd left at twenty. A record we were not proud of . . .

On our way out of town, we stopped to meet a couple of people.

ROBERT FORSTER AND THE SILVER SPOON

Connie Hoy, our first assistant director in Tucson, had worked with Robert Forster on a movie a year earlier and suggested him for the role of "Perk." We sent the script to Robert's manager. Robert read the script and wanted the role. We'd heard he was a great guy, but we'd also heard too many horror stories about difficult actors making the director's life hell. So before we could give him the role we needed to meet him, feel him out, see for ourselves.

During the first few days of filming the crew sizes up the director. Is the director a leader, decisive? Do the actors respect him or her? If the actors respect the director, the crew follows. If the actors don't, the crew probably won't either. And with first-time directors working with highly distinguished actors, this relationship was dramatically intensified.

We met Robert at the Silver Spoon restaurant on Santa Monica Boulevard in West Hollywood. He has his own table there. He greeted us as though we'd just walked into his house.

Robert is a throwback: classy, manly, and charming, self-possessed and confident. You immediately get the feeling that you can trust what he says. He treated us like established directors.

"This is my lucky table," Robert said. "A lot of good things have happened to me at this table. I figured it was a good place for us to sit. When I was at the lowest point in my career and thought I'd never work again, this kid tracked me down here and dropped a script on this table, said he loved my work, wanted me to read the script and see if I would be interested in acting in the movie."

The kid was Quentin Tarantino. The script was *Jackie Brown*. Robert was nominated for an Academy Award in that role. It resurrected his career.

"I really like your script, guys," Robert said. "You've got your foot on the audience's chest the entire time."

The waitress came over and refilled Robert's coffee.

"These young gentlemen wrote a terrific script," Robert said to the waitress. He introduced us. She poured us coffee.

Robert continued. "The characters are excellent. They're all different. You don't even need to look at their names when they speak, you just know who they are by what they say—really well-developed characters."

His praise was uplifting. Here was an actor we deeply respected, worked with Tarantino and John Huston, an old pro who's read thousands of scripts from the top writers in the business, and he was now complimenting *our* script.

The waitress returned.

Robert said, "Get whatever you want, boys. It's on me."

"Don't fight him," the waitress said. "It won't happen. Robert would never let me take your money."

We ordered bacon and eggs.

"So this character you want me to play, this 'Perk,' or rather, excuse me, this character I'd like to play," Robert said. "Is he modeled after a real-life guy? Someone you know?"

"Yes, sir," Noah said. "He's modeled after Coach Gough, a retired San Francisco cop and Khe Sanh Marine. He was like our surrogate father growing up, always real good to our dad. They had an understanding you know, both were veterans . . . You look just like Coach."

"What about the name? Why do you call him 'Perk' in the script?"

"We took the name 'Perk' from another one of our favorite coaches, Jim Perky."

We asked Robert how he got into acting.

"Well, I was in college at Syracuse and I saw this great-looking gal walk by . . . So I followed her and she walked into the drama department theater. They were holding auditions for a play. I figured this was a good place to be."

"Did you audition?"

"Yeah, and I got the role."

"What about the woman?"

"I ended up marrying her."

The Silver Spoon was filled with actors and actresses in their sixties and seventies, modest and polite, with color and high character, and Robert appeared to be the mayor of the joint. It felt like a small town coffee shop, where people come over to the table for a few minutes, good morning, how you doing, ask about the family, and then move on. We were in the heart of Hollywood, the capital of arrogance and rudeness, the land of inflated self-importance and distinction, but in here, there was none.

Robert was a bridge to the golden days. He told us about his first role. John Huston was the director. Robert was terrified, kept asking Mr. Huston when they were going to rehearse. Mr. Huston kept saying "soon."

Finally the day came for Robert to act. Still no rehearsal. He'd been going nuts in a Manhattan hotel room for weeks. He figured now Mr. Huston would surely take the time to instruct him, rehearse a bit. So Mr. Huston calls Robert over to the camera, tells Robert to look through the lens at the shot they are about to film. Robert looks through the lens, and Mr. Huston says, "Now . . . what do you think you need to do, Bobby?"

And that was it. He pushed Robert into the scene.

We talked for three hours, finished breakfast after lunch. Robert Forster was our guy.

BRAD DOURIF AND STARBUCKS

Next up was Brad Dourif. He told us to meet him at a Starbucks in Tarzana. We drove out there, our car packed for the top secret money-raising mission in Northern California. (Everyone, Ed, Robert, and Brad, and all their representatives assumed we had the money. Nobody, at least no rational human being, would take these steps without it.)

We walked into Starbucks and looked around, no sign of Brad Dourif—so far as we could tell. But there was a guy in the corner with a brown fedora pulled low, the line of customers forming a broken wall between us and him. He had a long ponytail and hair bushing out the sides.

We grabbed a table and sat down. A few minutes went by.

The guy in the corner with the fedora pulled low was studying us, sipping his venti coffee.

"Do you think that guy in the hat is Brad Dourif?"

"I don't think so . . . I told him to look out for the twins. If it was him, he would've come over by now."

Another couple minutes went by. And the guy with the fedora kept staring. At first, his staring wasn't that unusual. We're twins, a freak show, people always stare. But he was now crossing the line.

"That's gotta be him, that's gotta be Brad Dourif. If it's not him, I'm gonna ask the damn guy what his problem is."

We stood and walked over.

"You must be the twins?" the guy in the fedora said.

"Actually, we're cousins."

"And I'm Ed Harris."

Even the president of the Brad Dourif Fan Club would've had trouble picking him out of a lineup that day.

We sat down and Brad went cold, leery, suspicious of us. And he had good reason to be. Brad is an Academy Award nominee, taught acting at Columbia University, an astute and searching mind. A veteran of over a hundred movies from big-budget block-busters to B-movie horror flicks, he's worked with every stripe of director—Academy Award winners, dictators, thinkers, scream-ers, monitor jockeys, and first-timers. He wasn't about to jump on some miserable caravan across the Sahara with no water. He'd read the script and his agent said he wanted the role. But "wanting" is only the first step. "Wanting" is still a long ways from committing, which is an even longer road from a fully executed contract, which are still marathons away from showing up on set and putting *their* face in front of *your* camera. The meeting today was to decide if we were moving beyond the "wanting" stage.

We showed Brad the trailer. Like Ed, Brad understood the amount of work required to put beautiful images on screen. It gave us credibility, and he warmed to us. We weren't just two guys running around with a good script.

"Ed told us he's a huge fan of your work," Noah said.

This melted the last iceberg. Brad took off his hat, sighed, color rushed into his face. He rolled his eyes and ran his hands through his hair, feeling the pressure. "I gotta get my head out of the house . . . I gotta get to work . . . Ed Harris, shit . . . The guy's amazing."

"Yep, he's a big fan."

This wasn't some rinky-dink movie. Serious actors were on board. Brad would have to prepare, bring his A-game.

"I'm thinking that Clyde should be subtle, nothing over-the-top," Brad said.

"He's not a retard, and he's not Daniel Day-Lewis in *My Left Foot* either," Logan said.

"He's a poet," Brad replied.

"It's gotta be subtle, Brad."

"We'll rehearse as often as you like," Logan said.

"Good, 'cause I'm going to need it. I'm cutting my hair off for the role. *Deadwood* is over. I think Clyde would have short hair."

"He does. Good call."

Nuanced, eccentric, penetrating, that's Brad, a cross between a wizard and a vagabond. An avid astronomer, he's probably got an IQ of 180. He can shift effortlessly from an exhaustive commentary on nuclear physics and jet propulsion to the micronutrient properties of goat's milk. And he just might be able to read your thoughts.

We discussed his approach to acting, how he likes to observe and study people, find a subject, and assume its characteristics. While preparing for Billy Bibbit in *Cuckoo's Nest,* he hung out in mental hospitals and worked with an expert on speech impediments.

"I'm working on a few things with Clyde's speech, rolling of the tongue, lazy tongue, common with these types of brain injuries . . . I'm thinking he should also have some physical disability—subtle guys, don't worry."

"We gotta watch out for you actors," Noah said with a smile. "Make sure you don't *act* too much."

"I'm thinking that one of his hands should be impaired, doesn't fully function . . . Where's the real Clyde?"

"Don't know where he is . . . ," Noah said. We hadn't seen our uncle in several years. "When you're developing Clyde, keep this in mind: the audience needs to immediately discern that something is off with Clyde, but subtly. We don't want to bash them over the head. And that's difficult, hard to pull off. The risk of being too subtle is that the audience will think Clyde is just a deadbeat, some lazy artist. On the other hand, the risk of going too big is that they won't be able to understand what Clyde is saying, the wisdom behind his dialogue will be lost . . . We've gotta be somewhere between these polarities."

"You guys are also acting in it, right?" Brad asked.

"Yep."

"Shit." He grinned. "You guys are nuts."

HEAD NORTH, SON

WE DROVE NORTH in search of gold. The mission had to remain top secret, and nothing remains secret in Hollywood. It's one big mouth. So we didn't tell anybody why we went home. Only that we went. If Ed's agents or attorneys found out that we had no money—that we were living with our mom, searching for cash—our moviemaking charade would be over.

But as the winds of fortune would have it, Ed's people ignored us for several months. And we happily ignored them. If they had talked to us about Ed's contract early on, it would have been nearly impossible to prevent them from finding out that we were broke. One of their first demands would have been for us to escrow Ed's salary, a standard practice when dealing with unknown producers. And guess what? We wouldn't have been able to do it. Our bluff would have been called.

Yes, Ed gave us his word. But realize how theoretically flimsy this guarantee is in the movie business. At this point, we didn't know Ed, and he didn't know us. What if he was offered several million dollars to star in a movie in December, the same time we were going to film? Totally possible. In fact, highly likely. The pressure exerted upon him from his agents, attorneys, advisors, not to mention family and friends, would have been severe. Thinking about this scenario—and many others—made us neurotic.

Ed was the linchpin, the only reason our movie would make sense to a prospective investor. No Ed, no money. And no money, no movie. And we were all too aware of this terrifying fact. The devastating potential of Ed leaving our movie pressed against us constantly.

Constantly.

Three Academy Award–nominated actors were on board, with dates penciled into their calendars, and still we had no money.

We had no backup plan, no contingency, no "if this happens, we'll do this, and when that happens, we'll do that." We couldn't operate on contingencies. Life has never worked out that way for us. Our world never travels from A to B to C. It only works like that in business school models and self-help books. Our path has always been more pinball than bullet train. Know your end point and drive toward it. If you get knocked off course, tack your way back.

Like Yoda said, "Do or do not. There is no try."

Presumably, any savvy investor would want to see a signed contract from Ed before putting money into our movie. Problem was we couldn't *get* a signed contract from Ed until we paid him; his people would never allow that ink to touch that paper. It was an excruciating catch-22.

But we *did* have a shooting schedule. Pretend as if, and it shall become. And we were pretending as if we had the money.

It was so unheard of to have a shooting schedule *without* any money, that people just assumed we *had* the money.

It was mid-May. Because of Ed's schedule we had decided to break up principal photography (the actual filming of the movie) into two segments. Three weeks in September, break for two months, and then return in December and shoot for two weeks with Ed. And EVERYONE thought we were crazy to break it up. Yes, EVERYONE. "Shoot it all in November and December" was the advice from the experts. "Do *not* break up the shooting schedule. It's insane."

But we thought THEY were insane. From a conventional perspective, they were right. Dividing up principal photography invited countless disasters into our movie; so many that we won't begin to list them. It would become its own book. But we'll provide you with one of the more prominent considerations: CONTINUITY.

Let's say we have a scene at the quarry. The first part of the scene is with the brothers—Clint and Lane. The second part of the scene is with Charlie (Ed Harris). We shoot the brothers in September. It's hot and dusty. It's perfect. Then Ed shows up in December to shoot the same scene, and now it's raining, the quarry is a mud pit, the grass on the hills has turned from September Gold to Leprechaun Green. We'd be in big trouble. The scenes won't cut.

So you see the potential problem . . .

By breaking up the schedule, we placed part if not most of the scenes in this catastrophic jeopardy. All the brothers' scenes could be sunny. All of Ed's scenes could be raining—September Gold to Leprechaun Green. Ever seen a movie like this? No. You haven't. Because it doesn't work. It can't work. But this is what we were facing. It was supremely plausible and *very* real.

And we still thought the experts were wrong.

So we carefully examined every scene in our script, searching for ways to avoid continuity errors. We were filming in our backyard. We knew the land, the weather patterns, the sunlight of September, and the long shadows of December. We had explored the grassy hills and built tree forts in the mighty oaks, played baseball on every local diamond and horse pasture in West Marin, rode our bikes along the country roads, dug ditches and pulled weeds, slept in the warm grass in September and the cold, damp forests of December, stumbled home drunk on the dirt paths and through horse stables, driven past blooming flowers, cow pastures, and pumpkin fields. We knew every fold, stream, ridge, tree, rock, squirrel, scrub jay, raven, and person in these parts.

But of course, all this attention to the schedule was tied to the money. No money, no movie.

So we mass produced our business plan and distributed it widely, with the basic pitch:

"We're making a movie with Ed Harris. Do you know anyone who might be interested in investing?"

"Maybe . . ."

"Great, here's ten. Pass them around."

Tim Logan, our blood brother, built us a Web site. It contained the two-minute trailer, brief bios, the Panavision Grant, Kodak and FotoKem endorsements, and an article from a Tucson newspaper. Not too much information, just enough to spark interest, just enough to get us in the room with a potential investor.

We made a hundred phone calls a day. We needed to raise several million dollars in six weeks. Shooting in September meant that we would need to start spending money in July.

Gordon told us, "It's going to take you just as long to raise ten thousand dollars, as it will to raise one hundred thousand, as it will to raise a million, as it will to raise ten million."

We followed his advice. We weren't going to nickel and dime the financing by accepting ten grand here and five grand there. We wanted one investor, at most, four. It was all about getting in front of the right person.

Were we out of our minds for jumping the schedule to September, a full two months earlier than we needed? Ed was coming in December. If we waited, started filming in late November, and shot the entire movie in one chunk, then we'd have two more months to secure the financing. The self-imposed September deadline had increased the stakes in an already high-stakes game.

What were we thinking?

CAN YOU JUGGLE? YES, BUT ONLY CHAIN SAWS

Finding leads on money was easy. But getting money from them was damn hard.

Everybody wanted to sit down and "talk" to us about our movie. It was novel. It allowed them to pull up the curtain for a moment and peek at the mechanics behind their most cherished entertainment.

In effect, WE became their amusement for the day, perhaps the week. We would meet with prospective investors—at their office, their house, for dinner—all hope and enthusiasm. *This is the one!* But in reality, they had no intention of giving us a dime. We were their jesters, their twin fools.

We spent countless hours on phone calls and in-person meetings with people who were full of shit. Some of them were even dangerous.

THE POOL THAT COULD SINK US

It started as a harmless conversation at a pool party in Vegas. Alcohol was involved. The temperature was hovering at a pleasant eighty-five degrees. They were in the shallow end, strawberry margaritas in hand. He was splashing her. She was splashing him. They were smiling, giggling. He winked at her. She winked back. He was getting laid tonight. And we were about to get screwed.

He started bragging about our movie, about his involvement. Maybe he was producing it, who knows? He was trying his best to get laid, and movie producers, he presumed, get laid rather easily.

He refilled their margaritas with fresh slush, and they sat on the edge of the pool, feet in the water, all smiles and lust. The sun was setting. Turns out she's a conduit to BIG MONEY. HUGE

MONEY. She knows the Gettys or Rockefellers or some other whale of wealth. And you guessed it—they're looking to invest in a movie. He's hit the jackpot. Sex and money.

Now, this guy in Vegas is a buddy of a buddy. This doesn't imply that he's not a good guy, only that we didn't know him that well. And we had made the mistake of giving him a business plan.

"We should call my producing partners, the twins," he says. "You should talk to them."

"I'd love to," she replies, eyes sparkling in his.

He pushes himself up and stands at the pool's edge, offers his hand and lifts her up, balancing his drink marvelously. Then he dries his hand, winks at her again, and calls us on his cell phone, excited. He's gonna be a PRODUCER!

"Guys, you gotta talk to this beautiful woman here. She's a friend of mine. Pitch her on *our* movie. I think she could help *us* secure the financing."

So she gets on the phone and we pitch her on our movie. It was going good until . . .

. . . we mentioned Ed Harris—the star of our investment.

"Ohhhh . . . Ed Harris," she says. "I know his agent, Agent Man. I'll give Agent Man a call tomorrow and put in a good word for you guys. Let him know you're looking for financing. He can probably help."

NOOOOOOOOOOOOOOOOOOOO!!!!!!!!!!!!!!!!!!!!!!!!!!!!!!!!!

Put in a good word? Lady, you just put our neck in the lock of a guillotine.

CUT TO—PHONE CONVERSATION—DOOMSDAY TIMES TEN

(In our neurotic minds, this is how it might have gone down.)

POOL GIRL: I just talked to the Miller Brothers, you know those guys that are doing the movie with Ed Harris?

AGENT MAN: Yeah, I know those cocksuckers. What about 'em?

POOL GIRL: We had a great conversation. Nice guys. I'm gonna try to raise them some money.

AGENT MAN: For what?

POOL GIRL: Their movie, of course.

AGENT MAN: They don't have any money?

POOL GIRL: No.

Agent man is doing back flips across his office. All she can hear is gymnastics.

Agent man calls Ed. Agent man is more fired up than the day he moved out of the mailroom.

AGENT MAN: These guys are full of shit, Ed. They don't have any money. They duped you. Duped us. Duped everyone. Their movie ain't happening . . . Check out the script I just sent you, *Death Hunt 5000*. Universal is offering two mil, plus back-end.

BACK TO US

Our hearts knocked, creaked, pounded against our ribs. It sounded like the stressing of a submarine falling into the abyss, slowly imploding.

What had we done? What did we awaken?

Our survival right now depended on the immediate cooperation of brain and mouth. Noah thought quickly, then spoke: "You know, that's probably not a good idea to call Ed's agent."

"Why not? I love Agent Man. He's a great guy. It'll be great. I'll say how GREAT you guys are."

"No . . . Please don't," Noah said. "We're in high-level negotiations with Agent Man and his people right now, and your phone call could jeopardize the execution of a contract. There could be legal consequences associated with your actions that are beyond our control. If the deal unravels, our only recourse would be to sue you."

Our guy at the pool party tossed his margarita into the air—chances of him getting laid destroyed: "Whoa-whoa-whoa . . . What's going on here, guys?"

"Yep . . . We gotta be *real* careful. We're trying to close this deal. Our attorney's a killer . . ."

Silence at the pool in the desert. The margarita glass finally lands and shatters.

"Why don't we resume this phone call next week when the deal is signed?" Noah said. "Then we can disclose all the relevant details of the pending situation."

We hung up. Called Pool Guy back. "If she calls, you die."

Then we called our friend who recommended Pool Guy. "If she calls, you die too."

FIGHTING GHOSTS

It was 1:34 A.M. Logan couldn't breathe. He'd been waking up each night gasping. The stress was suffocating. He was fighting ghosts. *What if we don't get the money? What if Ed backs out? What if his agents and attorneys find out we don't have any financing yet?*

We'd crossed the event horizon. The tidal forces had grabbed hold and wouldn't stop pulling until we either *succeeded* or *failed*. All our credibility would be destroyed if we failed to raise the money. There were too many players involved now.

We had to close the ring.

Logan climbed out of his sleeping bag on the floor, sweating and gasping, turned on the lights and went into the bathroom. His face was drawn from stress. He washed it. He started taking deep breaths and long exhales, trying to calm his anxiety. After several minutes he turned off the lights, laid back on the floor, and tried to ease his mind by focusing on his breathing.

These episodes, waking in the middle of the night, gasping and heaving from anxiety, would be the norm for the next few months. It was just something Logan battled throughout the uncertainty of preproduction.

While Logan kept his stress internal, Noah raged. His stress was directed outward. He cursed all obstacles with the fury and defiance of an abolitionist sermon. Noah was in earnest. He would not equivocate. He would not excuse. He would not retreat a single inch. And he let everybody know it.

Noah made our fight apocalyptic, a fight for our souls, a fight for eternity—a fight for our father.

Grandiose?

Delusional?

Maniacal?

From a clinical perspective: YES, absolutely. But that's how Noah framed the struggle. And it worked for him.

What's your life worth?

How much do your goals matter?

What will you do to achieve them?

And sometimes Noah would go WAY out there. He would think of us as a river that had been dammed by some giant concrete wall, the water our knowledge and determination, continuously rising into this great reservoir of potential energy. Eventually it would burst. As long as we kept expanding our knowledge, the dam would break.

He drew confidence from one of the laws of thermodynamics: $KE = \frac{1}{2} mv^2$

The brotherhood was the kinetic energy. Each actor on board

increased our mass. And our velocity increased with every phone call we made, every investor we pitched, every location we scouted, every book we read, every person we consulted, every e-mail, positive thought, rewrite on the script, every atom of energy directed toward our goal.

Why wouldn't the laws of motion apply to our movie? Noah assumed they did. Either we were going to explode in a ball of fire or make our movie.

Then Noah started writing quotes on note cards and tacking them to the wall:

Thoreau: "Go confidently in the path of your dreams, live the life you've imagined." We couldn't think of any more powerful words to guide and fix our minds upon. "Live the life you've imagined" seemed to capture it all.

Emerson: "To be great is to be misunderstood."

Nobody understands us! We're doing a great job, brother.

Frederick Douglass: "For it's not light that is needed, but fire; it's not the gentle shower, but thunder. We need the storm, the whirlwind and the earthquake in our hearts."

Yes! We are a natural disaster!

Thomas Paine: "I like the man that smiles in trouble, that gathers strength in distress, and grows brave by reflection. 'Tis the business of little minds to shrink."

We weren't going to shrink. But damn if it didn't feel like we were in distress.

BOGGED DOWN IN THE NORTH

BY THE FIRST week of June, we had given business plans to friends, family, friends of friends, neighbors, practically tossing them out of our car like newspapers, and were quickly running out of leads. We'd met with several Bay Area movie investors and had been laughed out of the room. We'd been called "cocky and arrogant," told we needed "expert producers and an expert director," informed that "CAA will never let YOU GUYS direct Ed Harris," and asked "Why are you doing this? Why humiliate yourselves?"

We told them off. They could all go blow each other in the Land of Experts. We were fast building a reputation as a couple of stubborn kids who had "no idea how this business really works" by pseudoproducers who were more focused on hobnobbing with celebrities than putting out a quality movie.

We're not living in reality? Great! Fantastic! Best news we've heard in weeks. It must mean we're going somewhere. Drive it till the wheels fall off. Then yank the engine and throw it in a boat.

But no matter how defiant we were, each day brought us closer to September. And each day seemed to bring us further away from the money.

DRINK AND BE MERRY

We drove up Highway 1 to the Russian River with our blood brother Tim. We needed to get away for a few hours, forget about our frustration, hang out on the edge of things, float away on the winding roads, ocean cliffs, and redwoods, lose ourselves for the afternoon.

On our way up the coast we stopped in Bodega Bay and got a bottle of red wine and a loaf of sourdough, sat on the pier and hung out for an hour, breathing in the salty air, listening to the seagulls, watching the fishing boats chug into the harbor, the diesel rainbows on the tide.

We started to relax, a sensation dormant for months, the fermented grapes working their spell. Tim was full of wisdom and sound advice. He told us he knew we'd raise the money, that he didn't have a doubt in his mind we'd make the movie and that it was going to be terrific. His confidence was reassuring. This wasn't any bullshit. It was the conviction of someone outside the movie industry who was looking at the enterprise in simple terms. He said how much he admired our determination.

It was the remedy we needed; step outside, hear another voice besides our own, free ourselves from the tentacles of frustration, and receive the insight of a great friend.

The drive awoke old memories. It was a drive we'd taken many times with our father. He'd pick us up after work on Fridays, sweaty and brown from roofing dust, fingernails black with tar. We'd all cram into the front seat of his little truck and make the two-hour drive up the coast, chewing beef jerky and sipping Orange Crush. We'd arrive at the campsite along the Russian River after nightfall and gather wood along the bank. Dad would always bring a few wood shingles from the job site for kindling, cut shavings with his Buck knife, and in a short time we'd set up the tent in the glow of firelight. We'd rise in the silver dawn and fish all morning, and when it got hot we'd go swimming in the green pools under the willows.

The trip with Tim brought us back to those good times and dispelled the troubles and frustration we were having now. Later in the afternoon the sun warmed the redwoods above the Monte Rio Bridge and we jumped off the concrete slab and swam in the cool waters below.

THE SIX-YEAR MAC

WE BROUGHT ON casting directors Billy DaMota and Michelle Metzner to fill the acting roles that were still open. They gave us a considerable break on the up-front payment. Our movie was extremely appealing to them; Ed Harris, Robert Forster, and Brad Dourif would look great on their résumés. We retained them for a few hundred dollars.

In *Touching Home,* Mac is one of the brothers' best friends. He provides the comic relief, central to the dramatic rhythms of the movie. Without skillfully placed laughs, without scenes that lightened the audience, our movie risked being a linear descent into emotional ruin.

Six years earlier, our buddy Jeromiah Running Water Zajonc (you'll meet this champion soon) was working on a Showtime series called *Going to California.* Jeromiah invited us to a screening at the Directors Guild of America (DGA). There was one actor that caught our attention. He was onscreen for only a few minutes, but we felt he was the most talented guy in the show. His name was Evan Jones. And he *was* "Mac," though he didn't know it at the time. We remembered his name and followed his career over the years, always thinking that he would play Mac when the time came for us to make *Touching Home.*

So naturally, when our casting directors asked us who we wanted for Mac, we typed one name in the e-mail: EVAN JONES.

Billy DaMota knew Evan's agent at ICM and sent him the

script on Friday. Evan's agent called Billy on Monday and said Evan liked the script and wanted the role. So we flew Evan up to Northern California on a credit card and picked him up at the Oakland Airport.

We drove out to the country and visited our filming locations. We walked around Lunny Quarry—where Mac and the brothers work—climbed on the conveyor and rock crusher, sat in the tractors and other machinery, talked about the movie as the grit and dust settled Evan into the environment.

We told Evan that we didn't want anybody else to play Mac but him. We expressed Mac's importance to the movie, his comedy and humor, the contrast of his personality to the soft-spoken Brownie (another one of the brothers' friends), how Mac provides an offset to the brothers' determination and seriousness.

Evan asked us, "What's been the most difficult part so far?"

"Raising the money."

But of course, we hadn't raised it yet. And of course, we couldn't let him or our casting directors or anyone else know this dark secret.

In the fast approaching future, contracts would need to be signed, checks written for actors. Money would need to start flowing from our hands to other people's hands in exchange for goods and services.

It felt like we were slowly committing suicide.

We dropped Evan off at the airport. We would start rehearsing in a few weeks.

We should've been put in straitjackets.

DANCING AROUND THE FIRES OF GREED

WE HAD A conference call with a prospective investor the next day. He was some big shot lawyer who had apparently made fortunes in litigation. Prior to the call, we tried to anticipate the questions he might ask, put ourselves in his *legal* shoes, think about his motivations for investing.

He was a lawyer. He would surely ask the tough questions, search for inconsistencies. And he did, for two hours . . .

"Tell me about the movie."

We started our pitch with the usual cautionary preface. We told him that moviemaking was a speculative investment and that it's hard to find a riskier vehicle to sink money into. In fact, it's not even an investment, it's a gamble. Historically, it's hard to find worse. We were always up front with people about the hazards of investing in a movie. After listing all the pitfalls one might encounter even under the most thorough and exacting plan, we shifted gears and discussed some of the rosier dimensions of our movie, specifically, the investment *opportunities*. Remember, with enormous risk comes enormous upside. There's always a trade-off.

He started interrogating us with all the craft and sagacity of a hardened litigator, trying to draw out discrepancies in our pitch, expose inconsistencies in our business plan, reveal flaws in the investment structure. We assumed that such a thorough interrogation and expenditure of time from a man who bills out at $500/hour was a strong indication of his desire to invest.

There was a path to his questioning, a continuous chain of logic. He was quick of thought, quick to interrupt with another, deeper, more probing question, an extension to the one we were trying to answer. His intensity grew and his approach began to change. His freedom increased; his freedom to analyze and inquire, as though he were playing a new game. It was a blend of disciplined legal scrutiny and freewheeling street hustle, and as the conversation swelled and heated, his native tendencies and speculative desires fevered like a man on a hot streak at a back alley dice game.

We were his amusement for the day, a sideshow to break up the monotony of legal work, orally juggling his questions, tight-roping through the ignorant areas, swallowing the sharp questions and pulling out smooth answers while he, the circus master, barked orders and gestured fervently with his hands.

And the more excited he got, the more excited we got. Each question stoked our enthusiasm, and each answer stoked his, until we were all dancing around a bonfire of naked celebrity and movie madness. The flames licked and scorched *our* desires and *his* lust. We were three demons throwing fuel onto the inferno, swinging arm in arm around the blaze, howling and conspiring on our soon-to-be-famous deeds and imminent fortunes!

He then started name dropping. He had influential friends, men of high standing and high dollars, lions of the banking and computer industry. For all we knew he had the ear of Rupert Murdoch and held Warren Buffet's purse strings. We'd found our investor. The possibilities were intoxicating. Free at last, free at last, thank God almighty we're free at last to make our movie!

This was the one. This was the guy we'd been searching for. He talked about how electric the entire process of making a movie must be, how he's a big fan of the arts, how this is the type of investment he's been looking for, something that generated more than just money. He wanted us to meet his wife, wanted us over for dinner. Maybe he'd betroth a daughter to us.

So with our confidence flaming, white-hot now—he was ours—we asked the question that had been looming in our minds, the only question that really mattered.

"How much are you thinking of investing?"

By the way he was talking we figured he'd be good for at least 500 grand. Earlier, he had bragged about recently winning a $25 million settlement. Industry standard for his cut was 30 percent. He'd need a tax write-off for that windfall. And we were that exciting vehicle, or so we thought.

He became silent. A tense silence, as if we'd just kicked out his stained glass window. Then he began to speak, haltingly, squirming.

"If I was going to invest."

He placed considerable stress on the "if" and every "if" after that. No one was going to pin down this crafty pettifogger.

" . . . *If* I was going to invest . . . If . . . If . . . If . . ." He paused. "At the very most I would invest, remember, this is *if* I invest . . . would be somewhere between . . ." He paused again. A longer silence. He exhaled. "Remember, this is IF I was going to invest."

"Yes, we get the 'if' . . . We get the if. HOW MUCH?!"

"50 to 100 . . . thousand . . . At most."

He didn't even say dollars.

Fifty to one hundred thousand dollars sounds like a lot of money. And it is. But we needed several million. It would take twenty to forty nut-ticklers like him to bankroll our movie. That could take a lifetime to round up. Literally. Might as well hold a bake sale. Make brownies and chocolate chip cookies from now until the sun dies.

We hung up.

NO RALPH IN THIS NADIR

We'd reached the bottom. It felt like the bonfire jubilee with the attorney on that stifling afternoon in a room with no windows was the reading of our death sentence.

HANG THOSE TWINS FROM THE GALLOWS!

We weren't sleeping at night. We couldn't live with failure. All our ships were torched. We were barely sixty days from shooting and we had no money. We had everyone committed and ready to go. A million dollars' worth of contracts and commitments—and we had NO MONEY! Zip. We didn't even have the *prospects* of money. And this asshole attorney was wasting our time!—marching us up the steps to the rope.

It was a Minsky Moment. We were leveraged to the hilt. Our credit cards maxed. We had a good thing going and it was ALL about to collapse. Our demise would be infamous, a parable told in Hollywood about what *not* to do—a cautionary tale of unrestrained ambition. Our careers over before they started.

Noah said, "I'm so tired of begging for a chance, begging for an opportunity."

We needed to get out of the house and hit a workout, get the blood moving, endorphins pumping.

On the drive to lift weights, we thought about Dad, how he had died with nothing—an "indigent" according to the state. And it pissed us off. We felt like we were heading in the same direction.

Our movie wasn't going to happen.

We hit the iron hard in our friend Jasha's garage, throwing weights around in a 105-degree mechanic shop, breathing in the gasoline and oil fumes from dismantled hot rods. We blasted Judas Priest. The tension was primal. Jasha's pitbull hid under a fender leaning against the wall. She could feel the rage.

THERE'S GOLD IN THE JUNK

We drove home, dreading the return. It was 8:30 P.M., June 13. Logan started cooking dinner.

"Hey, Bro, I'm gonna clean up our bulk e-mail folder on Yahoo," Noah said. "Delete all of them."

"Why?"

" 'Cause we haven't cleaned them out in a few months . . . Probably got a couple hundred junk e-mails . . . It's not good for the computer, slows things down."

Why tonight? Who knows? But Noah felt compelled to erase the junk e-mails. Perhaps this trivial and mindless task would give him a sense of accomplishment. We didn't feel like we were in control of much right now and deleting the *Penis Enlargement* spam was something we *could* control, sort of like pulling cyber weeds. It's why people garden.

Noah opened the bulk e-mail folder on Yahoo and started deleting: Click, delete, click, delete, click, delete . . .

Noah stopped. One of the e-mails was titled "Winston." (The working title of *Touching Home.*) Noah didn't recognize the sender's name. First he thought: *How does some Nigerian spammer know about our movie?*

Then he thought it might be a conspiracy: *Is this a trap from the Hollywood agents?* He looked around the room, suspicious, as if being watched.

"Bro, come here."

Logan left the kitchen and walked into the room.

"You recognize this name?" Noah asked.

"No."

"Should we open it?"

"It could be a virus, blow up our computer."

"Let's open it. Who cares?"

We opened the e-mail. Here's what it said:

Are you still looking for money?
Brian C. Vail

That's it, the entire e-mail. No introduction, no "Hello, I'm Brian from Anywhere, USA, I'm a friend of so and so," or "This person told me to contact you about your movie."

It was strange. *Why didn't he introduce himself?*

We ran a search on the e-mail address, tracked it to a company server in Sacramento.

The only person we knew in Sacramento was Honest Pete Deterding.

In late-May, Pete had sent us an e-mail:

> **had an interesting conversation. too early to give**
> **details. i'll keep you informed.**

We hadn't thought much about Pete's e-mail until now.

Are you still looking for money?

Our reply:

Yes . . .

We called Pete at 6 A.M. the following morning. He's in construction. He gets up early.

"Do you know a guy named Brian Vail?"

"Yeah, that's the guy I was referring to in the e-mail a while back."

"He sent us an e-mail last night. It was kinda weird. He didn't introduce himself or anything, just asked us if we were still looking for money."

"Great. He's a busy guy. Call him."

Never wait for a phone call. So we called Brian Vail and left a message. "We're the movie guys. We believe we got an e-mail from you . . . You can call us back at . . ."

Our cell phone rang at 11 A.M. It was Brian. The reception was terrible and we lost the call after a few seconds. We ran over to our home line and called back.

"Hey, guys," Brian said. "Someone gave me a DVD of your trailer and a business plan."

"Pete Deterding?"

"No, I think it was someone else . . ." He paused. "Curtis Rapton, yeah, that's who gave it to me."

Pete had given a DVD of our trailer and business plan to his friend Curtis Rapton. A week later, Curtis went golfing with Brian and told him about our project. Brian said he'd like to take a look at it.

Brian watched our trailer, read our business plan, and now we were talking.

He continued, "Why don't you guys schedule an appointment with my secretary to come up to the office next time you're in Northern California . . . Where are you guys, L.A.?"

"We've been going back and forth quite a bit lately . . . But we're in Northern California now."

"Well, there's no rush."

But we were rushing. Brian's interest level seemed lukewarm; at least that's how he came across. But then again, all the *real* money men—the guys that actually have the big bucks and balls—appear that way at first, especially when they're a whale and you're a guppy.

He transferred us to his secretary.

"What's your schedule like?" she asked.

"How's tomorrow?"

"Uhm . . . Let me see. No, Brian can't do it tomorrow. He's booked."

Today was Thursday.

"What about Monday?" we asked.

" . . . Brian has an opening Tuesday morning at eleven . . . and in the afternoon at—"

"Eleven is perfect."

It was the longest weekend of our lives. We were the only guys in the working world praying for Monday to come quick. To all those people whose weekend felt mysteriously short, we apologize.

WE DIDN'T COME HERE TO FUCKING BARBECUE

WE SLEPT AT Bao's house in Sacramento on Monday night before the meeting. (Bao is Chau's brother, the woman who came to the Castro Theatre with us the night we ambushed Ed Harris. Bao is one of our best friends.) Sleeping at his house guaranteed we wouldn't be late. If our car broke down on the drive up there, we could ride the bus, walk, or hitchhike to Brian's office and still make it on time for our meeting Tuesday morning.

Brian's assistant escorted us down the hallway and into his office. The place was decorated with abstract sculptures and paintings. We had rehearsed our pitch all weekend. We were juiced.

Brian, and his CFO Mike Walker, stood up and shook our hands. They were in their early forties, wearing khakis and collared shirts. We got the feeling they weren't trying to impress anyone. They knew real estate, and they were damn good at it.

Brian and Mike are a contrast of personalities. Brian is highstrung, preoccupied, always moving, processes information with frightening speed. Mike is reserved, composed, an ex-marine with the core tattooed on his forearm. His contracts are impressively lucid and concise, with a skill in legal brevity that most attorneys lack. And he ain't even an attorney. They're a devastating team.

Mike doesn't sleep at night so Brian can.

"I hope you guys don't mind," Brian said. "But I got another guy that's going to join us in our meeting."

"Yeah, sure," we said.

It was his office. Who were we to tell him no? We figured it was another one of his employees. But it wasn't.

So the mystery guest walks in, fifteen minutes late, yapping on his cell phone, cool as iced lemonade on a hot summer day. He's got bling and pinky rings, a silk shirt, and gator-skin shoes; he might've been moonwalking above the carpet.

It turns out he's *also* a filmmaker, and by his own account, a very talented one, a rising star, someone to look out for. Let's call him "Iced Lemonade."

So Brian shows Iced Lemonade our two-minute trailer on the TV behind his desk, the trailer that's been getting everyone hot, melting fools.

Iced Lemonade watches, doesn't say a thing, nods and then sits down next to us.

Brian says, "Yo, Iced Lemonade, why don't you tell the Brothers here a little about your movie."

"Well, you see we shot dis movie, you see, and it's da shit. You know what I'm saying?"

We didn't have a clue.

Iced continued yapping and didn't stop for thirty minutes. For thirty minutes straight he bragged about how his movie is "da shit" and "my skillz" and on and on and on about what we needs to do to makes our movie "da shit" like his. And how he gots all these peoples wanting to give him millionzez for his next picture, and about how heez and Brians gonna raise fifteen millionzez to build a sound stage in Sacramento. (That's this much: $15,000,000.)

Meanwhile, Brian grabbed his putter and a golf ball and started putting around the room as Iced Lemonade, that prophet of moviemaking, rapped and rapped and rapped, and Mike sat stone as a Stoic.

We kept silent. To start rapping with him would only discredit us. Drinking the lemonade right now would've been like drinking the Kool-Aid.

This meeting was another dead end. Once again, we were someone's entertainment.

And the clock kept ticking.

For ten more minutes.

And Brian kept putting.

While Lemonade poured knowledge.

As Mike sat silent with his marine sniper's stare.

And we boiled in the mockery of the scene.

Brian was our last chance to secure the financing before the movie would be called off. And now, sitting there in his office watching this bizarre spectacle, our hopes were bludgeoned. Our optimism crushed.

We had given up. We were now out for blood. In a few seconds we were going to pick up Iced Lemonade by his saggy pants, rob him of his bling, and go Viking on his ass, when Brian set the putter against the wall, and said:

"Thanks, Iced Lemonade. That was great. We all appreciate it. I'm going to need you to leave the room now. We're going to talk business."

And that's when Noah put his fist on Brian's desk and said, "No shit. We didn't come here to fucking barbecue!"

The room slammed to silence.

Iced Lemonade walked out the door and things got cool.

Brian sat down, looked at Mike. Mike looked at him. There was a smile hidden behind their faces, as if Noah said what they wanted to say but their business etiquette muzzled them.

"Well, all right," Brian said. "Let's get down to business."

Mike placed a yellow notepad on the desk and removed a pen from his shirt pocket.

"Are you interested in investing in our movie or not?" Noah asked.

"I wouldn't have contacted you if I wasn't."

"What was that guy all about?" Logan asked. "He doesn't know his head from his ass." Frustration was polluting our manners. But maybe there was something in our candor that made a good impression.

Brian had apparently given Lemonade some money and felt Lemonade was mismanaging it. He'd called Iced Lemonade into the meeting to sort of "put him in check. He'd see your professionalism and realize how things are supposed to be done." But Brian's method didn't work. The problem was his method depended on Iced Lemonade having a rational mind. He didn't expect Lemonade to sour himself so easily.

"How much money have you guys raised?" Brian asked.

"We have three hundred thousand committed."

"Committed?"

"Yeah, committed."

"Is it in the bank?"

"No, not yet . . . It's from people we know . . . Friends. They're good for it."

"I'm sure they are," Brian said, amused. "Do you have a signed contract from Ed Harris?"

"No. Not yet."

"So how long do you think that will take?"

"He's doing our movie. He gave us his word. We shook on it."

Brian looked across his desk at Mike, skeptical. We were a couple of naive kids sitting in front of men who negotiate $100 million deals on vacation.

"Ed is doing our movie," Noah continued. "We shook on it. He's a good guy. A contract is only as good as the man's word behind it, and Ed is a good man. Anyone can sign a contract and then violate it."

"But it's better to have a contract than *not* have one," Brian said.

Then Mike asked, "How long will it take to get Ed signed?"

We knew this would come up. It had to if their interest was genuine.

"Ed shook on it," Noah repeated.

"Come on guys, a handshake?" Brian said. "This isn't 1850."

"How much would you be willing to invest?" Noah asked.

"I'll take down whatever you guys have left," Brian said in an offhand, nonchalant manner. He checked his watch.

"Whatever we have left?"

"Yeah, whatever you have left . . . So the total budget minus . . . what did you say you have committed, three hundred thousand?"

"Well . . . uhm, it's not exactly committed for sure . . ."

In theory, under the best circumstances and generosity, we could round up $300,000. These were informal commitments made to us by blue-collared folks, not savvy investors. *Could* they come up with their commitment? *Would* they come up with their commitment when the hour came? Fifty-fifty at best. We only said this because nobody wants to be the first money in the game—nobody, that is, except for a ballsy, confident, instinctive, risk-taking investor like Brian Vail. Guys like Brian Vail listen to their gut. They don't wait for the verdict, they make the verdict.

"Whatever it is, I'll take down the rest." Brian said.

"You're not blowing smoke up our asses, are you?" Noah asked. "We've had a lot of people blow smoke up our asses. We're choking on it. We don't need any more of it. "

The meeting had changed so abruptly that we questioned Brian's sincerity. In a few minutes it had gone from a nightmarish jabberfest to the genie rising out of the lamp.

"I'm serious guys. I think it's a great investment. With all the help from Panavision and Kodak, and all those other people, I figure I'm getting a lot on my dollar . . . And the chart on your business plan makes the investment even more attractive. Hey, I know it's risky."

He was referring to a chart listing the box office grosses of movies starring Ed Harris that we found on the Internet and inserted into our business plan. We felt the chart was one of our strongest selling points. Movies starring Ed Harris averaged $36 million in domestic box office receipts. The investment we were selling was a fraction of his average draw.

Brian checked his watch again. Mike was writing on his notepad, head down. "Guys, I got another meeting."

"So what's the next step?"

"We'll get back to you."

"When?"

"Soon.

SOON IS SOON

Two hours later Mike Walker sent us an e-mail.

The speed of their proposal shocked us.

The first salvo of the negotiation had been fired.

On our way home from Sacramento we stopped at a fruit stand along I-80 near Davis, ate some almonds, walnuts, and dried apricots under the shade of an oak tree, and stopped by our buddy's house two hours after we left Brian's office, not expecting to hear from Brian or Mike for at least a few days.

We checked our e-mail on our buddy's computer and saw their proposal. We said good-bye and raced back to our house. The speed of the negotiation would be dictated by our response.

We printed their proposal, marked it up with red pens and highlighters, and called Gordon to discuss. Some of their terms we could accept immediately. They had all the leverage and were being surprisingly fair with us. Movie financiers are notorious for cutting pounds of flesh from struggling filmmakers, and they weren't.

Most of their terms were win-win. They had a long-range vision for our relationship. But there was one condition that could potentially sink the deal: a signed contract from Ed Harris. This could take months. As our attorney Matthew Fladell said, "Ed probably won't be signed until next January."

CAA was not going to let Ed sign a contract until he was done filming. Why? Because the agency did not want him to do our movie. They certainly prayed he would pull out somewhere between now (late June) and Thanksgiving. The odds were in CAA's favor. If they waited us out, somewhere along the line we'd fail.

"Guys, you have a tough negotiation ahead of you," Gordon said, referring to Brian's proposed terms. "But this is a good sign . . . I would say you'll be lucky if you can close this in eight to twelve weeks."

"We don't have eight weeks. We got two, maybe three."

"It ain't gonna happen, guys. You have to let negotiations work through certain steps, rhythms. You have to be patient. Nobody closes this type of money with first-time directors *and* producers in two weeks. Nobody. I've never heard of it. So be patient."

"We have only two weeks, Gordon. We gotta close the financing in two weeks."

Gordon is the counterbalance to our financial impulses. He wasn't trying to discourage us. He's pragmatic, gives you the hard reality. And that's why we go toe-to-toe with him all the time. The volatile contrast between his personality and ours often erupts into a verbal slugfest. But we love him for it.

"Be patient," Gordon said. "It may take longer than that. It could take months . . . It most likely won't happen. That's the reality. You need to continue searching for other prospective investors."

"Gordon, this is our guy. We have to make it work. Have to. Two weeks is all we got."

"You're insane, guys. Get out of that dream world you live in.

You want to hang yourself? Closing financing is an intricate, tricky negotiation. You have to work through the steps."

"We got two weeks."

DRIVING TO BE HEARD

In order to drive the negotiation, we physically drove back to Sacramento the next day—220 miles round-trip. Of course, it was more convenient to conduct the negotiation over the phone or e-mail. But we weren't looking for convenience. We were looking to close the deal.

After our first meeting, Brian told us that Mike would exclusively handle the negotiation; we probably wouldn't talk to Brian again until we reached an agreement. And if we didn't, good luck.

We met Mike in the conference room and sat at a long wood table. There were abstract canvases on the wall and a huge six-foot-by-eight-foot satellite image of Sacramento, a patchwork of neighborhoods, golf courses, and industry. Brian Vail owned half of it.

We started going over the contract, point by point. For us, creative control was the most important condition, a nonstarter. We needed 100 percent. We couldn't have the financier interfering with our vision. "Hey, my cousin is an actor. He's gonna be the bartender," or "You need a sex scene. I want to see some tits." Whatever went on-screen started and ended with us. Good or bad. If the movie failed, we'd bear the burden. If it succeeded, we'd probably get another chance to make one.

"We'll let you guys do your job," Mike said. "Frankly, we don't know anything about making movies. We're investors. We invest in people and let them do what they're good at."

"We need to have creative control over the budget as well," Noah said.

"What do you mean?"

"We need to be able to allocate monies freely, to shift around cash and not be fixed to a specific amount for each line item. Some line items are going to be cheaper than our current budget indicates, and others are going to be more expensive. We may be able to get certain locations for free, locations that we've set aside several thousand dollars for. Other locations will cost more than anticipated."

There was a condition in their proposal that would not allow any line item in our preliminary budget to exceed 110 percent of its anticipated cost. This would have crippled us. Movie budgets are massive spreadsheets, sometimes hundreds of pages, with thousands of line items and figures. On a small budget like ours, non-union, everything was negotiable. We needed that economic freedom.

Noah said, "The budget needs to be viewed in the aggregate, not by each line item or department. These are just estimates, figures that we'll do our best to stay within. But so many aspects on the financial side shift daily. For example, if we have to shoot more film in order to get it right, then we will. We'll pull money from another department, and vice versa. This will cause some line items to exceed their initial estimate, some will be lower, and some will be eliminated entirely. The only thing that matters is that we don't exceed the entire budget, the aggregate. If we deliver the movie without overages, what does it matter how we allocate specific line items? It's the whole that counts. Ultimately, we are going to put as much money as possible on-screen. We won't pay ourselves a dime until the movie is finished. Nothing."

We weren't taking 10 percent in salaries off the top, a reasonable amount for writing, producing, acting, directing, raising the money, and everything else we were doing. They took comfort in knowing the only way we'd get paid was if we brought in the movie on budget.

The line item provision, however, was a sticking point for Mike. To him, it was a reasonable way to control the budget. But we couldn't produce the movie under that limitation. It was all improvisation. And we needed the financial freedom to improvise. An hour later he conceded the point.

Three hours later we had agreed on most of the terms. But we remained deadlocked on two issues: a signed contract from Ed Harris and the amount of interest we'd pay on Brian's money. They wanted a rolling interest rate. We wanted it capped.

Mike was worn out. So we ended negotiations for the day.

"I'll discuss the remaining issues with Brian."

"How long until you get back to us, Mike?"

"I'll get back to you tomorrow."

We called Gordon. He was shocked.

"I can't believe you guys were able to come to an agreement on most of the issues." He paused. No one pauses longer than Gordon on the phone. "Still, getting a signature and the money is a long ways off. Guys, you have to stay firm on the Ed Harris contract provision and the amount of interest you'll pay on the money. Keep hammering them. Let Brian and Mike know that it's unrealistic for Ed to be signed by the time you start filming. This is the way it works in Hollywood . . . Personally, though, I would never start a production without an actor signed, never did. But you guys are the producers, and in this case, I don't see it happening. Furthermore, you don't want to engage Ed's people at a precarious time like this . . . And regarding the interest, you're insane if you agree to a rolling interest rate. Insane. You have to cap it. Otherwise you may never pay it off. Stay firm. Remember, it's going to take resoluteness, integrity, consistency, and strength. Good show."

CAN'T TAKE NOTHING
FROM NOTHING

"YOU'RE INSANE IF you sign this contract," Gordon said. "Don't do it."

"Gordon, we have to."

"No you don't. You don't have to sign anything."

"We can't forget the ultimate goal here. We can't lose sight of that. The goal is to make our movie. And we need money to do that."

Two and a half weeks after our first meeting with Brian and Mike, they were ready to escrow several million dollars into a joint account at Borel Private Bank and Trust in San Francisco—*without* a signed agreement from Ed to appear in our movie. (This took a lifetime's worth of finessing.) However, Brian was not obligated to release *the full amount of money without* a signed contract from Ed. This was a huge concern of ours. We could shoot half our movie in September, and Brian could pull the plug at any time. It was a massive risk.

(Remember, we had elected to break up our shooting schedule: three weeks in September, without Ed Harris, then a two-month hiatus, returning in December for two weeks with Ed, Brad Dourif, and Robert Forster.)

Gordon and our attorney, Matthew Fladell, thought the deal would collapse. Gordon was most concerned with the rolling interest rate, which we hadn't managed to overcome, while Matthew was most concerned with the full release of monies contingent on a signed contract from Ed.

Here's what we heard from them daily:

Gordon: "Ed is a mensch. He's doing your movie. Stop worrying about Ed . . . But the interest rate is driving me nuts!"

Matthew: "Stop telling me Ed will show up and do your movie. You don't know that. He has not signed a contract. He's not legally bound."

"He shook on it. He's a good guy," we'd reply, attempting to convince him as well as ourselves.

Matthew: "A handshake doesn't mean shit in this business. You guys gotta stop being so damn naive."

Both Gordon and Matthew: "If Brian decides to pull the plug halfway through and fails to finance the entire movie because Ed backs out or you don't get him signed before, let's say, the real estate market tanks, or any number of variables, then you guys will be faced with the harsh and very real prospect of lawsuits. You will be sued! You will owe hundreds of thousands of dollars on unfulfilled contracts. What's more, Brian could sue you guys for fraud and misrepresentation."

What they were saying was true, but wrong.

"Who cares if we get sued?!" Noah yelled at Gordon and Matthew on a conference call. "We don't own anything. You can't take nothing from nothing!"

"I'm against you signing this contract . . . I strongly advise against it," Gordon said.

"It's taken us too long to get here," Logan said. "We gotta move now."

Mike had sent us a revised contract that morning. Brian was prepared to sign. We were sitting in our stifling room with no windows. Gordon was beating us up over the phone. "Insane!" We had come so far in such a short time, exceeding all the experts' wisdom and experience in negotiating the terms of the financial agreement. We had wrangled face-to-face with Mike almost every day, driving the 220 mile round-trip to Sacramento. We'd battled over the phone, been picked up and slammed down repeatedly. Mike is a fierce negotiator. His tactics are the opposite of ours. We use many words. He uses few. As we would get hot, he would get cold. We were on the brink of realizing our dream.

All we needed was the money. All we needed to do was sign the contract.

We called Mike one last time to see if they would concede on the interest rate. They were firm. It was a deal breaker for them. We stepped outside and went for a long walk in the woods. Our guts still contradicted our advisors. We felt that we were losing sight of our goal. Our goal was to make our movie. Three months earlier, if placed in this situation, we would have signed the contract the moment it was thrown on the table.

We sat on the ridge overlooking the valley. Oak trees and redwoods covered the hills and ravines. It was hot summer and the forest was quiet. About a half mile down we could see the patch of scotch broom where our dad's hideout was.

We remembered what he told us, sitting on his tailgate, eating peanut butter sandwiches when we were seven or eight years old, simple wisdom we've carried with us. It was a wet Saturday afternoon, wintertime, a light rain coming and going. Our dad had four dollars to his name. He pulled his truck into a grocery store parking lot and bought a loaf of bread and a jar of peanut butter to last us through the weekend. He let down the tailgate and made us sandwiches with a metal spoon he had in his glove box.

"I know it ain't much boys, but right now it's all we got," he said.

It started drizzling, and we sat there with our feet dangling off the tailgate, eating peanut butter sandwiches, hanging out with Dad. He wasn't drinking. And we were happy . . .

"So we gotta pay interest," Noah said. "So what? No money is free. And if we don't make any money off the movie, then we don't pay any interest. Don't see the problem there. We gotta look at the situation from our perspective. Both the guys giving us advice own homes, have lucrative careers, have lots of money. The interest rate is a rich person's problem, and the last time I checked, we were still broke . . . Their wisdom and experience is getting in the way . . . What would Dad say?"

"Make your movie."

"We can't forget our game," Noah said. "We've already gone all in, passed that point a long time ago. We don't know how to play the nickel-and-dime tables. It's not our style. We've never had any success that way . . . Signing the financial agreement makes our movie possible. And don't forget, we still owe forty-five grand from Tucson. We sign this deal and we pay that off, move out of Mom's house . . . Brian's offer is all we got right now and I'm damn happy we got it."

We walked down the hill and back to our room. The wooden box with our dad's ashes inside was sitting on the shelf.

We called Mike. "Let's do it."

AND AWAY WE GO

"We want to sign the financing agreement in person . . . Before Brian hops on the jet."

"He takes off at 9:30 A.M.," Mike said. "But he gets back at 3 P.M. Wouldn't it be a lot easier on you guys to just meet him at the office in the afternoon?"

There was no way we were going to risk Brian getting on that flight without the financial agreement signed. What if he crashed? As soon as we heard the word "flight" we became uneasy—head him off at the airport before the plane leaves the ground.

Of course, with modern technology and all its conveniences, we didn't need to drive to Sacramento and sign the agreement in person. We could have exchanged signatures by fax or e-mail. But we wanted to make sure Brian signed the financial agreement BEFORE he hopped on his jet. And the only way to guarantee that was to be in his face with the contract before he flew away. Brian certainly wasn't thinking about the grim prospects of his jet going down and the consequences that would have on our movie. But we were . . . Or, less tragic to Brian, but no less tragic to us, what if the plane didn't go down and Brian changed his mind by the afternoon—perhaps the stock market crashed or an investment of his went belly up and he no longer wanted to plunge into the dice game.

"We'll meet Brian at the airport," Noah said.

"You sure?" Mike asked.

"Absolutely."

Furthermore, we hadn't seen or spoken with Brian since the first meeting. Since then, he was a rumor. We'd only heard about him indirectly through Mike. We felt uncomfortable taking millions of dollars from a guy we would have trouble recognizing at the supermarket. We wanted to tell him thank you and also let him know what he could expect from us that was not stipulated in the contract; that we would give him the highest level of transparency, that we would protect his money as if it were our mother's retirement, that we would do everything we could to make the best film possible. Every dollar would go on-screen.

"I'll e-mail you directions to the airport," Mike said.

We packed our duffel bag, drove up to Sacramento, and spent the night on Bao's living room floor.

On our way to meet Brian the next morning we stopped at Starbucks for a cup of coffee. Bao came with us. There was a Sacramento magazine on the rack. Logan flipped through the pages.

"Check it out. There's Brian."

The title of the article was something like "People to Watch" or "The Most Influential People in Sacramento."

It felt like someone was watching over us. "Hey Dad-o," Noah said, smiling, looking up.

We arrived at McClellan Airpark at 9 A.M. and walked around. It was already getting hot. Heat waves shimmered on the tarmac.

McClellan is a former air force base turned private airport. Both of Brian's jets were stored there. Mike told us that Brian owned a "big jet and a small jet." The small one—which we initially thought was the big one—was idling on the other side of the fence, the captain inspecting it. We admired the jet through the chain links. The fence separating us from Brian was about to come down.

Brian drove up in his silver Land Rover, swiped his security card, and opened the door for us into the private lounge. Two women were sitting at computers behind the counter.

"You guys have the contracts?" Brian asked us.

"Yes, sir."

Brian walks almost as fast as he talks. His mind was already on the flight to survey a piece of land in the Central Valley.

He pointed at a table in the corner. "Let's sit over there."

Brian walked over to the counter. "Do either of you ladies have a pen I could borrow?" He looked over his shoulder and smiled at us, shrugged. "I forgot a pen."

We had expected Brian to sign the contract with a Montblanc or some other thousand-dollar writing utensil.

One of the women handed Brian a pen.

"Thrifty Car Rentals," Brian said, reading it. "This'll do."

Brian sat at the table with us. We handed him three copies of the contract, expecting him to take *at least* a few minutes to read them over. But no. Brian flipped to the back page of each contract and signed them without so much as glimpsing at a line or a clause. He could've been signing away his jet on the tarmac for all he knew. It was unreal. Here's this guy, who we've talked to for a total of twenty minutes, and with his signature, has just given us several million dollars—and doesn't even take a moment to see what he's signing. It was complete trust in action.

"Are we good?" Brian asked.

"Brian, we'd like to tell you a little about what you can expect from us," Noah said, trying to be very professional. "We'll give you as much transparency as you need. You're taking a huge risk and we want you to feel comfortable—"

"I'm already comfortable. I trust you guys." He checked his watch and stood up. "Guys, I gotta run. Good luck." He shook our hands.

"Can we at least get a picture?" Noah asked.

"Sure, but be quick," he said, looking outside at his jet, checking his watch again.

Bao snapped a photo of the three of us. Brian handed us two signed contracts, kept one for himself. He then rolled up his contract and stuffed it into his back pocket like Tom Sawyer with a spelling test, then strutted down the tarmac and climbed into his jet.

We treated our contracts as if they were the last two copies of the Declaration of Independence, placing them delicately inside a manila envelope and then placing that envelope securely inside our daily planners.

We walked outside and stood at the chain-link fence separating us from the runway. Brian was sitting shotgun with the pilot of his aircraft, window open. Brian waved to us, slid the window closed, and took off into the cloudless morning. We stared through the chain links and watched the white jet disappear, a portrait of an unbelievable drama; Bao Phung, a Vietnamese immigrant whose family came to this country from a refugee camp with only the donated clothes on their backs, and the Miller Brothers, his best friends, a couple nobodies from nowhere whose life thus far was a chronicle of failure and unrealized dreams, who months earlier were visiting their homeless father in jail, a veteran who lost his battle with alcoholism, a man who died penniless and incarcerated, and were now making a movie in honor of him, and Brian Vail, the self-made real estate tycoon whose signature just made the movie possible, flying off in his private jet. To those who no longer believe in the American Dream, read this, and say otherwise.

Then Bao said, hands on the chain link, "I guess that's how the big guys do it."

"Guess so."

It took less than ten minutes from the time Brian pulled up in his Land Rover to the time he hopped into his jet. The only time he stopped moving was for the photo. And even that's a little blurry.

We drove back to Bao's house and celebrated with cheeseburgers.

Gordon left us a message. "Guys, you did the right thing. The goal is to get the movie made. Congratulations. I'm proud of you."

Four days later, over one million dollars was wired into our movie's escrow account at Borel Private Bank and Trust in San Francisco.

We were now bona fide.

PART VI

CHARGING NAKED

MOTORBIKE KID AND THE ICE PRINCESS

WE HAD THE money to make our movie, so we headed back to L.A. to rehearse with our September actors: Evan Jones, Brandon Hanson, and Ishiah Benben—the Juvenile Crew. (Ed, Robert, and Brad were the Veteran Crew.) You've met Evan. Here's how we found Brandon and Ishiah:

SIX MONTHS EARLIER

Like most eccentrics, Carly Ivan Garcia, our lifelong friend and extraordinary artist, knows many things and many people, some of them actors. He called us. Here's what he said:

"You guys remember Brandon, the motocross rider I used to lift with at the gym?"

"Yeah, think so."

"Well, he's living in L.A. now. Just got done acting in some independent movie. He's a good guy. You should give him a call."

We called Brandon and left a message. He never called back. Then, coincidentally, we bumped into him at Gold's Gym Venice. He said he got our message and that he'd been meaning to call for the last two months.

"Let's go grab a beer," we said.

A few days later we drank some beers at an Irish bar in Venice. Brandon had been studying acting for a while and just completed his first role in a feature film. We told him we were making a movie. He asked if he could read the script. So we gave it to him.

He read it, called, and said he wanted to play the role of "Brownie."

Physically, he wasn't what we envisioned. But that didn't prevent us from considering the possibility of Brownie looking like Brandon. Why not? Why couldn't Brandon play Brownie? We thought about it for a few days, and the more we thought about it, the more interesting it became. Brandon was tall, thin, reserved, unassuming, a perfect counterbalance to a high-strung Mac (Evan Jones).

We told Brandon we'd give him a chance if he was willing to start rehearsing with us.

"No guarantees though," we said. "You're gonna have to earn it. If you wanna work on the role, we'll give you the time. Hell, we'll rehearse every day, twice a day if you want."

"Just give me a shot," Brandon said. "If it doesn't work out, cast somebody else."

THE ICE PRINCESS

"Have you guys seen Ishiah lately?" Jasha asked.

"No. We haven't seen her in years."

"She lives in L.A. now. Before that she was in Chicago at some big theater, doing plays or something. You guys should call her."

"What does she look like?"

Now, Jasha is a man of profound appetites, especially the physical ones. His hunger was felt through the phone. "She looks like a Russian ice princess."

He gave us Ishiah's number. We met her for coffee. She was stunning, overflowing with personality. Not in the bubbly, affected way they teach you in bad acting classes. Ishiah was pure and genuine. Quite rare in those parts.

A year earlier, Ishiah won a national competition to train with the Steppenwolf Theater Company in Chicago. It was a great experience, but afterward she found herself back home working at a bar in the small town where we all grew up in. Unsatisfied, she decided to move to Hollywood to pursue her acting dreams.

She had earned her stripes in theater and was used to the demands of performing night in and night out, weeks in a row. She was disciplined, studied the craft. She hadn't come to Hollywood hoping to get discovered by looking pretty at some trendy nightclub. She came there to work her way into a career.

She had a job at a wine bar in Coldwater Canyon and shared an apartment with a couple in Culver City, a French guy and his girlfriend. We told her living with couples was a bad idea, especially if one of them is a Frenchman.

"Yeah, I know. I'm trying to get out."

We gave her our script. She read it, called us, and now we were at Starbucks.

"I'll do anything to help you guys out on this movie," Ishiah said. "I'll brew the coffee, get the doughnuts, I don't care. Anything. I can't believe you guys are making a movie."

"What about Rachel?" Noah asked.

"You mean the girl in the script?"

"Yeah, her. You're an actress, right?"

"Yeah, but I've never acted in a movie before. Only theater . . . You guys have Ed Harris in this thing—holy shit—I can't believe you guys. I can't believe it!"

Whenever she got excited—which was 98 percent of the time—she would blurt out "Holy shit I can't believe it!" and then instinctively cover her mouth, hunch her shoulders, and look around, apologetically, realizing we were in Starbucks.

"Sorry," she'd whisper. "Oops." Then she'd giggle.

"Do you want to play Rachel?" Noah asked.

We felt Ishiah was perfect for the role. She wasn't famous, nobody knew who she was. She still had that small town feel, modest, humble, charming. We were concerned a big-name actress would take the audience out of the rural environment, out of the realism. Sure, we had Ed Harris, Brad Dourif, and Robert Forster, but it's different with a female lead. Can't explain it.

"I don't know if I can do it," Ishiah said.

"Of course you can. You're an actress."

"Movies are different. I've only done theater."

"How many tries do you get in theater, when the house is packed?"

"What do you mean?"

"Can you stop the performance when you flub a line, and say, STOP, let's do that again?"

"No."

"Well, when you're making movies you get to do it until you get it right. Don't worry. We'll rehearse. We're the directors. It's our job to make sure you do a good job. We'll get you where you need to be. Trust us. We won't let you down . . . What are you doing tomorrow?"

"I guess I'm rehearsing with you guys."

THE NAKED BUSINESS

We started rehearsing with Ishiah, Brandon, and Evan—individually. We didn't want to rehearse as a group until they felt comfortable with their characters, gained some confidence. Acting is a naked business. It can feel like that bad dream in which everybody else has clothes on. The key is to forget that you're naked.

So we started slow, simple, just reading the lines in the script without emotion. No acting, only reading.

"Don't put anything on it. They're just words on a page."

Start small and then build. The same approach we used with

success in Tucson, with people who had never acted. Cultivate the seeds of the performance: words, words before any choices, words before any direction, words before any intention, words before any camera starts rolling, words on a page, nothing more.

"We're just reading."

It was in these early stages of rehearsal that we took off our writers' hats and put on our directors' helmets. Each step in the moviemaking process requires different headgear. When you're writing the script, you wear your writer's hat. When you direct, you wear your director's helmet. And when you edit, you wear a hockey mask, and so on.

It's wise to be objective at every stage of any endeavor— whether raising children, cooking an omelet, or shaving your goatee. If you repeatedly hear complaints about your child being an asshole on the playground or your omelet could use more cheddar and less ham or your goatee makes you look like you've just been paroled, you should probably consider making changes. Unless of course, your intention was to raise a little asshole, botch brunch, and intimidate relatives.

We'd written the script, but so what? What worked on the page might not work once an actor tried to perform it. If a piece of writing didn't work we couldn't hold on to it because *we* wrote it. Rehearsals helped us discover what worked, and what didn't. And if it didn't work, we threw our writers' hat back on and figured it out. This doesn't mean that every time an actor struggled with dialogue we changed it. Sometimes we let them struggle, made them work, but tried to be smart about it, open-minded to the possibility that if a piece of dialogue or an entire scene continued to flounder, that it might not be the actor—it might be the writing.

We'd fail to realize our movie's potential if we held stubbornly to something that wasn't working. So what if it took us six years to write? So what if we considered it the greatest demonstration of forensic oratory since Churchill? The audience wouldn't care. They want the story to move. If it didn't drive the narrative, then we needed to cut it out of the movie. Cut it out of our life.

THE JUVENILE CREW

Evan and Brandon came over to our apartment. They had never met. (We kept Ishiah away for a few more days, keep the guys focused.) We drank some beers and read through the script.

Evan (Mac) and Brandon (Brownie) are best friends in *Touching Home*. The more time we could all spend together, the better the chemistry on-screen. The audience needed to believe these guys were friends since childhood, would have the other guy's back in a fistfight.

We were still at the reading stage. Nobody was "off-book" yet. (Off-book is when the actor has memorized his or her lines.) We had the time to take the time. So we took it slow. More important than the lines was getting to know each other, noticing the other guys traits, his mannerisms, like you know your best friends. Anybody can memorize lines. But chemistry—that's the good stuff. Making it appear as if you've known someone your entire life— that you love them—when you've known them in *real life* for only a week or perhaps a few hours, is one of the most challenging dimensions of acting.

We all started assuming our on-screen names. Evan was now "Mac" and Brandon was now "Brownie." And we became "Clint" and "Lane." It didn't matter what we were doing or where we were at; the bar, a coffee shop, or walking down the street together, we were now Mac, Brownie, Clint, and Lane.

Evan had worked on major studio movies, *Jarhead*, *8 Mile*, *Glory Road*, and yet had no problem coming over to our tiny apartment for rehearsals. He and Brandon worked hard developing their characters. We trusted them and we hoped they trusted us. In a few weeks, we were all going to be naked together in front of seventy people. Everybody else would have clothes on.

After rehearsing at our apartment one evening, we all went up to the Getty Museum and drank a bunch of wine on the grass above the topiary garden, laughed, and shared stories. It felt like we were a group of old friends.

Bro and I thought back to those nights on the roof of the roach apartment, years earlier, lost and desperate, unknown and full of desire, staring at the glimmering city we were now above, dreaming about a dream we were now living.

OUR BACKYARD

REHEARSING IN OUR apartment was adequate but not ideal. It was acting. Not living.

So we asked Evan and Brandon if they would come up north two weeks before shooting and rehearse on location. They thought it was a great idea and migrated with us. Ishiah came up a week later.

Filming where we grew up had numerous advantages. One of them was rehearsing on location FOR FREE. The acting would be better, no doubt. It would also increase our efficiency during principal photography when we'd be throwing bags of cash into a mulcher—all day, every day.

In the original screenplay, we went back home and worked as roofers with our father, just like in real life. But we were informed early on that filming on a rooftop would drastically raise the price of our production insurance. Furthermore, we were having trouble finding someone who would let us walk up and down their roof for two weeks without making us buy them a new one.

Plan B: Find a suitable blue-collar working environment that was hot, dirty, and gritty, only on the ground.

MONTHS EARLIER

"Have you guys checked out the quarry on our property?" Randy Lafranchi, our mom's boyfriend, asked us. "You might want to take a look at it, see if it'll work for your movie. We rent it to the

Lunny family. They're good people . . . I'll call Bob Lunny and let him know you're coming by."

So we drove out to the quarry.

Bob Lunny, the owner of Lunny Quarry and possessor of the county's firmest handshake, was waiting for us next to a two-story pyramid of gravel.

"Randy told me you're filming a movie," Bob said. A rancher by birth, straightforward and clean dealing; there's no B.S. to Bob. "Do you want to use the quarry?"

We were surrounded by giant earth-moving machines: tractors and dump trucks, excavators and loaders, gray rock piles, gravel pits, a conveyor, and a carved-out hillside. It was dirty, gritty, and hot; it screamed timeless Americana and the workingman.

"It's not as tough as roofing," Bob said. "But it'll look tougher in a movie."

"How does it sound?" Noah asked.

Bob smiled and walked us over to the rock crusher, a yellow Dumpster-looking behemoth of steel and horsepower that pulverizes boulders and spits out streams of gravel onto a thirty-foot-high conveyor.

Bob turned on the crusher. The electric pulse slowly whined thousands of horsepower into action, pistons gearing up, ominous, a violent upheaval building, surging, and then ten thousand jackhammers were shaking the valley, booming, thunderous, thrilling.

Bob was still smiling, yelled into the roar. We read his lips. "Loud enough?!"

We smiled, nodded. We were sold.

BACK TO NOW—REHEARSALS

We took Evan and Brandon out to the quarry every day of rehearsals and drove the heavy machinery. We'd eat lunch on the rock piles and then drive to another location. Sometimes Brandon would bring his dirt bike and ride around the hills; Bob borrowed it one day, expertly soaring off the gravel mounds and nearly scaling the wall of the quarry before stalling the bike feet from the top.

Ishiah would usually meet up with us in the afternoon or early evening.

By the time we started filming, we had walked through each scene dozens of times, taken road trips together, drove up to the Russian River and rehearsed under the Monte Rio Bridge, and went swimming afterward.

We were careful not to overwork each scene. We didn't want the acting to become stale. We wanted to save the freshness, the raw emotions for the camera. The object was to *live* like the characters, not *act* like them. Once living in their skin, all we needed to do was capture it on film.

Evan and Brandon hung out with our buddies, the guys their characters were modeled after. They fit right in. They had become one of us.

The effect this would have on the quality of the acting, not to mention our shooting efficiency, cannot be overstated. It allowed us to make our schedule each day. We averaged three takes per camera setup, substantially fewer than the industry standard. It's not uncommon for directors on a studio movie to shoot twenty, thirty, even fifty takes. They can spend days on one scene. They have the money and the time. We had neither. We couldn't spend more than a few hours on a scene. It was all the time we could afford, and in most cases, all the time we needed. Many times we nailed it on the first take, shot a second for insurance, and moved onto the next camera position. This was only made possible by the extensive rehearsal process—in our backyard.

YOU'VE MET LITTLE ANGRY, NOW MEET BIG ANGRY

HE CAME FROM the same tribe as Little Angry, only Big Angry must have stolen more anger from the mush bowl growing up. If Little Angry was a harmless dust devil, then Big Angry was a deadly tornado, so much more anger did he have inside. We were two weeks from shooting, and things were blowing down.

Big Angry's job was to oversee the entire production side of the movie so that we could focus on the creative side. He had done a decent job up to this point. But when we started hiring crew, and allowing them to express their opinion, he became a massive, puckering asshole. Every discussion was a golden moment for Big Angry to scream at somebody. His idea of effective communication was "Fuck you, bitch." Needless to say, it wasn't very effective. He was fifty years old, yes, FIVE-ZERO, and that's how Big Angry spoke to people.

Our days were unimaginably hectic. No other time would be as demanding, and yet half our day was spent playing peacemaker between Big Angry and everyone else he was pissing off; everyone else being a crew that was about to abandon the movie because of him. Thankfully, he would soon self-destruct, setting the stage for Jeromiah Running Water Zajonc. But that's a few weeks from now.

Right now was chaos, the clock spinning in free fall as we sped toward principal photography; each day we were rewriting the script, rehearsing, composing our shot list, learning our lines—don't forget we were also acting in the movie—negotiating deals with vendors and crew, reading actor contracts and location agreements, signing checks, ordering film and lenses, visiting locations, making hundreds of wardrobe decisions, hundreds of prop decisions, interior and exterior production designs, colors of paint, rugs, plates, beer cans, cereal boxes, artwork, furniture in the house, pigeons, bicycles, baseball gloves, baseball uniforms, lighting preferences, public relations, and a billion other decisions that all make a movie happen. And Big Angry was doing his best to make sure we failed.

In hindsight, we should've fired him early on. But in our inexperience, we thought we could work it out. Plus, we didn't know anyone at the time who could replace him.

(It should be noted that Big Angry wasn't all bad. He actually managed to hire two gifted people: his burnout buddy who thought it was totally acceptable to smoke weed and drink whiskey while shuttling Oscar-nominated actors from the hotel to the set, and a female medic with a mullet, who, after being paid $9,000 to treat one bee sting and hand out thirteen aspirin, decided to sue us for $18,000 in overtime. The court graciously awarded her $344.44 . . . if she promised to cut the mullet before it came back in style. So you see, Big Angry wasn't *entirely* bad. After all, he did hire these two Outstanding Achievers.)

BRING ON THE SAGE

It's impossible to express the value of a good editor. Try quantifying the value of your eyeballs. You get the picture. Editors are important. And we didn't have one yet.

Back in April, and long before that, the plan was for Pierson to edit *Touching Home*. We'd spent years talking about it. He'd witnessed its genesis on a notepad. But in June, Pierson was offered a job as a supervising editor on a reality TV show. It was a huge opportunity, worth ten grand a month. No more night shift. He'd been pulling night shifts for seven years and finally reached the Promised Land: humane hours.

But he was torn. If he took the job he wouldn't be able to edit *Touching Home*.

We talked in his garage until three in the morning, passing around a bottle of Maker's Mark.

"You can't pass this up, Pierson. Who knows what's going to happen with our movie? We don't even have the financing yet. Even if we do get the money, we won't be able to pay you what you're going to make on that show, not even close."

His wife, Annie, one of the great ones, would back whatever decision he made.

"You gotta take the job, Pierson," Noah said.

"I know."

After we lost Pierson, we met several established editors in L.A. They were all nice. Had terrific résumés. But our guts told us they weren't right for our movie.

So we took Gordon out to breakfast to discuss our problem; a week and a half from shooting and we didn't have an editor. Situation dire.

"I strongly suggest you boys get a Northern California editor. They have different tastes, different sensibilities that I think would be right for this movie."

"We called Walter Murch."

Walter Murch is an editing god.

"What did he say?" Gordon asked. "How'd you get his number?"

"From Richard Hymns . . . We called Walter and left a message. But he never called back."

That's no reflection on Walter. We would later become friends with him and his wife, Aggie. They became strong supporters, watched early cuts of *Touching Home,* and gave us valuable notes.

"Let me see what Robert Dalva is up to," Gordon said. "He's good friends with Walter. Dalva, George [Lucas], and Walter all went to USC together. They were all original members of Zoetrope. I'll give him a call when I get home. I think he'd be good for your movie."

This was a watershed in our relationship with Gordon. Before that morning, he never called anyone for us. But he had witnessed our progress, our determination, and now believed that we might have what it takes . . . might.

Twenty minutes after breakfast, Gordon called us. "I just got off the phone with Robert Dalva. He's not working right now. He wants to read the script. Get it to him as soon as you can. Here's his e-mail address."

We e-mailed Robert Dalva our script. He read it and called us the next morning as we were driving out to Nicasio to photograph the locations.

"I really like your script," Dalva said. "It's well done."

"Why don't we get together and talk about it?" Logan said. "You live in Larkspur, right? You know that little Italian bakery on the main street there?"

"Rulli."

"Yeah, that's it. How about lunch there today? Let's say two o'clock?"

"Sounds good."

We met Dalva at Rulli and talked for two and a half hours. He has a gray beard and long gray hair, looks like a wizard. In 1980, he was nominated for an Academy Award for editing *The Black Stallion.* His credits include *Jumanji, Jurassic Park 3, Hidalgo,* and *October Sky.* A baseball nut, he always wears a Giants cap. Fans like Dalva are the reason baseball players make millions a year.

But baseball was only a warm prelude to our conversation.

Dalva understood story. He was the first editor we interviewed who spoke about the central importance of driving the narrative. He quoted Aristotle as he gave us notes on our script.

A man of many talents, Dalva has performed just about every significant creative duty on a movie set—except acting; although his hands made a debut in an early version of *Touching Home,* and then, in an ironic twist of editing, met their death by those same hands. He's directed, edited, DP'd, gaffed, recorded sound, and is also a terrific camera operator.

Dalva came on board a week before we started filming and set up his editing gear in the downstairs room at our mom's house. We lived together for nine months, drank a hillside of Colombian coffee. Dalva is a true collaborator, philosopher, and teacher. We called him "Sage," "Scenus Adeptus," and later, "The Alchemist."

WEEK ONE

IT WAS TIME to roll film.

We put up our crew at the Novato Oaks Best Western, which might have the best waffles in the country. Scott Curran, the manager, cut us a swap-meet deal on the rooms. It's adjacent to the Wild Fox restaurant, which had a full bar to satisfy our thirsty crew after a long day's work.

Unlike Tucson, we now had a real production, a fleet of vehicles: a forty-foot eighteen wheeler, a Peterbilt grip truck, camera truck, art department truck, four passenger vans, three minivans, three stake-beds, four Starwagons, three picture cars—a '71 Ford Ranchero, a '71 Ford F-150, and the Perfect Car, which arrived from Arizona the night before shooting. When our production moved down the road, it was a half-mile long.

There were several days of anxiety surrounding the Perfect Car in the week prior to shooting. Because—

Big Angry shipped the Perfect Car from Tucson with some ragtag outfit. Bao had repeatedly volunteered to drive down to Tucson and bring it back on a stake-bed. Other than gas and the truck rental, Bao would do it for free. But Big Angry liked to make war with everyone and everything.

"I can handle the fucking job!" Big Angry screamed. "I don't need twenty people telling me how to ship a fucking car from Tucson to Northern California. LET ME FUCKING HANDLE IT!!!"

So we let Big Angry handle it, and he totally blew it. The Perfect Car was lost for three days. That's right, LOST. How do you lose a car for three days? It's doesn't seem like an easy thing to do, but he did it.

After Big Angry melted down on day two of the Perfect Car's disappearance, we gave the job to Bao, who said, "I'll take care of it."

If Bao hadn't found the Perfect Car, we would've been so far up the creek that not even Hiawatha could have paddled us back. Needless to say, as if we didn't have enough worries, the three days it was lost were mental earthquakes. At 2 A.M., the night before shooting, Bao delivered the Perfect Car to the Novato Oaks.

In the afternoon, we stood on the balcony outside the production office and looked over the convoy of vehicles and equipment occupying a football field in the hotel parking lot. We walked over to the Wild Fox, bought the boys a shot of whiskey, and called it an early night.

At 4:30 A.M., Bao, Claytus "Beowulf" Bertlesman, Dave Lifton, and a few other soldiers pulled the trucks out of the parking lot and onto Highway 101. Destination: fifty miles north to the Russian River and the Monte Rio Bridge. We were standing proud in the parking lot, coffee in hand, gave the vanguard a thumbs-up. They pulled their horns, loud diesel and candy lights in the darkness.

We followed a half hour later in a minivan with Ricardo and Connie and pulled into Monte Rio at 6:30 A.M. A ceiling of fog shrouded the redwood hills. We were concerned it wouldn't burn off. We needed sunshine for the fishing scene.

We walked around to every department, said good morning, making sure all their gear made the journey, when we heard the rising voices of distress, and turned around to see a look of alarm on Bao's face, an expression rarely seen. He's cool under pressure, as many people are from war-torn countries. But now he looked concerned. And his concern was for us.

We jogged across the parking lot and over to Bao's truck, which was idling beside Gary Beaird, our key grip.

"Gary, the list said that you'd be driving the Peterbilt," Bao said.

"I know. But that was a few days ago," Gary said. "I told Big Angry yesterday that I wasn't going to be driving my grip truck, that transpo would have to bring it up here. Big Angry said he was going to tell you. He said he would make the change to the transpo list."

"Well, no one told me."

They weren't yelling at each other, just trying to solve the problem. The grip truck was sitting back in the hotel parking lot fifty miles away. We could NOT shoot without it. Forgetting the grip truck was like forgetting the gasoline at the Indy 500; you can't win. Hell, you can't even begin.

Somebody had to go back and get the grip truck.

So good ole Bao and trusty Claytus immediately jumped in Jeromiah's convertible Porsche and drove 120 mph back to the hotel. And in just over an hour and a half they had the grip truck in Monte Rio in time for the first shot of the day, the only casualties being a few chickens that tried to cross the road. When they returned, Bao and Claytus looked like they'd just had face-lifts. Their hair was iron straight and launched back. They've never looked so young.

After that, the first day was a cakewalk. The fog burned off and the day was beautiful, a sublime time on the river. The acting was smooth, effortless, real. We got all the shots we needed, and the crew was happy.

As we were packing up, Taylor and Jeromiah gave us each a gift basket with a bottle of Knob Creek, a chocolate bar, and stainless steel flasks engraved with one of our favorite quotes: "We mutually pledge to each other, our lives, our fortunes, and our sacred honor."

To commemorate the day, we each took a long pull from the bottle as the sun set on the river. The whiskey heat swirled with the heat of achievement. We felt unstoppable. We were living life at its peak. The four of us had talked about this day for seven years—at Jeromiah and Taylor's UCLA apartment, at our crummy hole in the Gaza Strip of Hollywood, in the Mar Vista War Room, around the campfire at our spot in the desert, sharing a chew on the road through New Mexico on our way to Austin . . .

We drove along the river back to the hotel, passing rolling vineyards glowing shades of pink in the dusk as the redwood hills turned to shadows against the dying light behind them. We called Coach in Montana, and mentally prepared for Day Two.

DAY TWO: WATERLOO

It ran without time. It felt as if there would be no end to the bloodshed.

During principal photography, every director will have a day where he gets slaughtered. Some directors have several, while others never escape the carnage. Ours was Day Two.

There are three "DON'T'S" for first-time directors, and we were violating two of them on Days One and Two.

1. Don't shoot on water—which is what we did on Day One at the river.
2. Don't work with children—which we also did on Day One and were now repeating on Day Two.
3. Don't work with animals—which we would do extensively in December.

Day Two began at the Little Store in Forest Knolls, population, very few, a loud whistle from our dad's old shed. It was foggy and cold, just like the morning of Day One. Before we started shooting, Ricardo took us over to an oak tree in the park across the street. He looked serious, solemn. We put our backs to the crew.

"Give me your hands," Ricardo said.

Someone must have died; definitely, it was that kind of seriousness. So we too, with respect to the newly departed—whoever they were, we were about to find out—became serious, that deep, respectful seriousness of death. We gave Ricardo our hands and made a circle of three. He locked eyes with us, deeper, more intense now. *Half our crew has been wiped out,* we thought. Multiple deaths, for sure, perhaps it's bigger than that, a new war— America is being invaded. WE ARE IN TROUBLE. A movie? Trivial. We should be ashamed to be out here right now.

We bowed our heads, waiting, bracing . . . for . . . the inevitable . . . hoping it never came, but knowing it would . . . just give us the names, Ricardo . . . give us the news . . . be frank, we can take it . . .

"Guys, look at me," Ricardo said.

It's even bigger than we thought . . . A giant meteor is speeding toward earth. We've got a few minutes, at most.

"Pray for sun."

"Sun?"

"Yes. Sunshine. I've worked too hard for too long. So have you. We need beautiful sun. Sunshine. You got it? . . . This fog is crap. Now pray."

Ricardo bowed his head, closed his eyes, and squeezed our hands. He *was* right. We *needed* sunshine later in the day for a scene scheduled at Red Barn Road in Nicasio, just over the hill. It had to be golden sunshine, magic hour, a sweeping pastoral shot in the fading hues before sunset.

If we couldn't control the weather, what could we control?

So with heads bowed in a circle of three, we prayed for sunshine, begged, pleaded, offered our souls, held mass under the tree throughout the morning.

But the sun never came. Not even a peek. All day. Fog. Dense. Heavy. Leaden. Sometimes Mother Nature doesn't care about your plans.

But Mother Nature was the least of our afflictions.

We had ourselves to deal with.

For our first shot of the day we had concocted an elaborate and *unnecessary* crane move. Stupid, idiotic, first-time-director nonsense. Stupid! Let's display our skill, our artistic vision with this elegant camera move for a scene that could be shot with three simple setups. No, let's take the simple and make it complex. Why? Because we're young and stupid, green, smarter than everyone else, smarter than all that have come before us.

It took two hours to set up the crane. It should've taken thirty minutes. We were behind before we started. After each shot, it took fifteen minutes to get the crane back to its starting position. Furthermore, the crane was experiencing technical problems. So were the young actors, twin boys playing us as kids. They were enamored of the crane, couldn't keep their eyes off it, wanted to take it home and make it their pet. The crane would creep down the side of the building and sweep around the corner and find the boys, and each time—whammo—they would look directly into the camera, forgetting that we were making a movie.

"Cut."

"Let's go back to one."

It took us eight hours to shoot two hours of work. But it wasn't the kids' fault or the crew's fault or even the crane's fault. It was *our* fault! The twin directors' fault, dumber than most, smarter than the rest.

Our afternoon filming at Red Barn Road was canceled. We had grim visions. If we proceeded at this pace we'd run out of money, never complete the September shoot. At the end of Day Two, we were a half day behind. And our schedule was only getting tougher.

But we rallied on Days Three, Four, and Five and made up the half day we lost on Day Two. We finished the first week on schedule, a massive pivot in the course of battle. We ended Friday at Red Barn Road, the sun golden, prayers answered.

Jeromiah brought out a cooler of beers for the crew. It was hot September, everyone sweating, beer-drinking weather.

We handed out the frosty Lagunitas IPAs and congratulated each person for a job well done. They were all fired-up. The crew is like a pack of sled dogs. They enjoy working hard, love to complete the schedule. When they don't, they get down, lose confidence in the movie. We had turned the week around from a disastrous Day Two and were now ending the week one scene ahead.

But the celebration was short-lived for us, didn't even have time to drink an IPA.

Ricardo, Connie, Taylor, Jeromiah, and Bao walked over.

We were flying. They were not.

"Guys, listen. Big Angry is outta control," Jeromiah said.

"He left the exposed film in the lobby for two days," Connie added. "Two days!"

Our happiness died.

Connie continued, "Last night when we walked into the lobby after shooting, I looked over and saw our cans of film sitting on the couch, unguarded. I couldn't believe it. I asked the woman at the front desk who left those there. She didn't know, thought they had been there all day."

The exposed film represented every penny, every line of dialogue, every person's salary, every ounce of contribution to the movie—our seven years of work! IT WAS THE MOVIE. What you record in-camera is EVERYTHING. It cannot be replaced. And it was left in the lobby—for TWO DAYS!

"So me and Katie took the film up to our room. Then I called Big Angry to ask what's going on, why the film is sitting in the lobby . . . and he says, 'Fuck you, you dumb bitch. Don't talk to me that way. You're below me, you cunt!' and then he hung up."

Connie was in tears.

"You guys gotta do something," Ricardo said. "Or else he's going to ruin your movie."

"Bao, Taylor, Jeromiah, let's get back to the hotel," Noah said. "We need to take care of this."

We jumped in a minivan and drove to the hotel.

The first week had been shot on rural locations: the Russian River to Point Reyes to Nicasio. For economic reasons, we'd been staying at our mom's house; it saved the production over $100 a day. We were the first ones on set each morning and usually the last to leave. Consequently, we hadn't stepped foot in the production office at the hotel during the first week of shooting, which is where Big Angry spent the working day.

Jeromiah and Taylor also informed us that one of our financier's had seen Big Angry's burn-out buddy taking shots of tequila on Day Two in the bar across the street from where we were filming—during work hours—and then driving actors from set to the hotel. One actor refused to let Burn-out drive her and her children. Burn-out was also getting high in the production trailer, leaving his bag of weed on the desk as if it were a paperweight. What's more, Big Angry had never been authorized to hire this guy. He hired him behind our backs, put him on the payroll. These were not the type of people we wanted representing the Miller Brothers.

NO MORE ANGRY

We walked into the production office. It looked ransacked, like someone had emptied a file cabinet and then turned on a leaf blower. Important contracts, bills, invoices, and various other documents were strewn across the desk and floor, intermingled with pizza boxes, soda cans, candy bar wrappers, and Chinese takeout.

Big Angry and his smoked-out partner were at the end of the table with $10,000 in cash, dividing up the crews per diem. A few other people were in the room.

"We need everybody except Big Angry to get out of here."

Big Angry's buddy slithered out of the room.

We sat down. So did Bao and Jeromiah.

Big Angry slammed a handful of money on the table and then stomped over to a file cabinet. "If I'm going to be on trial, then I'm going to show you my evidence!"

"Big Angry, your buddy is fired. Gone. Send him home. He needs to pack his shit and get out of here now. Either you tell him, or we're going to throw him out," Logan said.

"If he's outta here, then so am I," Big Angry said.

Great, we all thought . . . On the drive over, we had discussed firing him—thought it was necessary—but were concerned he would try to sue us. So before we fired him we were going to run it by our attorney. But Big Angry saved us a $300 phone call. His anger had finally paid off for us.

Then he started yelling, packing his gear, unplugging his laptop. "I've given everything to this project! Everything! This movie is in economic ruin, and I'm not going to stick around and watch it crumble. You're on the road to bankruptcy!"

It took the greatest angels of our nature to keep us from ripping him apart.

"This project is doomed," he said, grinning. "Doooooomed . . . You're going to run out of money in a few weeks. You're fucked. Good luck."

THE DELUGE

FOR WEEKS, WE'D been asking Big Angry for a cost to date—a report listing how much we'd spent and the projected costs for the remainder of the movie. He never produced one. As a result we knew very little about our financial condition. Did we have ten thousand in the bank, one hundred thousand? Were we bouncing checks?

The financing was held in escrow, disbursed to our movie bank account on a drawdown schedule. On September 7, a certain amount was released into the movie account, on September 21, another amount was released, and so on at intervals that corresponded to our budget. This demanded fiscal responsibility. We couldn't outspend the drawdown schedule. Nor could we exceed our overall budget. Not knowing where we were at financially was a dangerous position, especially on a low-budget independent film. There was no studio to hit up for more money. Once the budget was exhausted, that was it. We had a crisis on our hands, and it demanded immediate attention and action.

First step: organize

The production office was so messy you couldn't think inside.

It was 9 P.M. We all started cleaning up the room.

"Jeromy . . . Do you think you're ready to be a line producer?" Noah asked. "No bullshit, here. Can you handle the job?"

"Absolutely."

"Good, you're hired."

It was a battlefield commission. Jeromiah had just vaulted from private to colonel.

A month earlier, Jeromiah was selling life insurance in San Francisco. He was making six figures a year. When we finally raised the money for *Touching Home,* we called with the good news. It was just an update. NOT A JOB OFFER. Mind you, he was making *six figures a year*. We thought he might be able to help us out on weekends, volunteer a few hours on Saturdays and Sundays.

Thirty minutes later he fired us an e-mail:

i'm giving my two week notice tomorrow. i'm coming to work for you guys.

We called him back immediately. "Whoa, whoa, whoa, Jeromiah. We can't pay you much, maybe five hundred a week. And we already hired a line producer . . . You'll be a P.A. or something—far below your ability."

"Guys, I've already made my decision. We dreamed about this day back in the War Room in L.A. I'm in. I've always been in. I don't care what my job is or how much I make—I just want to be a part of it."

JEROMIAH RUNNING WATER ZAJONC

Jeromiah Running Water Zajonc comes from good stock. His father, Bobby-Z, is a renowned helicopter pilot and aerial cinematographer. Bobby has filmed movies all over the world for the world's most celebrated directors: Spielberg, Zemeckis, Howard, etc. He learned to fly choppers while dodging rockets and gunfire over Vietnam, logging over one thousand combat hours during his tour.

After Jeromiah graduated from UCLA he started working for line producer Paul Kurta, and writer/producer Scott Rosenberg. Back then, Jeromiah and Taylor were renting a house together in the Mar Vista neighborhood of Los Angeles. When one of their roommates moved out, we moved in. The four of us turned the garage into the War Room for movie production. But nothing materialized when we were living together. After a few years, Jeromiah moved back to the Bay Area but never lost his love for movies, always planning to return to the business one day. And one day had now arrived.

ACCOUNTING FOR THE UNACCOUNTED

Our eyeballs were burning tangles of red veins, looked like someone squirted Halloween juice in them. Yet this bastard telling us that we were doomed, and snickering about it, rallied us. A bunch of bad energy had been dumped south.

By midnight, we had cleaned up the production office. It was far from organized, but at least you could walk around without squishing a slice of pizza into a contract.

"Get your asses down here and have a beer with us," Evan Jones said over the cell phone. "Take a break."

The crew was down at the Pint Size Lounge celebrating the first week. They were having a loud time when we arrived. There was a wonderful cohesion; the grips, the electricians, transpo, hair and makeup, camera, the actors, all the departments were drinking together and enjoying life. They gave us a hearty toast and loud cheer. We told them that Jeromiah was now the line producer. And an even louder cheer erupted. They had our backs, and it felt good.

We drank a couple beers with them and then drove back to the production office with Jeromiah and Taylor and worked until 3 A.M., crashed on the production office floor, and started working again at 7 A.M., mainlining coffee, chewing tobacco, and drinking Red Bulls and Rockstars, with an occasional handful of peanuts and party mix.

We needed to find out where the movie was financially. None of us had any experience in accounting other than balancing a checkbook—and the only time we did that was high school math class. We made a few calls to movie production accountants. Their estimates for coming in and balancing our books were far too expensive. We needed a solution, and the solution was us.

"I think the first thing I should do is go over the deal memos," Jeromiah said. "It will help us figure out the daily burn rate."

Two hours later:

"We don't have one signed deal memo," Jeromiah said. "I can't believe that . . . Actually, there is one for Burn-out . . . We need to find out what we're paying people each day . . . Worse, we could be violating labor laws. This exposes us to a bunch of bad things."

So . . .

One by one, we called each crew member into our production office—Room 4207—and asked them what deal Big Angry had screamed at them. Over the past few months, we (Logan and Noah) had personally brokered the deals with our department heads—the Keys. But it got tricky with the rest of the crew, around fifty people. Some of the wages Big Angry had orally promised were excessively high, as if designed to bankrupt our movie. Rudimentary mathematics—somewhere between first- and second-grade level—could have figured that out. On the other hand, there were deals Big Angry brokered that threw people into the poorhouse—so who knows what he was really thinking. But either way, we had to correct the math. So we increased some salaries and reduced others.

The negotiation was fairly straightforward from our end: either we modify your deal so we can finish the movie, or we have to let you go. WE ARE completing our movie, with a crew, or without a crew. To their credit, the crew was willing to work within our budget. Everyone loved our energy, proud to be part of *Touching Home*. Even at that dire moment, the crew believed in us. Jeromiah drafted up deal memos and had everyone formally employed by the end of the day.

We then sent unnecessary gear back to vendors in L.A., brokered new rates with caterers, and persuaded the hotel to reduce its price. While the crew slept and barbecued out by the pool, caroused in San Francisco, or tasted fine wines and fine cheeses in Napa Valley, we worked each night until 3 A.M., crashed with Taylor and Jeromiah on the production room floor, and attacked the workload again at 6 A.M. (Jeromiah slept both the September and December shoots in the production office, such was his dedication to *Touching Home*.)

Those two days off from filming gave us time to get the machine back on track and streamline the budget. Our burn rate was now approximately $40,000/day, down from nearly $55,000/day. In addition to wages, we provided two catered meals (around $2000/day for the entire crew), a hotel room with a pool and hot tub, complimentary breakfast ($88/night), and $20 per diem, plus gas money. Craft Services, a hot truck stuffed with sandwiches, breakfast burritos, muffins, doughnuts, cookies, cakes—a fossil-fuel-guzzling-diabetes-inducing-snack-shack—cost roughly $500/day. Food overflows during principal photography. Most of the crew gains weight and carries home a notch or two of guilt—just like a Caribbean cruise.

We were physically and mentally smashed. But not beaten. We just needed two more strong weeks like the first. It was time to reflect on the road behind and envision the road ahead, remember why we were here. So in the dawn before we resumed filming we jogged to the top of the hill above the hotel to clear our heads and talk to Dad.

Growing up, we used to ask him, "When are you gonna teach us how to put on a roof?"

We were always the grunt labor, tearing off and loading the roofs for him or whatever contractor he was working for; our tool was a crowbar, his was a hammer. We destroyed, he created. Even though it's backbreaking and brain-melting hot, we wanted to learn, wanted to know what Dad knew.

"Never . . . ," Dad would say. "I'm not ever going to teach you how to put on a roof . . . I don't want to give you this to fall back on . . ."

If we'd had something to fall back on after baseball, we never would have started writing, wouldn't be making this movie—NO WAY. It was too far from us, too far from everything we knew, which could be summarized in the educated world as—next to nothing, miles from nowhere.

Our dad never gave us any path to follow. And so we made our own. Perhaps that was his intention.

"I've seen how stressed you guys were handling the production issues," Jeromiah said when we got back from our run. "I don't want you to worry about them again until we're done shooting. Let me stress. I can handle it. Focus on what you do best and direct this movie."

We blazed through Weeks Two and Three and completed our shooting schedule on time. We averaged twenty-seven camera setups a day, nearly double the industry average. We had worked with massive quarry equipment, baseball action, rain machines, kids, built a carnival and populated it with over three hundred extras—not easy scenes to orchestrate.

For a day, we felt accomplished and then started worrying about December.

SLEEP-DIRECTING

A psychotic disease fell upon us when shooting ended. We thought we'd never fight our way out. We called it Sleep-Directing. And we have the terrifying scars on our hearts and minds to prove it.

Here's how it attacked:

It would start out as a nightmare and then morph into a hallucination once we opened our eyes. Actors didn't know their lines, the camera was chewing apart film, the crew had food poisoning and the outhouses were locked, someone embezzled our financing and fled to Mexico, packs of wild dogs were mauling extras, swarms of locusts were eating our props, and giant eagles were carrying off actors.

The hallucinations were so intense that it would take several seconds for one brother to slap the other brother back into reality. One haunting night, Noah woke up shouting, "Where's the camera going?!" and threw his pillow at the wall, then ripped off his underwear and threw them at the ceiling, screaming "WE CAN'T MAKE A MOVIE LIKE THIS!" Another night Logan woke up and started punching holes in the air, believing that someone was trying to steal the Perfect Car.

The Sleep-Directing nightmares and hallucinations gradually dissipated over several weeks. But they occurred both in September and December. Interestingly, they never occurred in April 2006 (when we filmed for four days in Arizona) and in April 2007 (when we returned to Arizona for two more days of filming). This led us to conclude that the intensity of principal photography compounds in the brain. The swelling increases each day until your mental immune system breaks down and Sleep-Directing takes over, somewhere after Day Ten. Of course, this depends on the individual. Some directors probably never experience this affliction. Some have never been cured.

ROCKIES ROAD AND THE MIRACULOUS RECEPTION

IN DENVER, MEN were loading hunting rifles. They wanted our hides.

"Guys, you may be receiving a phone call from the Rockies," P. J. Carey said. If you remember, P. J. was the head coach of the Colorado Rockies extended spring training. He continued:

"Apparently, some people in the front office are upset with me for allowing you guys to come out and film us in spring training. Look, I told them you're good kids and that I thought it was a great experience for our players . . . You guys had insurance, right?"

"Yes, sir. One million dollars' liability, and a permit to film at Reid Park."

"That's what I thought . . . I remember you guys showing me the paperwork . . . Look, I think everything is going to work out. They're just a little upset that you didn't talk to them first."

"How pissed are they?"

"They're pissed . . . But they're more pissed at me, I think . . . Look, the guys in the front office are good people. They just want to figure out what's going on, who you guys are, and what sort of movie you're making."

"Who should we call, P. J.?"

"I think they're going to call *you*."

"Maybe we should call first. That way it doesn't look like we're hiding."

"Greg Feasel is the guy to call. He's the senior vice president of business operations."

"Hey, we understand their concerns. If we were working for the Rockies and we found out that some movie guys had filmed on our fields without asking us, we'd be pissed too."

"You guys did ask. You asked me. And I stand by my decision. It was a lot of fun for everyone . . . But it still needs to be cleared with the top guys. Look, call Greg, tell him about the movie, and I'm sure everything will work out."

It was a bad thing we always saw coming and put off until the hour of reckoning. Now the hour was here. We prayed they would forgive us. We prayed they would let us use the footage.

THE MIRACULOUS RECEPTION

So we called Greg Feasel in Denver. Hal Roth, the Rockies head counsel and CFO, joined him on the call. And like P. J. said, they weren't happy with us, weren't happy at all.

Greg and Hal told us to send them our script, a DVD of the spring training footage, and any other relevant materials. They'd review and get back to us. Lawyers were now involved.

If the Rockies didn't let us use the footage, the consequences would be disastrous. We had no way of replacing what we had filmed.

But somewhere on the heavenly ceiling, Michelangelo was mixing plaster and preparing to paint a new story of divine intervention: *The Miraculous Reception.*

That weekend our buddy Tony Shapiro was getting married. Tony is a blessed breed, a six-foot-three Viking-Jew. He can hit a 450-foot home run and murder you at chess. His bride, Evelyn, is an El Salvadoran and German goddess, one of those true beauties we all wish we could find but never do.

Greg Feasel and Hal Roth called us back on Friday, a day before the wedding. The Rockies, and now, Major League Baseball—the steel-nosed attorneys in New York who had final say on the usage rights—were not warming to our movie. In fact, it appeared our request to use the spring training footage was going to be denied. We might even get sued. New York was livid.

So we go to Tony and Evelyn's wedding at a mansion in the rolling hills south of San Jose, Steinbeck country, put business on hold for a few hours, eat, drink, dance with lovely women in lovely dresses, all that delicious stuff.

After the vows were given, there was an hour of drinks and socializing, followed by a formal dinner, assigned seating, name cards on each table.

"Hey, guys, I don't know where you're sitting," Tony said. "It's completely random, a chance for both families to get to know each other."

Both Tony's and Evelyn's mothers are immigrants, Sweden and El Salvador, respectively. Many of the guests had never met one another, due to geographic and linguistic barriers.

It was a buffet-style feast. We loaded up our plates, refilled the wine, found our name cards, and sat down. There were ten people at our table, didn't know any of them, or so we thought.

"I'm Gary Hughes," a sturdy, confident man in his fifties said. He reached across the table and shook our hands. "It's nice to finally meet you guys. Tony has told me a lot about you over the years. I hear you're making a movie."

"Yes, sir. We just completed the first half of filming."

No business for a few hours, right?

Well, like we said, miracles were being painted on the ceiling. There were 250 people at the wedding, some twenty-odd tables. We could've sat next to anyone. But no, we were sitting next to Gary Hughes.

And well, Gary Hughes is a very influential man in a line of work that was causing us great mental pain and distress. Coincidence? No, it's miraculous. You see, Gary Hughes just happens to be the special assistant to the general manager of the Chicago Cubs. That's right. THE CHICAGO CUBS. His son, Sam, also sitting at the table, is the clubhouse manager for the Florida Marlins. They're a baseball family. They know quite a few people in the business of baseball.

"Tony said you guys did some filming with the Rockies," Gary continued.

"Yeah, they're pretty pissed off at us right now, might not let us use the footage. We sort of filmed without getting permission from the front office."

"I used to work for the Rockies."

THE COLORADO ROCKIES!? Noah coughed up a shrimp; Logan shot cabernet out his nostrils.

Then Gary asked, "Who have you been talking to?"

"Uhh . . . Hal Roth and Greg Feasel."

"Hal Roth is a great guy, a very close friend of mine. You don't meet better men than Hal. I'll call him tomorrow. Tell him I know you guys, straighten everything out."

Gary looked over at Tony and Evelyn, who were saying hello to each table. "I love Tony like a son. He's always had great things to say about you guys. I know how much he loves you . . . You won't have any problems with the Rockies."

He raised his wine. "Here's to Tony and Evelyn, and your movie. Cheers."

Everyone at the table chinked wineglasses and beer bottles.

Gary called Hal the next day. Then Gary called us and said everything was going to work out with the Rockies. "If there's anything else I can do for you, let me know. Good luck with your movie, boys. Take care."

Michelangelo, high on the celestial scaffolding, applied the final touches to *The Miraculous Reception*. The man who had commissioned the work was waiting below. Michelangelo put down his brush, climbed down the scaffolding, stood beside our dad, and asked his opinion. "Well, done."

CALL ME ISHMAEL

THE DAYS WERE getting short. Dark winter approached. Every day was page one of *Moby Dick*.

Despite the drastic cost-cutting, our economic position was still bleak. The movie was driving toward financial death. More harsh measures would need to be taken. One of our conclusions: we could not resume shooting in December with a Los Angeles crew. It would bankrupt the production. We needed to hire locally. This was an extremely difficult decision for us. (Not the local issue, but having to replace people.) We had a great crew. We wanted to bring them all back in December.

Including mileage, plane tickets, hotel rooms, and per diem, each person on our September crew from L.A. cost us a premium of $1,500/week. By hiring locally in December, we could save in excess of $100,000. But it wasn't just about hard costs. Hiring locally would expose us to another potential hazard—a strong union presence. We'd avoided the union in September, largely because we'd *hired* an L.A. crew for a Northern California shoot, effectively operating outside the L.A. union's reach. Northern California and Southern California have different unions, so hiring a local crew for the December shoot would now put us on the Northern California union's turf. And, well, just like in someone else's neighborhood, you're gonna get tested.

Here's how hiring the crew typically works: the director hires the director of photography (DP). The DP then hires the gaffer (the electrician), dolly grip, key grip—with the director's approval, of course. But most of the time it never becomes an issue. However, Ricardo, our DP, was in L.A. It was now up to us and Jeromiah to hire a Bay Area grip and electric department, script supervisor— the most underrated position on set—props, and anyone else we could replace from L.A.

Hiring locally was a fiscal necessity. It had to be done. So we did it. But we weren't proud of it. For three weeks in September, our crew had bonded. They had devoted themselves to the movie. They couldn't wait to come back and finish in December. We had become especially close to our key grip, Gary Beaird. Blue-collared, ex-roofer, huge baseball fan, we had much in common. He was the first grip on set each morning and the last one to leave each night.

So we started the process of hiring a new crew, just like we had twice before. After dozens of phone calls and meetings, we hired Joseph Edward Scott as key grip, Jon Fontana as gaffer, Carol DePasquale as script supervisor, and Karen Bradley as hair and makeup, all Bay Area movie veterans.

Perhaps the most agonizing dimension of the hiatus was trying to put together a workable shooting schedule for December, a schedule that underwent hundreds of permutations. We could never complete the puzzle without having a few pieces left over.

Moreover, we were trying to play God by trying to control the weather. December in Northern California can be a torrential nightmare for anyone who makes his living outside. It's not uncommon for it to rain the entire month. Also, there's the dreaded absence of light. We needed to plan for these adverse filming conditions.

Typically, you have backup locations called "cover-sets" in case you get rained out during filming. For instance, if you're scheduled to shoot at a baseball field, you also have a cover-set at an indoor location so you don't lose a day of shooting because of the rain. But what if it's raining the entire time? Exactly, you guessed it, you eventually run out of cover-sets. What if all your scenes are outside? Then you have *The Rain Movie* that was written as *The Sunny Movie*.

An overwhelming majority of Ed's scenes took place outside. Rain throughout December would destroy us. One night in early October, we awoke to the pattering of rain. In our neurotic state, this was a portent of doom; utter disaster and catastrophe awaited us. It would rain from now until March. The next biblical flood had arrived, only an ark wouldn't save us this time. We didn't sleep for the rest of the night. Each raindrop on the roof was a nail hammered into our coffin.

By shooting much of the movie in September, we had already established the weather for a great number of scenes that we would need to complete with Ed in December. For example, the first day at the quarry, Mac (Evan Jones) walks over to the brothers at the rock crusher and starts talking to them. This was shot in September without a cloud in the sky, eighty-five degrees, hot and sunny. Now, in December, we needed to shoot two other parts of that scene (same day in the movie); Ed climbs into a loader and goes to work, then, at the end of the day he asks his boys in the quarry parking lot if they want to have dinner with him. Did this gap in scheduling overexpose us to risk? Yes. Did this defy industry convention? Absolutely. But there was no other way to do it. Our gut said, get it while you can.

Further tormenting us were the negotiations with Ed's people. After the conclusion of the September shoot we had time to engage them on the contract. Without an executed contract, we sensed that Brian Vail was getting worried that we might have misrepresented Ed's participation in *Touching Home*. Brian was already a million dollars in the hole.

Why wasn't Ed signed yet? He said he was doing your movie, right? That's the investment you sold me?

If *we* had financed the movie, these were the questions we'd be asking.

Hell, our entire crew thought Ed was signed. The only person besides us and Gordon aware of this vulnerable secret was Jeromiah.

As mentioned, Brian was not obligated to release further monies until Ed was signed. What's more, this handicapped us in negotiations with Ed's representatives. We couldn't disclose this clause to them. It would give them substantial leverage. They would own our movie by the time they were through.

All this uncertainty—the weather, the impossible schedule, the financing, not having Ed signed—made the two months off mentally unbearable.

Then, as if we weren't sick enough, other wonderful poisons began to enter our system.

An even greater concern than the weather, and similarly, one that was constantly changing, was the actors' schedules. Only the forecasting of this hasn't evolved with the accuracy of Doppler radar. This is as unpredictable as an earthquake. It's like juggling babies over a volcano.

Our little movie did not have the money to book Brad Dourif, Robert Forster, or any of the other actors for the entire two weeks in December. We had to book them by the day, which meant that our schedule needed to be perfect—and perfect, as anyone knows, is impossible. Any changes to an actor's schedule during filming would cost us huge dollars.

But here's what happened to us repeatedly over the break (October, November). We'd finally figure out the shooting schedule, this intricate network of logistics, locations, people, gear, geography, permits, traffic, state and federal ordinances, area codes, zip codes . . . And sure enough, when all looked rosy, one of the actor's agents would call, and in the sweetest of tones, inform us that his actor COULD NOT work on a specific date—who knows why, 'cause it was the actor's dog's birthday. Fine. We'd rework the schedule. The world would be at peace. Dogs and owners blowing out candles on fruitcake. A day later, another agent would call and tell us that *his* actor COULD NOT work on a specific day either. Fine. Rework the impossible. It was a merry-go-round of lunacy.

Then came the biggest missile.

Months earlier, Evan Jones had shot a TV pilot for ABC called *October Road*. In September, when Evan was filming with us, it appeared that *October Road* would not get picked up for the season. But during our break it did . . . And they would start filming new episodes in November and continue through the New Year. Great for Evan. Disastrous for us. We needed Evan in December. But ABC owned him. And guess what? We weren't gonna be able to use him.

Evan tried to find time to come back. We tried. But the demands of *October Road* prevailed.

So we had to figure out a way to finish the movie without Evan, one of our central characters. How do you do that? We didn't know yet. And it was keeping us up at night.

PART VII

THE RESURRECTION

BETTING IT ALL ON ED

BY EARLY NOVEMBER we had reached a stalemate with Ed's people.

We weren't budging. They didn't have to. Their e-mail responses became increasingly delayed. They had essentially shut off communication.

The possibility of Ed not showing up seemed VERY REAL to us.

"They are not going to sign under these terms . . . These guys are sharks. They're not going to settle on this," Gordon said. "More importantly, your financier is not going to release further monies without Ed signed. You need to fly out to New York and sit down with Ed in person. The same way you got him on board. Bring the contract. Tell him his people are being assholes and that you need him to sign the damn thing."

Ed was in New York, performing a one-man show at the Public Theater, seven shows a week. We had been corresponding through e-mail. He was upbeat, always wishing us the best, signing off with *I'll see you in December,* or some other encouraging words.

"Gordon, we want to keep our relationship with Ed strictly creative," Logan said.

"Bullshit. You ambushed him in the first place."

"We know. But once he committed to our movie, once we shook on it, he told us to take care of everything through his agents. They would handle the business side. We need to honor that out of respect for Ed and work through the proper channels this time around."

"Then you probably won't have a signed contract by December. It's insane, guys. Insane . . . You can't start shooting with him without a signed contract . . . What does your financier say?"

"We told Brian the reality, told him that Ed probably wouldn't be signed, but that he was doing our movie . . . We hope he trusts us enough to release the funds from escrow."

"It's insane, guys."

Our gut told us that Ed wouldn't let us down. Who cares about all the agents and attorneys? Ed had given us his word. We shook on it. *Ed's going to show up*, we convinced ourselves. *He has to.*

SCARE IN REDWOODS

It was the day before Thanksgiving, less than a week from shooting. Physically, we had survived the dreary weather; mentally, we were shaky, self-medicating with nicotine and chocolate bars—chocolate of all kinds, any chocolate to mix with two cans of chew a day. A legal speedball, not advised for those wishing to live past fifty . . . but it eased the stress at the time.

It was supposed to rain over the weekend. Then sunshine. For ten days straight. It appeared the gods were in our favor, but like any great odyssey, as soon as you get confident, the divine winds decide to blow you off course again.

We were scouting with Ricardo in the redwoods of Samuel P. Taylor State Park when we received an e-mail from Jeromiah on our BlackBerry: *call me asap*. We knew this could only be one thing: EDWARD HARRIS.

We tried calling Jeromiah, but we were buried in the forest and couldn't connect.

"Ricky, we gotta go back to the hotel."

With our world unraveling, we raced back to the hotel and ran into Room 4207, our makeshift production office where Jeromiah was living.

"Guys, I got a phone call from Ed and his agent, asking if we could push our shoot to January."

"January?! Are they nuts?! It's November twenty-second!"

Noah was a little excited. The strain of battle will do that to you.

Mind you, we were six days from shooting. Most of the crew was already working and on the payroll. Gear and trucks were arriving by the hour. Brad Dourif was flying up in two days.

Jeromiah continued, "I told them 'no way.' But Ed's agent said that Ed was exhausted from New York. He'd been home for only a few days. I don't think it was Ed so much who wanted us to push, but I think his agent really does . . . Ed said for you guys to call him as soon as you can."

So we immediately called Ed at his house. He was cooking with his family, pots and pans clanging in the background, knives cutting carrots, sounded like a good time.

"Yo, boys," Ed said, happy to hear our voices. "So Jeromiah tells me there's no way to push, that you guys are ready to go."

"Yeah, it would be impossible for us to push right now. Impossible."

"Fair enough . . . I didn't know exactly where you guys were at as far as shooting was concerned, didn't know if everything was in place or what not."

"We based everything around you, Ed. We're ready to go."

"Great. I just had to check . . . I didn't mean to scare you guys."

We laughed. "Well, you sure as shit did!"

Ed laughed too. "Can't wait to see you guys. We're gonna have a good time."

"We got your plane ticket booked and everything."

"Is it refundable?"

"Yeah."

"Good, then I'm driving up on Monday. I don't want you guys spending that kind of money on a plane ticket . . . Plus, coming up a few days early will give us a chance to go over the script, rehearse a bit. I really haven't had much time with the material. This isn't how I like to work."

"Don't worry, Ed. You'll be great."

" . . . Well, I'm gonna drop my daughter off at school Monday morning and then hit the road and drive up to you boys . . . Jeromy, could you e-mail me directions?"

"I got you covered, Ed. I'm doing it right now."

"See you boys Monday."

"See you then."

Our world would survive a few more days. We could eat turkey tomorrow and be thankful.

MAJOR MAJOR

"WE HAVE A major problem," Jeromiah told us as we walked into company headquarters. "You guys need to go up to Brad Dourif's room—right now."

"We just dropped him off at his room a minute ago," Noah said. "No joke. A minute ago. What do you mean *major*?"

"Major."

"Major?

"Yes, major."

Pause . . . Silence. Us staring at Jeromiah.

"All's I know is there's a major problem," Jeromiah said, pacing. "Bao said that Brad has a *major* problem and that you guys should come up to Brad's room right now . . . Bao doesn't know Brad."

"Neither do we!" Logan said, throwing up his hands.

Brad was the first actor to show up for the December shoot. We hadn't seen him since our meeting at Starbucks in May, the first time we met.

So we ran up to Brad's room, a mixture of panic and manic. "So what's going on, Brad?"

Bao was standing in the doorway with Brad's suitcase, unsure what to do.

"We have a major problem, guys," Brad said. "A major problem."

"So I've been told . . . What is it?" Noah said in a calming tone.

Brad was looking at the TV. He walked over and tapped the top of it with his index finger. "Guys, this television isn't Hi-Def."

"Yeah? . . ."

"I need a Hi-Def television for my Xbox 360 . . . I only play on Hi-Def . . . It's not gonna work on this TV."

"What do you mean it's not going to work?" Noah asked. "Give me the damn thing, I'll plug it in."

"No, you don't get it, it's not going to work, guys."

The major problem was a TV? We thought it was going to be something serious like a death in the family, a contractual dispute, a clogged toilet, a bloody horse head in the bed, or I want to make my character a transsexual—but a TV?

"Brad, you want a Hi-Def TV?" Noah asked.

"I *need* one."

Brad's attitude was not that of a pampered movie star. It was more like a scientist with the wrong equipment.

"What size TV do you want, Brad?" Noah asked.

"It's gotta be *Hi-Def*," he said, emphasizing *Hi-Def* as if we'd never heard of it.

"Yeah, Brad. Hi-Def. As in *High-Definition*. I got it. We have them up here too. It's not an exclusive L.A. product . . . Bao, can you go get Brad a High-Definition television?"

"No problem," Bao said. "I'll run down the street to Target. They got a fourteen-day return policy. I'll buy it and then return it when Brad's done filming."

"That's terrific, cool man," Brad said, looking at Bao in the doorway, who was still holding Brad's suitcase. Then Brad turned to us. "Can we go see the pigeons now?"

PIGEON STARS

It rained earlier in the day. The pigeons were cold, didn't feel like flying.

Back in August, we bought the pigeons for $8 apiece from a guy named Jerry who lived in the Mojave Desert. We paid Jerry $224 for twenty-eight birds. He put them in a cardboard box. Then we put the box in our backseat and drove up to Northern California with the pigeons cooing and flapping the entire trip, six hundred miles' worth. By the time we arrived, our car wreaked of pigeon piss and dirty plumage.

Raccoons ate five pigeons the first week; mutilated them, feathers and tweety heads thrown about like savage artwork. Then we fortified the cage, and the raccoons went elsewhere for dessert. From August to November we trained the surviving birds with Bao. And they were now ready to become movie stars.

Brad has a natural way with animals. Animals like who they like. It's immediate. Some people have the gift. Some don't. Brad has it.

"The birds are trained to fly around their feeding schedule," Logan told Brad. "If you try to fly them after they've eaten, it won't work. They get lethargic. They won't budge from the floor of the coop."

"I'll start feeding them each day, get to know them." Brad said. "These are my friends in the movie. We gotta get to know each other. Be comfortable."

We walked Brad through the feeding process, just as our dad had taught us when we were kids: how much seed to give them, where to put it, showed him how to open the cage, how the pigeons fly, what route they usually take.

"Watch out for the hawks," Logan said. "Check the sky before you let out the pigeons. Also check the taller trees and telephone poles, the high points, the hawks like to perch there. They'll snatch the pigeons if you're not careful."

We hung out with the pigeons for an hour and then drove back to the hotel. We wanted to rehearse with Brad, see what he'd developed for Clyde. We had only spoken to Brad a few times over the phone since our first meeting.

"Where do you want to rehearse?" Noah asked.

"My room," Brad said.

Brad sat at his desk and opened his script. We sat on the bed.

"Now, this is just an example, guys," Brad said. "But I think Clyde has a bad left hand, impaired."

Good. Nice touch.

"And he speaks with a lazy tongue," Brad added. "Like we discussed."

"Let's see what you got," Noah said.

Brad went into character and started speaking.

Now, Brad is keenly perceptive, one of the great actors of our time. You can't pull the "*I like it*" fake smile past him. He stopped midway through the scene.

"You guys don't like it, do you?" Brad asked.

"It's a start . . ."

"It's not ready yet," Brad assured us.

"We have time, Brad." Noah said. "We'll work on it."

Then Brad stood up, started pacing, head down, thinking, growing agitated.

"My girlfriend loves it. It's too late to change . . . What don't you guys like about it?"

"Who says we don't like it?"

"Don't bullshit me guys . . . Your faces . . . You don't like what I've created."

"What do you like about Clyde in the script?" Logan asked.

"He's wise. He's the only person in the family who's got his shit together . . . He's a natural poet . . . Everything he says is lyrical."

"Well, the audience will never know that if they can't understand what he's saying," Logan said.

"Guys, I'm not like Ed Harris." Brad's voice grew louder, frustrated. "I can't just snap my fingers and make a change to my character. These things take time. I've been working on this for months. I need to observe someone, a subject, model my actions after them. It's too late to change now, guys. We start shooting in what, two days?"

"We do . . . But you're not scheduled to start shooting for five. We got five days until Clyde needs to be ready."

"Guys, it's too damn late," Brad said. He walked over to the window and stared at the hotel pool below. "Besides, my girlfriend likes it."

There was no point in waging a creative battle with Brad on his first day in town so we drove home. It was cold and dark, late November in the north. We were tired. But again, like so many other nights during this journey, we had trouble sleeping.

How could we shape and alter Brad's interpretation? We needed to be gentle, considerate. But we needed him to make a major adjustment in a short time. We barely knew the guy. His contract wasn't even signed.

"We gotta be smart about our approach. We need to build his trust," Logan said. "We don't want to frustrate him. We're just a couple of first-time know-nothings right now who happened to write a good script. That doesn't mean we can direct . . . We need to build his trust . . . He could leave anytime and fly back to L.A. Then we'd really be screwed."

There was a stubborn intelligence about Brad, a natural shield against stupid directors. He'd worked with a ton of good ones and many more bad ones. He didn't know yet which category we'd fall under.

The next morning we picked up Brad at the hotel and took

him to Starbucks. Then we drove out to the country to feed the pigeons.

"Do you guys feel better about Clyde now?" Brad asked.

In fact, we felt worse. No sleep, caffeine—delusion and neurosis were beating us up.

Then an Archimedes moment.

"What if we took you over to our friend's house to observe his uncle?" Noah asked, behind the wheel. "Would that help you?"

"What about *your* uncle?" Brad asked. "I want to meet your uncle, the real-life Clyde."

"We don't know where he is."

"Guys, look, it's too late to make a change to Clyde. It's too late."

"Brad, you said you need to observe someone, right?"

Silence.

Brad was getting frustrated with us. He just wanted to drink his damn coffee. And here he was, an Academy Award nominee, a veteran of over a hundred movies, a genius, being chauffeured down a twisting country road, badgered by a couple of first-time directors half his age telling him that they think his character needs to be reshaped, that it won't work.

Brad gets paid because he KNOWS what works. Brad works all the time because HE knows.

Brad was getting carsick. Coffee was spurting out the hole in the lid.

"Sure, call your friend," Brad said. "Just get me off this damn road. It's insane."

"It's straight where we're heading."

Noah dialed our friend's number. He was in the navy, stationed in San Diego.

"No problem," our friend said. "My uncle is at my grandma's house. Just drive on over there. I'll call and let them know you're coming."

Our friend's uncle was waiting on the porch when we arrived twenty minutes later. We'll call him "Woody."

Woody is in his fifties and still lives at home with his mother. He's rail thin, glasses, perpetual bed-head, looks down at his feet when he walks. Now, it don't take a doctor to notice that something ain't normal with Woodrow. Not sure what the clinical diagnosis is, but let's just say the room upstairs is missing some furniture.

Brad Dourif has a cult following; being the voice of "Chucky" will do that for you. And it just so happens that Woody is Brad's number one fan. Number one. As we walked down the hall to his room, Woody started randomly quoting lines from Brad's movies, asking about scenes that Brad didn't even remember filming.

"Want to see my drawings?" Woody asked, opening the door to his room.

"We'd love to," Brad said, enjoying the attention.

Woody took a box from the shelf. It was one of those kits that teaches you how to be an artist, the kind you see advertised on TV at three in the morning. It was filled with Woody's charcoal and colored pencil drawings. They were excellent.

He rifled through them, flashing them in front of us before flinging them onto the bed.

"This is Captain America," flash drawing, fling. "This is a barbarian," flash drawing, fling. "Viking Lord," flash, fling. "Martian Invaders," flash, fling. Flash, fling, flash, fling . . . And so on until his bed was covered with heroes.

Brad was studying Woody . . . Everything was working beautifully. We were thinking *this is perfect:* Brad has found his subject. We felt as confident as a beer league slugger on steroids.

That is, until we got into the car.

"Later, Woody," Brad said, waving good-bye as we drove away.

Brad rolled up the window, smiled, prompting us to smile—*he finally has it, he's found Clyde!*

"Was Woody a great study or what?" Noah asked.

"Guys . . ." Brad paused. "He's completely normal."

"Normal?!" Noah hit the brakes, pulled the car to the curb. "Normal?! He's out of his gourd! He's fifty years old, lives at home. He's got a dentist appointment later today, and he doesn't even know how he's getting there, who's picking him up, or where the office is—this has been his dentist since he was a kid. Normal?!"

"I saw and spoke to an articulate, intelligent, and perfectly normal individual," Brad replied.

Noah was white-knuckling the steering wheel with both hands, rocking in his seat. We drove back to the hotel in silence.

We all went up to Brad's room to rehearse again.

Brad put his script on the desk and got into character.

"I think I know what you guys are looking for."

Then Brad read the scene.

It was beautiful.

It was Clyde.

He saw our smiles.

"You guys like that, huh?"

"Don't know what adjustment you just made, but it was great."

"You guys wanted less, more subtle . . . ," Brad said. "You should've just said that yesterday."

Brad closed his script, turned on his new Hi-Def television, grabbed his Xbox controller, and plopped on the bed. "Are we done? . . .'Cause, like I got some things to do."

THE MESSIAH IN A BIG FORD TRUCK

IT WAS CHILLY and clear. We were waiting in front of the hotel for him, all nerves and caffeine. We could see his smile through the windshield as he pulled his diesel in front of the lobby.

"Where should I park this thing?" Ed asked.

"Throw it in the waiting area right there," Noah said, pointing.

Ed parked. His truck took up a space and a half.

"How's it going, boys? . . . Sorry about the scare the other day," Ed said, stepping out in faded Wranglers and a white thermal shirt, stiff from the drive. He was still smiling.

"No worries, Ed."

He gave us strong hugs.

We helped him with his things: duffel bag, backpack, cowboy boots, baseball glove, a couple of dumbbells in case he felt like hitting a quick workout in the hotel room, and some clothes he thought might be good for his role. We checked him into his room and introduced him to Jeromiah.

"Ed, you feel like going out to the locations?" Noah asked.

"Sure, I'm here for you guys. Whatever you want."

We drove out to the redwoods in Samuel P. Taylor State Park. It was dark and bone cold in the woods.

"This is where our dad lived, off and on for the last fifteen years of his life. We ate lunch and dinner with him at this campsite many times, raviolis and cream corn out of the can, cooked hamburgers on an iron skillet over the fire . . . And now we're going to be filming here."

Ed listened thoughtfully, observing the towering redwoods, the picnic table, the creek we used to catch crawdads in with our dad when we were little, the spigot where he used to brush his teeth and shave.

Then we drove to the Winston House in Nicasio, the family home in the movie. Roy Rede and Tom Power were dressing the interior of Charlie's truck (Ed's character). Roy and Tom had done a bang-up job. Ed was impressed. Then we drove out to Love Field. A decade earlier, our buddy Tyler Love and his family converted their hay field into a baseball diamond, and now we were going to use it for our movie.

We had some good conversations with Ed as we drove along the country roads. He was generous and open. He was playing our father and he wanted us to feel comfortable around him.

"I really appreciate you guys sharing your dad's letters with me," Ed said.

A short time before our father died we received a large manila envelope in the mail containing letters and stories he'd written in jail. We were living in Los Angeles at the time, and when we returned north a few weeks later and saw him, he asked with a big smile if we had read what he sent us. We told him, "No . . . We'll get to them." His smile left. He was proud of his letters and stories, and we had let him down. There was something he needed to tell us that he could only convey through writing.

"Please read them . . . ," he said. "Please. They're all true. " It was sweet hopefulness and desperation.

"We will, Dad, promise . . ."

He'd sent us letters before. Most of the time they were drunken talk, incoherent ramblings that were painful for us to read. Over time, we stopped. But once he died, we felt a great deal of guilt and sadness about not reading them. He'd given us a gift and we had rejected it. We sat down on our carpet, tears forming, and opened the manila envelope. There were several letters, written on jailhouse yellow notepads, neatly folded and fastened with hand-made paper clasps. They were humble and spare, written with the simplicity of one who has come to terms with mortality. It was the bare honesty and plain expression of a man reflecting on his life, unable to hide. The mirror was there. There was nowhere to go but inside.

"The Killing Attempt" was the first letter we read. These are our father's words:

> *The time was Xmas eve 2001. 8:00 evening. The place Olema Campground. The victim was me. The killer was me . . . I had given up on me. I had given up on you. I had given up on everything. I was tired of search-ing, scraping, and grasping for a sliver of any hope. I was tired of living in my truck for 10 years, dodging police, being arrested, going to jail, paying fines, doing programs, basically living like shit . . . I knew I was lost in my space unable to communicate . . . The invisible bridge from me to the world I could not cross . . . I felt fairly easy about giving up, and ending life now, on my own terms. We're born, we live and suffer, struggle, and then we die. Most people, even with a plan, have no idea . . .*

He went on to describe how he tried to kill himself by attach-ing a rubber hose to his exhaust pipe and pumping the fumes into the camper on his truck where he was lying down. He felt like an even bigger failure afterward. Life was hard, death was easy, and he couldn't even do that.

There was always an emotional distance between us and our father, a remoteness we never managed to bring close. Those let-ters exposed us to the man across that distance, to the man who had been so far.

When Ed came on board we made copies of the letters and gave them to him.

"The Jeep and the Angle" was another letter. He meant Angel, but our dad couldn't spell that well. He compensated for it with an unschooled imagination.

"The letter about the ambush, about the angel was really powerful," Ed said. "It helped me get a good understanding, I think. Losing your buddies like that in war, right in front of you has gotta be hard."

"His jeep had thirty-six bullet holes in it and he didn't get a scratch . . . He said the angel saved his life."

We were driving through the redwoods of Lagunitas, a stone's throw across the creek from the first place we called home. The car stayed quiet for a while as we reflected on our dad's letters and how we had all been brought together by this man who believed his life was not worth living, the man whom Ed Harris was now becoming.

"You guys know where we can get a good burger around here?" Ed asked, breaking the silence.

"One of the best places in the world is right down the road in Fairfax. It was our dad's favorite."

We stopped at M&G's and ate Louie burgers, milk shakes, and fries—thick style with ridges.

"Guys, I know what you're up against," Ed said. "I took on the same responsibilities on *Pollock*. It's a huge undertaking. We only made one of our shooting days on *Pollock*, and it was something like day fifty-six, the second-to-the-last day of filming . . . I want you to know that I'm here for you boys. Whatever you need. The crew is going to be watching, seeing if you guys are in control. You're the directors. If you don't like something I'm doing, or want me to do it again, just say so, and I'll do it . . . I'm here to help you realize your dream."

In one brief expression between the bite of a cheeseburger and the sip of a chocolate milk shake, Ed Harris relieved the months of anxiety and sleepless nights and dispelled the uncertainty that had been haunting us. He made us feel like we could kick through a castle wall and eat the stones without breaking our teeth.

Ed still wasn't signed, however, wasn't contractually obligated to our movie. But damn if he wasn't on our team. Those were the best cheeseburgers we've ever had.

GETTING READY FOR DAD

The next morning we read through the script with Ed. He had lots of questions about our dad that weren't answered in the letters or the previous day's conversations. How he walked, his posture—was it upright like this, or hunched like this?

"By the end of his life he was a broken man, beaten up by life," Logan said. "He'd lost everything, his pride, his self-worth, his friends, and most of his family . . ."

"So his posture was more like this?" Ed said, rounding his shoulders, looking as though his joints were aching.

"Yeah, like that."

"What about his cadence when he spoke? Was it like this . . ." Ed read a few lines of dialogue. "Or like this?" He read the same lines again, modulating his voice, the intonation and rhythm.

After an hour and a half we took a break. It was Ed's birthday and our mom had baked him a carrot cake. We each ate a slice—it was damn good—went outside for a shot of tobacco.

Brad Dourif was outside on the patio. He and Ed had never met. We introduced them and they talked for a bit. There was a mutual respect between them, a tone of admiration, two masters who had studied each other's work for decades and were finally working together.

Ed finished his cigarette.

"Let's get back to it, boys," he said. "See you tomorrow, Brad."

"All right, Ed. See you then," Brad said, then to us, "you boys take it easy on your father here . . . It's his birthday."

Three hours later Ed felt confident with the material. Tomorrow we'd capture it on film.

FROM PAUPER TO KING

It was twenty-three degrees when we arrived at Love Field at 6:30 A.M., a thick layer of frost covering the grass, puddles iced over.

The first two scenes were shot without Ed, who was getting worked on in the hair and makeup trailer. Mary Mastro, Karen Bradley, and Ginger Damon, the hair and makeup artists, had taped several photos of our father to the mirror for reference. We walked into the trailer the day before, unaware of our dad's photos. Seeing his face and looking into his eyes brought all the pain and emotions back. It was hard for us to go inside again. So we waited for Ed out on the field.

"Whoa, guys," Jasha said, walking over to us, tears in his eyes.

Jasha is no softy. He's six feet high and 260 pounds of tattoos and muscle, a former national champion Olympic weightlifter and disciple of Coach Gough. He lost his mom to a heroin overdose when he was fifteen, bounced around from home to home. Nothing has been easy for him. He knows tragedy and raw emotions and wasn't afraid to bear his. "Man, I just saw Ed. He's on his way over here. I gasped when I saw him, thought I saw the ghost of Dan Miller. Just giving you the heads-up. He looks so much like your dad it's scary."

Several of our lifelong buddies were on the set that day. None of us grew up around the movie industry, and what we were doing was a very cool thing to them. So they hung out, ate a bunch of good food, and hit on the girls in our crew.

We were shooting from the pitcher's mound when Ed walked onto the field. His walk was our dad's walk. He was wearing a red jacket and backpack, just like our dad the last day we saw him walking down the road. The set went quiet. There were lots of people out there who knew our dad, and Ed had become him. Our father had been resurrected.

"How do I look, boys? Do I look like him?" Ed asked.

We nodded, choked up, couldn't talk, turned our backs, and walked over to the side of the field and gathered our emotions. We took the time we needed and then went back to work. We finished the day at Love Field playing catch in the sunset with Ed. Then we drove to Samuel P. Taylor State Park and filmed Logan having dinner with Dad in the redwoods one last time.

JOHN FORD, MOVIE STAR

IT WAS THE season of cold feet. We filmed outside the first four days. It never got above forty degrees. At night, it hovered in the twenties. The crew froze. In the movie, when Ed is shivering down by the creek, he's *really* shivering. That ain't no movie shiver. That's real shiver, living-outside-in-the-winter shiver.

Salvation arrived on Day Five. And the army said Hallelujah as we moved inside to shoot Ed playing poker at the Papermill Creek Saloon in Forest Knolls, a rustic den with old-growth redwood beams running down the ceiling, a milled log for the counter, a mixed bag of neon signs, Christmas lights, old funky mirrors, a couple of nude paintings, and a wood-burning stove. It was a place where our dad blew many a dollar.

For the poker scenes, we didn't want to cast a group of well-known actors. We wanted men full of hard living, faces with character, creases of laughter and weathered skin.

We held a casting session at the hotel a week before shooting. We saw thirty-two actors and chose five extraordinary talents: James Carraway, Richard Conti, David Fine, Rod Gnapp, and George Maguire. We tried to find time to rehearse prior to shooting, but the demands of preproduction intervened. So we told the fabulous five to know their lines and that we would rehearse the day of filming. It's tough to work like this, but that's the way it was.

A big concern: the poker game had to move. It couldn't get

bogged down with shuffling and dealing. It had to look natural. All the actors swore they were avid poker players, said they could play at whatever pace we needed, no sweat. But we also knew that actors will tell you they can do no-handed handstands in order to get the job.

"We gotta find a dealer," Noah said after the casting session. "A professional, someone who can keep the pace moving so that the scenes feel natural, like a real game. Not an actor that's a dealer, but a professional dealer, a guy that does it for a living. He won't have to say anything, just deal, keep the flow."

We called Bao. He plays cards all over the Bay Area. He said we should come on over to Casino San Pablo and meet John Ford, a house dealer, see if we like him, see if he'd be good for the movie.

John Ford is in his midfifties, ruddy skin, gray hair, and thick gray mustache, a guy you might see dealing cards in a Cheyenne saloon.

Now most people won't admit it, but nearly every American hopes, dreams, envisions the day when some producer or director—anyone associated with a movie—walks into his life, recognizes a skill of his, and says, "You . . . yes, you. You're really good at what you do. Really good . . . How'd you like to be in a movie?"

John Ford had been tossing cards most of his adult life. Destiny in every hand, though never in his. Destiny was always across the table. But now, finally, the winning hand was right in front of him. His talent had been recognized. He had dealt himself destiny.

We asked John if he wanted to be in a movie with Ed Harris.

All we had to do was say when . . .

We pulled into the Papermill Creek Saloon, early morning, coffee in hand. We'd be filming here the entire day and late into the night. But the prospects of us completing the day—a day that looked impossible on paper—looked even bleaker when we showed up.

The bar was supposed to be prelit by the electric department. Meaning, the electricians show up early, and by the time everybody arrives on set, the place is ready to shoot.

But there had been a miscommunication. The electric department was now arriving with the rest of the crew. As a result, we were three hours behind schedule before we started.

"Guys, I just don't think we can make this day," Connie said, sitting on a barstool, studying the schedule. "I'm not trying to be negative. I'm just trying to be realistic." She laughed at the odds. "It's impossible, Bros . . . You know I love you."

We gave little Connie a big hug. "We'll make it, Connie. Why? . . . Because we have to."

We threw in a chew of tobacco and searched for a solution. There wasn't much we could do to speed up the electric department. They were already moving their gear off the truck; if we tried to help we'd only get in their way.

So we took the actors out back and started rehearsing at a rotting wooden table on a deck above the creek. John Ford, our dealer, hadn't arrived yet. He was thirty minutes late. We'd live or die by his dealing.

"Bao, have you heard from John?" Logan asked over the walkie-talkie.

"I spoke to him this morning, said he was coming."

"How well do you know John?"

"He'll be here."

We continued rehearsing out back. The actors took turns dealing. It was failure, complete and total. It was thirty-seven degrees and we started sweating. The "avid poker players" hadn't dealt a card since Jimmy's bachelor party in '78. It was interfering with their acting. A two-minute scene was a clumsy and awkward five-minute molasses guzzle. Ten minutes passed and Noah jumped on the walkie again: "Bao, where the hell's John Ford?"

"He's probably lost. He don't ever come out this far."

We prayed John Ford, our savior, was speeding to the joint with the full force of his foot.

"Let's get rid of the cards, guys," Noah said, reaching across the table and gathering them up. "Let's just work through the mechanics of the scene without them."

"We're just getting the hang of it," one of the actors said, believing he was.

"Look, you guys are superb actors and that's why you're here. But you're not card dealers. So let's just try the scene without the cards for a while. Okay?"

So we took the cards away and worked through the scene, men sitting around a table drinking and gambling, trying to upset the confidence of their opponents.

Connie came out back, worried. "Where's your dealer? The electric department is almost ready?"

"He's on his way," Noah said softly, stepping back from the rehearsal table.

"Did you talk to him?"

"No . . . He'll be here, Connie. Don't worry."

Truth is, Noah was in a world of darkness.

And then the light came as the saloon doors swung open.

And John Ford arrived, looking like the Electric Horseman, smile blazing, prepared to deal all night, forever if he had to. He was carrying decks of fancy cards and a set of antique poker chips, had a .38 Derringer in his breast pocket, "in case we got some cheaters."

John Ford, a professional dealer at a Northern California Indian Casino, was shining. Tonight was his night. He'd taken his character preparation and wardrobe ideas to a level of towering enthusiasm.

Connie turned to Noah and said under her breath, "He's kidding, right? He can't wear that shirt."

Noah walked across the saloon and gave John a mighty handshake. "John, love what you've done with the outfit, truly, it's remarkable . . . But you gotta go to wardrobe."

"You don't like the shirt?" John asked, deflating. It was a $300 glowing white cowboy shirt with blue and red tassels running down the sleeves, a mixture of disco cowboy and Buffalo Bill in all his American glory.

"Dude, I love the shirt. Love it. It's just not right for this movie."

"What about these?"

John set his antique poker chips on the table, stacked several columns, and fanned a deck of cards across the felt. The chips were vivid blue and red, with a regal-looking emblem in the center, and made a rich sound when dropped on the table. These chips had character, history, like the saloon and the guys at the table.

"The chips and cards are perfect," Noah said.

John's smile blazed anew.

"Now go run to wardrobe so we can rehearse . . . And put the gun back in your car."

John Ford ran out of the saloon and returned with all the beam and gleam of a man ready to be a star.

The electric department finished lighting the bar and we moved the actors inside for a camera rehearsal. The place was tight. We were shooting with two cameras, which made it even tighter. John Ford started tossing cards around the table and the scene started flowing. We rehearsed a few more times and then rolled film.

Everybody was having a blast. The place was warm, filled with extras, surging with energy, a real fire blazing in the fireplace. It made you wanna pour a whiskey and drink it hard, yell YEEHAAA, grab the Derringer and shoot the ceiling. But we had to keep our wits, had to stay focused. So we stuck to the coffee and chocolate and climbed the electricity of the joint.

THE TRANSFORMATION

It was early evening. Noah was inside the saloon next to the camera, studying the performances. Logan was out back on the deck watching the video monitor. We were shooting the third poker scene of the day. We'd already shot Ed's close-up and were now working our way around the table, shooting the other poker players.

The camera was on Rod Gnapp. Ed was speaking to him off camera. Problem was we weren't getting any reaction from Rod when Ed spoke to him. Rod seemed to be preoccupied with his lines, only thinking about what he was going to say next. He was not listening to Ed.

Listen and react, that's all it is.

In the scene, Ed grows belligerent and tells Rod to "Shut up." We needed to see a natural reaction to this on Rod's face. But we didn't want to tell Rod to give us a certain look: mean, scared, frightened. Directing of this kind smacks of inexperience. It's hard for an actor to do that. The reaction appears forced, contrived, unnatural, and dishonest. And most importantly, out of respect for the actor, you don't want to depreciate their creativity in front of forty people by saying "Do this."

So Logan runs inside and whispers in Ed's ear, "Ed, this time when you say shut up, yell it as loud as you can. We're not getting anything from Rod, and we need some reaction. I think we're going to want to cut to Rod, or the other players' reactions, after you say shut up."

"It's kinda cramped in here . . . ," Ed said. "I'm not going to yell, but don't worry, I'll get a reaction outta him."

"Okay."

We shoot Rod's close-up again. Ed says "Shut up" and Rod doesn't react. Nothing. So Logan runs back inside and whispers to Ed again.

"Ed, we're not getting anything. He's not giving us a reaction. Scare the shit out of him. Yell SHUT UP as loud as you can. Please."

"I'm not going to yell. Well, a little bit. Don't worry. I'll get what you want."

Logan runs back outside. We shoot the scene again. Ed says "Shut up" a little louder this time. Nothing scary, just a firm "Shut up." And still nothing from Rod.

Logan runs back inside.

"Ed . . . do you trust us?"

Ed grins, "Yeah . . . I trust you guys."

"Then will you PLEASE yell as loud as you can. Scare the shit out of him. Yell 'Shut up' with all the force of your soul, all the man in your power . . . We need his reaction and we ain't getting it."

"Okay. Okay. Okay . . . I'll yell."

Logan runs back outside. Sits at the monitor. Puts on the earphones. The camera starts rolling. The actors start working through the scene, ridiculing Ed, giving him a hard time. And then Ed yells "SHUT UP!" with all the terror of his barbarian ancestors. The bar rumbled and collapsed in silence. Logan's earphones exploded. And the reaction was there. Rod's face dropped. His fear was real. His toothpick lifted when he clenched his teeth. An expression you couldn't manufacture. For a moment, which was all we needed, Rod, and the rest of the players at the table, thought Ed was going to stab them with a poker chip.

It shocked everyone, even the crew. Most of them thought, from watching us whisper to Ed in the corner between takes, that we'd gotten into an argument with him.

Logan ran inside, elated. He'd just watched playback on the monitor. We had what we needed for the editing room.

Noah said, "Swing around the camera . . . We're shooting Ed's close-up again."

Ed's intensity on that take was riveting and we needed to recapture it.

We moved the camera and reshot Ed's close-up. He yelled, louder and fiercer than before. This explosion of rage, this booming, knife-edged roar transformed the arc of his performance. It gave it a higher peak. It was an emotional turning point for Ed's character. All his guilt and remorse, self-loathing, exploded onscreen. But what turns the scene is not the emotional height, but the emotional chasm it then falls into. Ed swings from an object of anger to an object of pity in one breath. You hate him the moment he slams the money on the table and then feel sorry for him when he pulls out the creased photo of his boys from his tattered wallet. It was a clinic on acting. We were all Ed's pupils. And everyone in the bar that night felt privileged to be there.

YOU CAN'T ARGUE WITH SUCCESS

Noses were running. Half the crew had the flu. Interest and enthusiasm were now stolen by the dream of a warm bed and a bottle of NyQuil.

It was 3:30 A.M. Tonight's shooting was supposed to take four hours, a half night of work and then a day off. It was now hour twelve.

Ed was in the Perfect Car with Logan and Ishiah, parked in front of the Fairfax Theater, rehearsing. The scene in the movie is hysterically sad: Lane (Logan) and Rachel (Ishiah) are on their first date when they run into Charlie (Ed), who is so drunk he can't remember where he parked his truck. (This happened many times in real life.) Lane throws Charlie in the car and they drive around searching for his truck, but have no luck. Rachel comes along for the ride. Frustrated and embarrassed, Lane slams on the brakes in front of the Fairfax Theater and turns around to Charlie in the backseat, who, at the end of the scene tells his son, "You can't argue with success."

Jeromiah ran over to Noah, who was standing next to the camera, lining up the shot.

"You gotta go talk to Ed," Jeromiah said. "It's serious."

The night had been a technical and mental disaster. Everything that could have malfunctioned did; the camera iced up, the forty-foot tower of lights blew a circuit and the street went black, a generator died, the batteries fried in the wireless video monitor, a semi got a flat, and perhaps the most debilitating, we ran out of coffee. Then two goons from the San Francisco union—a world away—showed up and threatened to shut us down. What's more, we had closed down the main street of our hometown. The entire population had crawled out of the hills and creeks, even the shut-ins put down the remote to come watch the filming and steal all our food. It was a partying soup kitchen. *Work? Who has to work tonight? The Miller Brothers are making a movie! Honk your horn! Don't worry about interfering with the scene. Honk, yell, whoop, and holler, then march over to the food table and dive in! Support the Bros!*

Yes, it's good to be loved. But we had a crew to feed, and there was nothing left for them after the town stopped by.

And now there was a problem with Ed. Bring it on, everyone else is. Let's deal with it all tonight!

"What's the problem?" Noah asked Jeromiah.

"Ed's driving home as soon as we're done shooting."

"I thought he was flying home for the day off? I thought you arranged for someone to take him to the airport once we wrap?"

"I did. But Ed said he wants to drive."

"No way he's driving back to L.A.! No way! That's a suicide mission."

"I know. It's like a seven-hour drive. It's nuts, he'll fall asleep and die. I can barely stay awake myself."

"If he crashes, we're done. We'll probably get sued too. We can't okay that."

Then Mary Mastro and Karen Bradley, the hair and makeup queens, hurried over, wrapped in black shawls like mourning widows. "Noah, you have to do something. This is your responsibility."

"Ladies, thank you for your concern. I'm aware of the situation, and I've got it all under control."

Noah walked over to the Perfect Car. Ed was lying in the backseat, in character, drunk, giddy, having a party with himself. Logan and Ishiah were in the front seat, laughing at Ed.

"Ed, you can't drive home tonight," Noah said, thrusting his head through the open rear window.

Ed chuckled, staying in character.

Logan, alarmed, whipped around. "You're driving home, Ed?"

Ed chuckled again, amused at our concern, our hovering attention.

"Seriously, though, Ed," Noah continued. "I mean, come on. You've gotta be exhausted. Look, Bao is going to drive you to the airport as soon as we're done and you'll be in L.A. an hour later. There's no way you're driving home tonight."

Ed guffawed . . .

Continued laughing . . . for a while . . . Then:

"Look, I'm a grown man. I'll be all right. I got a sleeping bag in the back of my truck. If I get tired I'll pull over on I-5 . . . Relax, guys." He chuckled some more. "Do you think I want to kill myself?"

"Of course not, but come on, Ed. It's almost four A.M. We gotta work again in thirty-six hours. It's nuts . . . Hell, we're not even done shooting tonight . . . No way, Ed. I can't okay it."

The more concerned we became the more amused Ed became.

He laughed. "Bros, you can't argue with success."

"Come on, Ed. Quit screwing around. This is serious."

"I know it's serious . . . and that's why I'm being serious,

Bros . . . Seriously, I'll be fine," Ed continued, drunk. He still wouldn't break character. It was all fun to him. Our moment of career-ending concern was his moment of drunken amusement.

Noah dropped his head, turned, and walked back to Mary, Karen, and Jeromiah, who were waiting with emergency room suspense.

"What did he say?"

Ed sat up in the backseat and then stuck his head out the window, and hollered, "You can't argue with success, Noah!" Then he hit the side of the car and laughed heartily and dropped into the backseat.

"I did my best . . . ," Noah said.

And that was that. Ed wanted to spend his day off with his family—and he wanted to get there by driving his truck.

"What a stud," Jeromiah said. "You want a coffee, Noah?"

"We're out."

"Right."

"Connie, you want to call action?"

"ACTION!"

Ed drove back to L.A. at 4 A.M. to spend time with his family and then drove back north a day later. How he found time to sleep is a mystery. But he made it back and forth safely, a thousand-mile round-trip.

AND THEN IT RAINED FOR THE REST OF THE TIME

The endless wet and gloom of a Northern California winter, the months without sunlight, the time of drip and drain, of wind and storm, had arrived. It was Week Two. Our plan to shoot the exterior scenes in Week One had miraculously worked out.

We solved the Evan Jones problem with a hat, a wig, and a rewrite to the script. Even Evan doesn't know he wasn't there.

For the most part, we were now filming inside a farmhouse in Nicasio on the Lafranchi Dairy, the actual house where our mom was living. We still had a few more scenes to shoot outside, but the rain would give them a nice contrast to the rest of *Touching Home,* help express the passing of time, the changing seasons. Producers pay big money for rain machines. We got ours for free.

Then the actors started heading south.

Robert Forster was the first to go. He is an effortless craftsman—dignified, trustworthy, handsome, kind, and wise. The man on-screen is the man in life. He does not wear makeup or have his hair groomed by professionals before he goes on camera. He would step out of the car each morning and onto the set ready to deliver. Directing him is not a job; it's an observation, at most, a casual conversation. Learned and philosophical, a handsome exterior opens to a profound mind. He left us with this:

"It's taken me some time, and a lot of living, and, well, I've made my own three-step program that I try to live by. Some days are better than others of course. But I'm still learning, like all of us . . . ONE: accept all things. That gives you a good attitude. TWO: deliver excellence—right now. That gives you the best shot at the future. When you deliver excellence right now you get the reward of self-respect and satisfaction. And THREE: never quit. You can always win it in the late innings. You can win right now."

We were standing on the porch, rain driving into the night. Bao had the car running, waiting to take Robert to the hotel.

"Fellas, it was a pleasure working with you. I really think you're onto something special. Working with Ed was a real treat for me."

"It was our treat," Noah said. "We learned a great deal from you."

"The pleasure was mine, fellas. You guys did all the work. You wrote a great script and I just played the part . . . Give me a call when you're back in L.A. and we'll have breakfast. Thanks for the opportunity. So long . . ."

Brad Dourif finished shooting the following night. (And Bao returned his Hi-Def television to Target the next morning for a full refund.) At first, Brad viewed us with distrust. By the end, he was deeply moved when the entire crew stood and clapped for him after he finished his last scene in the cramped living room of the farm house.

We hugged Brad and he left. He was going back east for the holidays, to his house in upstate New York, look at the stars with his telescope, and hopefully, take a break from the Xbox 360.

And a day later it was Ed's turn.

He finished around 2 A.M. Rain was blowing sideways.

"I'm really glad you boys talked me into this . . . I really am . . . I think we did some great work here."

We didn't know how to respond. He had made our movie possible. He had taken a huge risk on a couple of nobodies, put his reputation on the line, believed in us when few did. And now he was praising the work.

We didn't know what to say, how to thank him.

Ed leaned forward slightly, his brow wrinkled, searching for a response, searching for approval.

But there was just the sound of the rain.

"Right? You guys think we did some good work, don't you?" Ed asked, as though he was growing unsure of his performance as our dad.

This was Ed Harris. Four-time Academy Award nominee. An American icon, hailed by many as our greatest living actor, and here he was, asking us if we thought that he/we had done good work. There is no higher compliment.

"You became our dad . . ." Noah said. "You gave us a chance to say goodbye to him . . . We'll forever be grateful to you . . . Thank you, Ed . . . Thank you for everything . . ."

"I want to keep in touch with you guys. I mean it . . . I want to have you boys over to the house for dinner some time, when things slow down for you."

We hugged. Ed climbed in his truck and drove into the night. We watched him go, taillights disappearing down the dark country road.

THE DAY AFTER

IT WAS PAGE one of *Moby Dick* again.

The next morning we found ourselves walking down the frontage road alongside Highway 101, kicking rocks, post-shooting depression, no purpose to life, rudderless, insignificant, aimless. Filming was over. The intensity had vanished. What to do now?

Where were we walking to anyways?

We drank a vineyard of wine the night before, and the down and out, next morning blues of a hangover wasn't helping us feel any better about ourselves. We were just trying to keep the rocks going straight, hadn't kicked rocks down the road since we were nine or ten. And here we were, grown men, lost and forlorn. One pathetic duo.

The cars whooshed by as if they were angry with us. The sky was heavy, looked like it might rain.

"We should get outta here . . . Let's drive to Montana," Noah said, kicking a rock and watching it tumble.

"When?" Logan asked, kicking a rock and watching it go.

"Right now."

It sounded like a good idea. It was better than kicking rocks. So we called Coach and Gale and asked if we could come see them. They told us to hurry up, "But drive safe, damnit."

Thirty minutes later we were on our way to Montana, speeding east on Highway 80 in a rented Chevy Tahoe borrowed from the production. Jeromiah was hesitant about us taking the Tahoe;

we had already damaged three rental cars during shooting. First, Noah fell asleep behind the wheel of a minivan in the hotel parking lot after a night of filming. The minivan was in reverse, not park, and it rolled backward through the lot and into an oak tree that did not move, blowing out the back windshield and door, waking Noah, sort of like an exploding alarm clock. Next, a rock flew into the windshield of a Jeep we were driving and spider-webbed the glass. Then Logan, driving the camera truck through the quarry, sideswiped one of the passenger vans, damaging both. So actually, we had cosmetically impaired four vehicles, not three.

"We had a lot on our minds when we were shooting," Noah said to Jeromiah. "Don't worry, we've reinvented ourselves since then."

"Are you sure you don't want to fly?" Jeromiah asked.

"Driving's better."

We stopped that night in Winnemucca, Nevada. It couldn't have been more than fifteen degrees inside our hotel room. Someone had left the windows open and the heater was busted. But we were too tired to go downstairs and get another room. So we froze all night.

We hit the road at 5 A.M. the next morning. Noah's toes were black.

Montana was the silence we needed. The land was dormant, frozen and white. Each morning we lifted weights in the garage with Coach, the door open to the negative temperatures, the steel bar icy and rigid, like our joints, calluses burning in the cold, straining, grunting, cleansing, Coach yelling, "Get up, you puke!" as a 330-pound squat tried to bury us. After the beating, we'd walk through the snow down to the pasture and feed the horses: Teddy, Fuji, and Spanky the pony. For three days it never got above twenty below zero.

We were in the mountains, away from people, away from the overstimulation of filming, away from the sensory explosion and mental overload.

It gets noisy. It gets tiring. Not saying we don't love it, only that it gets noisy and tiring.

Sometimes you gotta quiet up to figure it out.

Montana allowed us to quiet up.

KEEPING THE VOW

When we got home we drove out to the field where the old oak tree stood to spread our dad's ashes. We'd kept him with us for a year in a small wooden box and weren't going to lay him to rest until we'd completed the vow. Now we could set him free under the old oak tree we used to drive by when we were little, the old oak tree that stood alone in the field, the one he used to point to and say, "Boys, when I die, spread my ashes under that old oak tree out there."

"Don't talk like that, Dad."

"Bring me a sandwich every once in a while."

"Don't talk like that, Dad."

"It's all right, boys . . . We're just here for a short time and then we go home . . ."

We'd never be able to hug him again.

We parked alongside the road and crawled under the barbed wire fence and walked across the field. We poured our dad in a circle around the trunk and the tears started running down our faces. The ash that was now him, gray and dust, was all that was physically left of our father. We remembered the good times, fishing on the Russian River and playing baseball at the park, camping in the woods, eating hot dogs with American cheese melted on top, watching movies on rainy days, working hard in the long summer sun, how he had once been young and strong, a man with dreams, and how far those dreams had run away from him, the pain and tragedy of his final years, now spread under the mighty oak that stood alone in the field.

We stood under the tree and talked with our dad all morning. And when the sun got high we wiped our tears and walked across the field and back to the road.

For the first time in a long time there was no urgency, no anxiety; a freedom had been unleashed. We had suppressed our emotions for much of this year-long journey in order to focus on the enormous undertaking, and now we thought about our dad with unreserved reflection, a life that was lived with all its difficulties, with all its struggles.

Perhaps it was our father's struggles that made his life profound. Perhaps his difficulties pushed his soul deeper and made the man more. Perhaps truth comes through struggle. And our father's truth, stripped down from alcoholism and guilt, was often painful: deeply flawed, conflicted, poetic, and human.

The journey of our father's death brought us closer to him in life. His spirit was there with us, at every moment. His final gift was himself. He was the movie and the movie became him. If we ever saw him again we could tell him, "We did it, Dad. We made our movie . . ."

EPILOGUE: FULL CIRCLE

IN JANUARY 2007, Robert Dalva started editing *Touching Home* on an Apple G5 in the downstairs room of our mom's house. Days bled into weeks and weeks bled into another life. We never saw the sun. We got so depressed we thought about moving to Sweden. In June, composer Martin Davich and music editor Michael Mason delivered a beautiful score. In July, we went to Skywalker Ranch for three weeks to do the final mix. And then it was time to show the movie.

On April 26, 2008, the San Francisco International Film Festival held the world premiere of *Touching Home,* the same place we had cornered Ed Harris in an alley two years earlier. We had come full circle. *Touching Home* was the first sellout at the festival. Ed and his wife, Amy Madigan, came up to celebrate. We did several interviews and an onstage Q&A with Ed in front of 520 people. The following Tuesday we had a second screening, a 12:30 P.M. matinee in which 800 people showed up for 520 seats. The audience reaction was affirming; they were laughing and crying, profoundly moved by our story, two standing ovations.

Walking off the stage after the Q&A, Ed told us that his wife thinks this might be his finest performance.

And now we're here. Wherever that is. Somewhere between obscurity and the rocket-ride.

ACKNOWLEDGMENTS

DEAR READER,

Let us start with a fact: This was the most difficult part of the book to write.

Why?

Because we know this: We are going to leave out good, honest, hardworking, loyal, deserving, and loving members of this journey. And knowing that we've screwed up before we've started is, well . . . crushing.

So here we go.

It took a team of devoted and intelligent people to put this book in your hands. They have guided and inspired us along the way. While it's nearly impossible to list them all (as a result of our failings), here are a few: Mom, for always being there. Grandma, for always caring. And all our buddies, for being the most loyal, conflicted, emotionally troubled, medicated, and crazy friends any brothers could hope for. We love you. Thanks for not being normal.

To our brother Bao, for getting us here.

To Jeromiah Zajonc and Editorro, for reading numerous drafts, challenging our choices, and not putting up with any of our bullshit.

To Coach Gough, for teaching us that character is built, not bought. And Gale, for loving Coach.

To Tess Uriza Holthe, for her encouragement and conviction.

To our beautiful and loving agent, Mary Ann Naples, for believing in us. And showing us New York City. We never thought we'd get there. . . . She's also really smart.

To everyone at Collins Publishing Group: Steven Ross, Bruce Nichols, Matthew Benjamin (our editor—big thanks, amigo), Jean Marie Kelly, Paul Olsewski, Gretchen Crary, Doug Jones, Margot Schupf, Carla Clifford, Jessica Ko, Kimberly Chocolaad, Jessica Deputato, Amy Vreeland, Beth Silfin, Ariele Fredman, and everyone else in the building. Thank you for breaking us in. It's been a lot of fun so far.

To Kristin Bowers, for her passion, friendship, and dancing spirit. Thunderous hugs.

To Amy and Lily for sharing Ed with us. And Ed, for becoming our friend.

No money, no movie. And no movie, no book. So here's to the people who put money into our hat: Brian Vail, most of it; Lance and Debra Logan, some of it; Pete and Dee Deterding, the rest of it.

To the entire cast and crew of *Touching Home*. Your efforts allowed us to write this book. Thank you.

Ric Halpern and Bob Harvey at Panavision, Lorette Bayle at Kodak, Alan Tudzin and Debbie Eldridge at FotoKem, and Amy Peterson at Avid for starting the snowball.

To Gordon Radley, for his wisdom and mental beatings—it's painful, but we love you for it.

To all the Jedi at Skywalker Ranch, whose efforts, for the most part, were left out of these pages. If we're able to write a longer version, you're in. Bet on it. Josh Lowden, Glenn Kiser, Richard Hymns, Mark Berger, Chris Boyes, Pascal Garneau, Marilyn McCoppen, Frank Clary, Chris Gridley, Terry Eckton, Frank Rinella, Sean England, Jana Vance, Dennie Thorpe, Ellen

Heuer, Jonathan Greber, Phil Benson, Eva Porter, Big Mike, and many more.

To Chrissie England and ILM.

To Tom Sherak, for his wisdom and generosity.

To Bruce Snyder and Bert Livingston. Time will prove you right.

To Ethel and Stan Seiderman, Linda Nackerud, and everyone at the Fairfax San Anselmo Children's Center. You helped raise us.

To all our mother's friends, who helped raise us too.

To the Sanders family—the whole clan—for giving us shelter from the storm.

To our attorney, Matthew Fladell, for his counsel, patience, and flexible rates.

To Bill and Kathy Shine, for taking care of us. And Alycia Paletta for dealing with all our crumpled receipts and poor bookkeeping.

To Sue and Mercy and the team at Borel Private Bank and Trust. Thank you for making banking easy.

To Catherine Olim and Alicia Mohr at PMK/HBH. We appreciate all your help thus far.

To Tony Magee and Pat Mace at the Lagunitas Brewing Company. You brew gold.

To Major League Baseball.

To Jack Bair, Sara Hunt, and Sue Peterson of the San Francisco Giants.

To Hal Roth and Greg Feasel of the Colorado Rockies. Thanks for not taking a bat to our heads.

To P. J. Carey, for opening the gates.

To Graham Leggat and Hilary Hart of the San Francisco Film Society.

To Stefanie Coyote and the San Francisco Film Commission.

To Steve Berringer and the College of Marin baseball team.

To Victoria Cook, for guidance, love, and support.

To Coach Soto and the Pima Junior College baseball team.

To Hooman, we know your name. And the team at Alice radio.

To all the local media: Joe Bayliss and Fernando and Greg at Energy 92.7 FM; Jeff Bell at KCBS; Paul Hosley, Rich Walcoff, and Jon Bristow at KGO.

To Dave Albee at the *Marin Independent Journal,* Jesse Hamlin at the *San Francisco Chronicle,* and Jacoba Charles at the *Point Reyes Light*.

To the Fab-Fivers, for their love, dedication, hard work, and unflinching loyalty. We are blessed.

To the independent booksellers at the Frantoio dinner: Sheryl Cotleur and Karen West (Book Passage), Ty Wilson and Stephanie Deignan (Copperfields Books), Barry Rossnick (Books Inc.), Melinda Powers (Capitola Book Café), Joyce Ripp (Northern California Booksellers Association), Laura Tibbals (Moe's Books), Michael Barnard (Rakestraw Books).

To David Sondheim and all the teachers in Marin County and beyond, whose early support of the book started the blaze.

To Dr. Donnis Taylor, for not kicking Noah out of class. You said I could write. I just thought you were being nice. Thanks for believing in me.

To Paul Fradelizio, for feeding us the greatest Italian food west of the Atlantic. And Bill Booth, for being the best boss ever.

The entire town of Nicasio and the LaFranchi Family.

To everybody in Fairfax and West Marin and the outlaws and the time that was. . . . The redwoods still rise and the mountains are still free . . .

Who else? If you're still reading—YOU.

The Bros
The House of Winter
February 2, 2009